Policy and Education

Written specifically for education studies students, this accessible text offers a clear introduction to education policy. It aims to help the reader understand what is meant by educational policy, how policy can be made and the main discourses that have driven education.

Capturing the essential aspects of educational policy over the last 30 years, the book provides an overview of political themes in education demonstrating how education policy has progressed and the effect this and politics have had on schools. It then covers key themes such as performance, choice and professionalism to show how education policy is constructed and implemented and how this has impacted on education in practice.

Features include:

- activities that can be undertaken individually or as a group to promote discussion
- annotated further reading lists
- chapter overviews and summaries.

Part of the Foundations in Education Studies Series, this timely textbook is essential reading for students coming to the study of education policy for the first time.

Paul Adams is a lecturer at the University of Strathclyde, UK. His interests are in education policy, the politics of pedagogy and social and educational inclusion.

Foundations of Education Studies Series

This is a series of books written specifically to support undergraduate education studies students. Each book provides a broad overview to a fundamental area of study exploring the key themes and ideas to show how these relate to education. Accessibly written with chapter objectives, individual and group tasks, case studies and suggestions for further reading, the books will give students an essential understanding of the key disciplines in education studies, forming the foundations for future study.

Research and Education
Will Curtis, Mark Murphy and Sam Shields

Policy and Education
Paul Adams

Forthcoming titles

Philosophy and Education
Joanna Haynes, Ken Gale and Mel Parker

Sociology and Education
Richard Waller and Chrissie Rogers

Policy and Education

Paul Adams

Routledge
Taylor & Francis Group

LONDON AND NEW YORK

First published 2014
by Routledge
2 Park Square, Milton Park, Abingdon, Oxon OX14 4RN

Simultaneously published in the USA and Canada
by Routledge
711 Third Avenue, New York, NY 10017

Routledge is an imprint of the Taylor & Francis Group, an informa business

British Library Cataloguing in Publication Data
A catalogue record for this book is available from the British Library

Library of Congress Cataloging in Publication Data
A catalog record for this book has been requested

ISBN: 978-0-415-69757-6 (hbk)
ISBN: 978-0-415-69758-3 (pbk)
ISBN: 978-0-203-13875-5 (ebk)

Typeset in Bembo
by Swales & Willis Ltd, Exeter, Devon, UK

Contents

Introduction

It is true to say that over the last 30 years or so there has been increased emphasis placed on educational policy and education policy-making. The activities involved in such matters have come to the fore academically and most would now maintain that policy study is a vital part of any education studies or related programme. Whilst the opportunities for such study may have diminished on initial teacher training courses, on education studies, related degrees and masters level courses there has been a surge of interest and application. Indeed, policy and politics are now often seen as another of the underpinning disciplines of education alongside philosophy, sociology, history and psychology. Added to this, governments now pay more attention than ever to education; it is seen as one of the most important aspects of government. It has been transformed from relatively unimportant to vital in the drive for increased profitability and the renewal of society. Consequently, policy announcements are often forthcoming, and dealing with these has now become part and parcel of the work of those involved in education and related services. Importantly, education has attained a political currency like never before. This added to the fact that the education system has, in the last 30 years, undergone systemic change on an unprecedented scale, means that the study of education policy has a great deal of interest and currency.

This, book is about the 'big P' of education policy and is written for those who are studying education policy as part of an undergraduate degree course. Such study might be part of an education studies degree, or as part of a sociology or related discipline-based degree that has the study of education policy as part of its makeup. It sets out to examine some of the political thinking that has been involved in education policy-making over the last 30 or so years. Its main focus is from the rise of Margaret Thatcher through the years of Tony Blair and Gordon Brown to the present Coalition government. The discourses that abound during such times are examined along with the ways in which political thinking came to drive education policy. By the time the reader has finished with the book, they should have a good insight into the main discourses that have driven the development of education policy over the last 30–40 years. They should be able to identify the main ways in which education policy has progressed and the effect this and politics have had on the nation's schools.

When writing a book such as this there is a need to provide some sort of rationale for the adoption of certain elements and organisational features. As I have examined education policy from the rise of Thatcherism through to the present day, it would seem pertinent for the prevailing discourses and arguments to take centre stage. In this way I have chosen the chapters I have as I believe they capture some of the essential aspects of educational policy over the last 30 years. Thus, chapters include choice, markets, professionalism and performance. These seem to be the main discourses that have driven education during the time period in discussion. Readers will no doubt be able to identify other discourses that have influenced education, and in one respect this is good. If you are able to challenge some of the ideas herein with reasoned argument and careful research, then you will be 'doing' educational policy work. Perhaps there are other chapters that I could have included, but for brevity and cohesion, I have adopted the ones I have. Whenever a book is written, there is an element of author choice. I hope, though, that I have captured the main planks of educational reform. Additionally, I have tied the book to statutory age schooling: chapters are provided that cover primary and secondary education.

There are things which this book does not discuss. It does not discuss the ways in which higher education has altered over time, certainly since the 1960s and the first expansion of the sector. Neither does it deal with early years, the sector that has seen so much growth during the last 15 or so years. This is deliberate: to try to integrate all of these would have meant that the book would have been less cohesive. In only discussing statutory age education through an examination of that which has happened in the primary and secondary sector, the book, hopefully, has a better rationale.

With this in mind, this book is set out in three parts. Part 1, *The Context,* identifies political and policy theory so that an understanding of what the study of policy might mean can be gleaned. Chapter 1 discusses the ways in which government since the Second World War has been positioned. The welfare state is briefly outlined with the chapter analysing the politics behind the drive for change that ensued during the 1980s and 1990s under successive Conservative administrations. Neoliberalism is detailed alongside neoconservatism as the underpinning ideologies of this time. The Third Way is outlined and all are noted for their impact on education. This chapter seeks to identify how and why politics is intimately tied into the development of educational policy and policy-making. Through the identification of how politics has changed over the last 30 years, the chapter signals the mechanisms by which education has been influenced politically. Chapter 2 discusses what might be meant by policy and how policy can be developed and studied. From this chapter the reader should be able to see the particular line that is adopted for the rest of the book: the ways in which discourse drives educational policy-making.

Part 2, *The Phases of Education,* examines statutory-age school changes. Chapter 3 identifies the ways in which secondary education has changed since the inception of the welfare state. It notes the way in which the system has developed over time and the main mechanisms governments have deployed to effect change. Chapter 4 does the same for the primary sector. Both chapters bring the reader up to the policies of the current Coalition government. They make apparent the ways in which the political ideologies of the time drove the development of education policy.

The third part, *Political Discourses,* examines the discourses that currently drive and have driven educational development. Chapter 5 examines the idea of educational markets and takes the reader through the development of a system that is predicated on market reform. Chapter 6 discusses educational choice and diversity; the ways in which the education system has been forced to adopt different structures and ways of working so that market rhetoric might be achieved. Chapter 7 discusses the thorny issue of teacher professionalism. Here the history of the concept as well as its theory is examined so that the reader might be able to understand the ways in which teachers have been positioned with regard to professional status for their work. Chapter 8 considers performance in education; what it might mean and how it manifests. The rise of the performance indicator is outlined through an appreciation of aspects such as SAT scores, Ofsted inspections and teacher targets. All of these chapters deal with education policy up to and including the policies of the current Coalition government; they detail the Coalition's rise to power and the way in which education is now positioned politically; the policies of Michael Gove are discussed as are the ways in which the government seeks to drive a particular version of education.

This book can be used in a variety of ways. The most obvious is to start at the beginning and read through to the end. In one sense this is the most beneficial as the reader would gain an insight into the various aspects of education policy. The chapters do intertwine somewhat, so such a reading might be propitious. However, it is also the case that the book can be 'dipped into'. It might be that as part of your course you are looking at educational choice. The chapter titled 'Choice and diversity' would be an obvious one to read. This said, it is probably wise to read Part 1 to gain an understanding of what can be meant by educational policy and how policy can be made, along with the political discourses that have influenced education.

The book also has a number of activities throughout. These are meant to stimulate conversation and debate and should enable to you engage with the text more clearly and with much greater focus. The tasks can be undertaken individually or as a group.

When reading this text it is important that the reader understands that in many cases an examination of policy is an examination of the positions one would adopt. Whenever one 'reads' a policy one is placed by one's thoughts, beliefs and ideologies as well as one's history. It is vital, therefore, that readers do not simply take everything in this book at face value, but that they examine and challenge the interpretations herein. No book can be completely comprehensive and if anything has been left out that is entirely my fault.

The context

1

Political ideology

Purpose of this chapter

After reading this chapter you should understand:

- what is meant by ideology;
- about the main points of the political ideologies of:
    - the post-Second World War welfarist settlement;
    - New Right thinking;
    - neoliberalism;
    - neoconservatism;
    - the Third Way;
    - the Coalition government.

Linking politics and education

Since the mid to late half of the nineteenth century, education and politics have been inextricably linked. Laws have been passed that have guided and governed education. Such orientations have mirrored social and political ways of viewing the world. So, for example, the 1870 Education Act was introduced at a time when liberal and conservative doctrines were in ascendance. This meant that education was subject to particular ideologies, both political and social. It is, therefore, necessary to explore the links between education and politics. To do this, certain aspects must be considered, namely, the nature of ideology and the ways in which political parties position themselves regarding social matters. This chapter identifies what is meant by ideology and then goes on to explore political orientations and the ways in which these have given rise to certain forms of educational policy. Such considerations are necessary if the reader is to understand the ways in which education policy has both altered and continued under different governments.

Ideology

Before considering the interaction between politics and policy it is necessary to consider what is meant by ideology. This is a difficult term to pin down. Apple (2013: 34) suggests that:

> Most people seem to agree that one can talk about ideology as referring to some sort of 'system' of ideas, beliefs, fundamental commitments, or values about social reality, but here the agreement ends. The interpretations differ according to both the *scope* or range of the phenomena which are presumably ideological and the *function* – what ideologies actually do for the people who 'have' them.

According to Hartley (1983) the essential characteristics of ideology suggest that it consists of values, beliefs or ideas about the state of the world and what the world should be. These cognitive (thoughts) and affective (feelings) elements form a framework. Ideology thus consists of some relatively systematic structuring of thoughts and ideas; it represents the ways in which individuals and groups think about the world. Importantly, ideologies concern social groups and social arrangements that, in turn, develop and maintain the groups and arrangements themselves. There is, then, a link between the individual and the group: individuals have ideas that influence the group and the group's identity influences the individual. It is these links which provide justification for behaviour. We can say that ideology is:

> a broad interlocked set of ideas and beliefs about the world held by a group of people that they demonstrate in both behaviour and conversation to various audiences. These systems of belief are usually seen as 'the way things really are' by the groups holding them, and they become the taken-for-granted way of making sense of the world.
>
> (Meighan and Siraj-Blatchford, 1997: 180)

Thinking about ideology has a history that started around the time of the French Revolution. It has been thought of in a variety of ways (Meighan and Siraj-Blatchford, 1997: 179):

- the science of ideas;
- revolutionary thinking: the term ideological became synonymous with those who opposed the prevailing political order;
- false consciousness: an 'abstract thought about human society which was fake';
- a group philosophy: this is a more sociological approach.

Political thinking and ideology

Political positions can be thought of as ideological, in as much as they can be said to be views of versions about the good life (Bartlett and Burton, 2012); political positions are inclined as they are due to the ways individuals feel that society should be run. Politics is a way of defining what is best for society so that everyone can live a full and fulfilling life. Politics is ideological in that it forms broader political programmes and social movements (Apple, 2013: 34).

Politically speaking, a left/right dichotomy can be identified as a rough classification of political ideologies, although this is rather simplistic. However, it is possible to locate different political parties on this spectrum although their position will alter over time and as policies shift and change to meet economic, social and political need (Bartlett and Burton, 2012). Bartlett and Burton (2012: 135) highlight the general positions held by those on the left and those on the right. Those parties traditionally seen to be on the left of the political spectrum generally have values associated with:

- social equality;
- social justice;
- the redistribution of wealth;
- the promotion of state ownership of key industries; and,
- state provision of a range of services.

Those parties traditionally seen to be to the right of the political spectrum generally have values associated with:

- the defence of individual rights;
- the promotion of private property, capitalism, free trade and the free market;
- the promotion of traditional values to pursue social stability;
- strong leadership and a reduction in state bureaucracy.

Bartlett and Burton go on to note that ideologies are useful tools to enable us to compare and understand change over time. However, care should be taken not to assume that they are a rigid set of principles to guide our political or, indeed, educational thinking. For example, in the 1960s and 1970s many felt that both Labour and the Conservatives had become centrist in orientation; in a sense the traditional ideological positions of the two parties had been disregarded, leading to similarity. Both parties supported the welfare state, a change in the position of the Tory Party from that which had existed prior to the Second World War. The consensus between the two parties was such that both believed in maintaining welfare state apparatus as a means to ensure that society met its obligations to its citizens. Whilst this shift was less dramatic for the Labour Party, for the Conservatives this broke with the traditional view that 'man' should be the definer and architect of 'his' own endeavours.

Care should be taken, however, when considering education policy, for such policy derives from sources other than just political ideology: e.g. educational ideology, pragmatism, negotiation and compromise. Ideology and policy are not necessarily welcome bedfellows; sometimes muddling through or political compromise drives policy and it is not always the case that policy is a result of ideological position (Trowler, 2003). It might well be, for example, that necessity drives the adoption of certain policies and these may cut against the traditional ideological position of the party in power. For example, the introduction of academies under New Labour was ideologically not in keeping with traditional Labour views. Furthermore, as will be seen later in this book, Tony Blair was at pains to maintain that New Labour was not ideologically driven. It is also the case that the current Coalition government has had to manage the process of governing by compromise and negotiation. A clear example of this is the increase in tuition fees for university students agreed by both the Conservatives and Liberal Democrats, something the latter were opposed to whilst in opposition.

The political context relating to ideology and policy

From the 1940s to the 1980s education was part of the welfarist settlement (Trowler, 2003) and was, for the most part, an amalgam of socialist and social democratic thinking during the times when the Labour Party were in power, and Conservative thinking during the Conservative years. Although traditionally ideologically different, the two parties promoted the idea of *distributive justice*; that a more democratic society with more equal access to public provision would lead to greater involvement in the workings of democracy itself (Gewirtz, 2002). What was sought was cooperation rather than competition. Everybody was seen to have a role in society. Even though each person did not offer the same resources and skills, active membership was desired.

As Gewirtz and Ball (2000) note, such welfarist settlement orientations for public services were based on a public-service ethos where decisions were driven by a commitment to 'professional standards' and values such as equity, care and social justice. The emphasis for relations was collective, cooperative and collegial, maintained, in part, by strong trades unions. Consultation was a key feature of this system and managers had been socialised into the field and specific values of the sector in which they worked by 'passing through the ranks'.

Further, in the 1950s, social scientists argued forcibly that both capitalism and communism in their contemporary forms had failed. There was a need, they believed, to instigate a new form of political intervention which would blend state, market and democracy so guaranteeing security, inclusion, well-being and stability. The belief was that the state should focus on full employment, economic growth and citizen welfare and that the state should intervene in the marketplace if and when required. The instigated changes to welfare and state intervention were designed to prevent a return to the conditions which led to the great slump of the 1930s. Social democratic states such as Britain removed sectors of the economy, such as education from the marketplace in the belief that they provided basic human needs and should not, therefore, be determined by ability to pay (Harvey, 2005).

The welfare state sought to combat the deprivation and want of the years preceding the Second World War. Welfarism, the theoretical basis for the welfare state, is an ethical theory which posits that the outcomes of actions, policies and rules should be based on the impact they have on the welfare of those residing within the particular state. Thus, the original premise of the welfare state was to eradicate the five giant evils of the time: squalor; ignorance; want; idleness; and disease. The introduction of the welfare state, paid for through the introduction of national insurance contributions, sought to ensure that public services would be free at the point of delivery. No longer would people's welfare be determined by their ability to pay. Education was part of this endeavour and, as will be seen later on, meant that schools would change to meet the new requirements. The main premise of the welfare state is the redistribution and intervention of services to meet public and social need (Heckman and Smith, 1998). In essence a social contract ensued between the individual and the state. The former is required to work, if possible, and pay taxes and national insurance, whilst the latter seeks to ensure the continued welfare, education and health of state citizens. The focus is on delivering a fairer society where those who can afford to pay do so through a progressive taxation system but that those who are unable to make large financial contributions are not penalised.

Welfarism and the welfare state seek to enshrine collective responsibility as the cornerstone of civil and social society. It is, in this ideology, unacceptable to simply look after oneself; it is the duty of all to provide for others in need, albeit indirectly through the mechanisms of state apparatuses for matters such as education and health care.

However, by the 1960s this consensus was beginning to break down and a period of stagflation (high inflation and unemployment coupled with low economic growth) ensued which lasted well into the 1970s. Further, worldwide economic downturns and US and UK financial and policy changes made the economics of the welfare era unsustainable (Olssen and Peters, 2005). Welfare settlement economics was blamed and the global market gradually gained the upper hand. Economic survival became the key measure of national and individual success. As Davies and Bansel (2007: 251) note,

> Individual survival became attached to national survival, and both were tied to the market. 'Survival' was, and is, routinely constituted in economic terms dictated by the market, and this has the double force of necessity and inevitability.

The welfare state was never universally welcomed though. Some, notably the *Financial Times*, presented the welfarist settlement as stiflingly bureaucratic and a major contributor to the bleak years of 1970s stagflation (Harvey, 2005).

The shift from Welfarism

In 1979 Margaret Thatcher was elected to power. It was her party's view that 'supply-side' monetarist policies should be pursued due to the perceived failure of the post-war welfarist settlement. Politically, those on the right felt that the original evils the welfare state sought to eradicate were still prevalent. This and the belief that contemporary economic and social problems were due to the failure of the proposed individual-state contract led to the adoption of economic and social theory driven by a desire to increase national output and consumption. To achieve this, barriers to production such as income tax and capital gains tax were lessened. The idea was that if people were empowered to produce more, then economic growth would ensue; goods and services could be provided at lower prices and both consumption and production would thus increase. This meant confronting trades unions and the power of professional bodies, however, as it was believed that they stifled invention and creativity in the production process. Additionally, the welfare state was rolled back and many state-owned assets such as the rail service and gas and electricity supplies were privatised. Britain was portrayed as 'business friendly' in an effort to win foreign investment and trade. Indeed, 'all forms of social solidarity were to be dissolved in favour of individualism, private property, personal responsibility, and family values' (Harvey, 2005: 23).

It was during this period that New Right thinking came to the fore. From 1979 Conservative governments had their origins in nineteenth-century thinking which espoused individualism, freedom and enterprise. Grounded in the ideals of neoconservatism and neoliberalism, such thinking sought to reorient public and social policy along business lines. This New Right thinking, particularly in the 1980s, demonstrates tensions between neoliberalism on the one hand and neoconservatism on the other.

Neoconservatism

On the one hand, neoconservative thinking holds that government must intervene to ensure morality and social order with 'custom', 'tradition' and 'order' as key words. Neoconservatives are suspicious of local government and people's freedom to choose: they are centralist in orientation and believe that strong central direction should be provided by government (Trowler, 2003).

Neoconservatism, as a right wing political movement, shares some similarities with neoliberalism in that it believes in elite government and the maintenance of market freedoms. However, it differs in that it seeks to engender social order in place of the chaos of individual interests, and in its belief in an overweening morality as social glue (Harvey, 2005). Neoconservatism seeks to provide specific dictates for life in areas such as lifestyle, sexual habits and orientation, self-expression and, with regard specifically to education, the canons of society which should be taught and learnt (Harvey, 2005). In this regard, and as an educational example, the first National Curriculum offers a clear guide:

> If pupils are to make the most of [the opportunity that schools offer] they must attend school regularly, and be given a clear moral lead by the governing body, the head teacher and the staff of their schools. Pupils must be helped to recognise their responsibilities to themselves and to others.
>
> (DfE, 1992a, quoted in Trowler, 2003: 108)

Neoconservatives advocate tradition and order. They bemoan 'progressive' teaching methods which they believe lead to a decline in standards, and they advocate traditional values and traditional subjects.

Neoliberalism

It was the case, though, that throughout the 1980s and 1990s, social and public policy was increasingly aligned with economic imperatives and meeting the needs of the economy. Whilst the neoconservative argument supports the view that people are motivated by individual not collective gain, it is neoliberalism which particularly argued that contemporary values were warped and needed redefining, particularly amongst the poor and the working class (Apple, 2009). Again, such thinking was not new. As far back as 1954, Polyani noted that the doctrines of Welfarism were being attacked by the right as removers of essential freedoms.

Neoliberals believe that market forces are the most efficient way to run an economy. In this view, producers produce goods and services which people want. If they cannot do this to meet the expectations of those purchasing or if they cannot do it efficiently, then they will go out of business. These resources are then released to those who can operate in efficient terms. Neoliberals advocate minimum interference by government. The consequences of government input is inefficiency and a need to support certain industries that become protected (Bartlett and Burton, 2012).

Arguably it is the neoliberal agenda which has been the main political driver for social and public policy for at least 30 years. Giroux (2002: 425) maintains that neoliberalism is 'the defining political economic paradigm of our time' and refers to 'the politics and processes whereby a relative handful of private interests are permitted to control as much as possible of social life in order to maximise their personal profit'. Neoliberalism presents the market as common sense and favours individual property rights and the rule of law; personal and individual freedom in the marketplace is held as sacrosanct (Harvey, 2005). It holds that 'trickle-down', whereby wealth creation eventually flows to those with less, will occur through the creation and maintenance of free markets and free trade and the generation of wealth for the few. Within this doctrine the individual is responsible and accountable for their own actions and well-being. Success and failure are, accordingly, interpreted in terms of entrepreneurial virtues or personal failings rather than through any systemic failure (Harvey, 2005). Thus education, for example, is seen as the province of the individual and, as such, failure in this endeavour is down to personal shortcomings, not the system. Democracy is viewed with suspicion by neoliberals, but tolerated where there is a strong middle class to ensure political stability. Neoliberals favour rule by experts and elites and judgement by judicial decision-making rather than democratic and parliamentary decision-making. Harvey (2005: 5) notes that in choosing individual freedom as its basis, neoliberalism supports the very fabric of civilisation as we know it.

> The founding figures of neoliberal thought took political ideals of human dignity and individual freedom as fundamental, as 'the central values of civilization'. In so doing they chose wisely, for these are indeed compelling and seductive ideals. These values, they held, were threatened not only by fascism, dictatorships, and communism, but by all forms of state intervention that substituted collective judgements for those of individuals free to choose.

Neoliberalism shares many characteristics of classic, nineteenth-century liberal thinking. Both believe in the dominance of the economically self-interested individual who is a rational optimiser and best judge of his or her own needs. The free market is held to be the best way to allocate resources and opportunities due to its more efficient and morally superior mechanisms. Both are committed to laissez-faire: a reduced need for government regulation and a distrust of governmental power alongside a commitment to free trade with the abolition of tariffs or subsidies and other forms of state-imposed support (Olssen and Peters, 2005). This said, neoliberalism does differ in a number of respects: whilst in classical liberalism the state was seen as anathema to individual flourishing, in neoliberalism the state is seen as the key to creating appropriate market conditions. And whereas in classical liberalism the individual is seen as having an autonomous nature, neoliberalism seeks to create the individual as enterprising and competitive.

As Lynch (2006) notes, what neoliberalism does offer is a critique of rights-based approaches for it does not wish to guarantee state-based rights in education, welfare, health care and other public goods. Rather, the citizen is glorified as a consumer able to make market-based decisions. Well-being is seen as an individual, not state-based, issue (the state is no longer responsible); the state merely exists to facilitate individual choice and decision-making. The individual is required to think only of him- or herself. Neoliberalism locates the individual as a rational decision-maker and ignores the interdependent nature of human existence, preferring instead to extol the virtues of economic individualism. It seeks to remove cost from the state, passing it instead to the individual.

From the 1980s neoliberalism has been touted as the only way to solve economic and social problems. It introduces free-market thinking, competitiveness and deregulation and is now the driving force behind globalisation. Neoliberal agencies pronounce that everything is subordinate to the economy.

> By 'neoliberalism' we mean a philosophy of political economy that emphasises private property rights, free markets and free trade and allows the workings of markets to provide solutions to social and economic problems (Harvey, 2005). Neoliberalism is then more than policy and ideology. According to Dean (1999: 210) it refers to a specific style or a general mentality of rule and can be understood in terms of what Foucault (1991) referred to as 'governmentality', which is specifically about controlling or guiding the relationship between individuals and their relationships with social institutions and communities.
>
> (Pick and Taylor, 2009: 69–70)

Neoliberalism and individualism promote life as a 'project' in which 'the self is the subject of continuous economic capitalisation' (Pick and Taylor, 2009: 78). In short, neoliberalism has meant the 'financialization of everything' (Harvey, 2005: 33):

> Under neoliberalism, both government and society have taken up, as their primary concern, their relationship with the economy. What was called 'society' has been reconstituted as the product of earlier mistaken governmental interventions, shaped by the unaffordable systems of social insurance, unemployment and welfare benefits, social work, state education and the 'whole panoply of "social" measures associated with the welfare state' (Burchell, 1996: 27).
>
> (Davies and Bansel, 2007: 249)

The neoliberal state produces the individual as an economic entrepreneur and the institution as the creator of such individuals who, in turn, produce docile individuals who see themselves as free but who are, in fact, tightly controlled (Davies and Bansel, 2007). At the same time the workings of government are made more opaque.

What is particularly of note is the way in which democratic values steadily give way to commercial ones. Social visions are dismissed as hopelessly out of date and the entrepreneur becomes ascendant (Giroux, 2002). Civic responses give way to commercialism, privatisation and deregulation. The individual is defined through the mechanisms of individualism, competition and consumption (Giroux, 2002). The person is seen not as a social being, but as an individual consumer with attendant rights. For neoliberals 'the end goals of freedom, choice, consumer sovereignty, competition and individual initiative, as well as those of compliance and obedience, must be constructions of the state acting now in its positive role through the development of the techniques of *auditing, accounting* and *management*' (Olssen and Peters, 2005: 315). Accordingly, markets come to be seen as key to the success for the public sector.

Neoliberalism and education

Regarding education neoliberalism holds that (Trowler, 2003):

- social planning is impossible due to the selfishness of individuals and the complexity of society;
- community institutions hold producer capture, that is, they decide who has and does what and when, rather than the consumer deciding, based upon sound judgement and good information;

- local education authorities, etc. are not needed as the market will sort out schooling for the common good;
- schools should compete with schools;
- parents should be defined as, and have the benefits of being, consumers;
- diversity within the system should be encouraged.

Neoliberalism orients the individual as self-regarding and a consumer: competition is seen as a necessary factor for entrepreneurship. It ignores that the fact that living conditions are an important basis for educational success. It sees as unproblematic the possibility that profit might be gleaned from the provision of educational services.

Problematically, the language and policies of neoliberalism support the definition of 'we' (defined as the law abiding and hard-working populace) and 'they' (the lazy, immoral and permissive, usually marked out according to social status) (Apple, 2009), even though many policies are specifically designed to alleviate underachievement in poorer areas. In particular what often occurs is the gentrification of the educational landscape; the marking out of 'middle class values and practices' as those to emulate, with associated policies. This amounts to what Apple (2009) calls 'middle-classing': the lauding of specific behaviours seen to be more deserving of support and celebration. Furthermore, policies for the 'they' are often downplayed due to their cost. Whilst measures are put in place to attempt to raise standards for example, real poverty reduction mechanisms are not used to achieve these targets. The neoliberal agenda of financial judgement marks out educational success in terms of simplistic measures not entirely related to dealing with the issues which cause educational underachievement. For example, national standardised test scores indicate whether policies have been successful in one sense only; nor do they indicate whether or not children's housing standards have risen. The mechanisms by which education is judged are specific to the classroom and any relationship to wider social and political forces is usually underplayed. Neoliberal thinking posits that:

> educational policies should centre on removing schools from state and bureaucratic control; enhancing privatisation and marketisation; weakening the power of teachers and their unions; and reconstructing a people's character largely based in individual and entrepreneurial values.
>
> (Apple, 2009: 23)

ACTIVITY 1.1

How might the shift from Welfarism be a productive one? How might it engender greater efficiencies in the system?

The contradictions of New Right thinking

A summary of right wing and left wing ideology and corresponding educational policy can be found in Table 1.1.

TABLE 1.1 Right wing and left wing ideology

Ideology	Right Wing		Left Wing	
	Neoconservative	**Neoliberal**	**Social Democrat**	**Socialist**
	Conservative		**Labour**	
Key beliefs	Traditional values leading to a healthier, more stable society.	Market forces and individual freedom leading to greater economic efficiency.	Opportunity for all and responsibility for all.	Social equality for all. State ownership of major utilities and industries.
Education policy	Discipline, school uniform, 'proper subjects', traditional assessment.	Parental choice leading to competition between providers. League tables.	Choice and variety of schools within a strong state framework.	Free education provision. Abolition of public schools. A comprehensive education system for all.

Source: From Bartlett and Burton (2012: 137).

Neoliberalism and neoconservatism, then, seem to demonstrate contradictory thinking:

■ the individual versus strong government;

■ freedom of choice versus social authoritarianism;

■ a market society versus a disciplined society;

■ laissez-faire government versus hierarchy and subordination;

■ minimal government versus the nation.

As Trowler (2003) notes, the contradictions in New Right thinking are between the internal ideas of neoliberalism and neoconservatism. Thus the 'solid' sounding term 'New Right' actually represents a particular point of view. This means that that policy cannot be read off simply as 'New Right'; care should be taken to consider its leanings. It should be noted, then, that the New Right is more of an amalgam of ideologies rather than a coherent political ideology of its own; neoliberalism and neoconservatism emphasise different things.

Despite inherent contradictions in the two ideologies, neoconservatism and neoliberalism became welcome bedfellows in the New Right thinking of post-1979 Conservative governments. Held together by a shared distrust of socialist principles, a mistrust of professions and professional groups and strong leadership in Margaret Thatcher, the New Right agenda, as an amalgam of neoconservative and neoliberal thinking, sought to enact policies that, at the same time, pandered to free market principles whilst being somewhat traditionalist in orientation.

A good educational example of this contradictory thinking can be seen in the drive to both provide parents with information about school performance so that they might choose schools for their children, whilst at the same time mandating what it is that schools are required to teach through the National Curriculum. The former demonstrates key neoliberal thinking in that pitting school against school supposedly engenders increased performance and efficiency within a meritocratic regime. The latter holds up certain subjects deemed important in the education of the nation's children, some of which, at least, will be so classified due to their cultural heritage and traditional place on the curriculum. However, such state control of the curriculum was seen as necessary to engender free market ideals; give parents a level curriculum playing field and it will be easier for them to make their choices. Conservative reforms were designed to implement the neoliberal market whilst at the same time instil neoconservative traditional values.

The Conservative government of the 1980s and 1990s increased consumer power through the insertion of parental choice and differentiated schooling. However, whilst the means for schooling was devolved to schools, output requirements were set centrally.

Education and the New Right

In the 1980s, as part of this New Right agenda, review and control mechanisms became commonplace in an effort to instil an accountability culture (Henkel, 1991). This sits in contrast with the 1960s and 1970s where public services such as education were professionally led and where state control operated along persuasive rather than coercive lines. The 1980s saw the introduction of 'objective' evaluation driven by the key tenets of efficiency, effectiveness, performance and value for money; a drive towards deploying statistical measures, usually gleaned from test results, to determine whether or not education was 'improving'. This 'shift towards quantitative knowledge reinforced drives for certainty, for clear priorities and for conceptualising performance in terms of tangible outcome' (Henkel, 1991: 134).

It is important to note how the New Right more broadly and neoliberalism more specifically orient the individual. Here is seen the 'active' citizen with rights, duties, obligations and expectations; the citizen becomes an active social and moral entrepreneur (Davies and Bansel, 2007: 252). In this way the social sits in opposition and deference to the economic; in support the economy is restructured and privatised and the labour market likewise.

> There is no longer a conflict between the self-interest of the economic subject and the patriotic duty of the citizen: the newly responsibilised individuals fulfil their obligation to the nation/state by pursuing economic well-being for themselves and their family, for their employer, company, business or corporation.
>
> (Davies and Bansel, 2007: 252)

There is an emphasis on enterprise and the shrugging off of collective responsibility. The citizen becomes the middle class consumer. This positions the individual less favourably with regard to state intervention.

> As the state withdraws from welfare provision and diminishes its role in arenas such as health care, public education, and social services . . . it leaves larger and larger segments of the population exposed to impoverishment. The social safety net is reduced to a bare minimum in favour of a system that emphasizes personal responsibility. Personal failure is generally attributed to personal failings, and the victim is all too often blamed.
>
> (Harvey, 2005: 76)

And education is seen as merely a tradable service like any other: a better education can be exchanged for a better job. Whereas in the welfarist settlement, education was seen as vital to generating public good, under, particularly, neoliberalism, the public good carries no currency. The New Right orients the individual as self-regarding and a consumer: competition is seen as a necessary factor for entrepreneurship. It ignores that living conditions are so important a basis for educational success. Profit can be gleaned from the provision of educational services.

It is important to note, though, that Thatcher did not find it easy to dismantle the state apparatuses of, for example, education, the universities or the judiciary. What she did manage to inculcate, however, was a culture of entrepreneurialism, accountability and productivity. Although her party desired to privatise education through, for example, activities such as a voucher system which would pass choice of school completely to parents, she was never particularly successful.

The market state

For Ainley (2004), the move to competition rather than cooperation was manifest in the shift from Welfarism to a market-state. This marketplace discourse provided the basis for social, economic and political change. In the market-state, law gives way to the market and management gives way to capital; the emphasis for public services ceases to be the operationalisation of Welfarism, replaced instead by a concentration on customer needs and efficiency. A world market was created which operated independently of states. The nation-state ceased being the centre of attention; instead, markets and business became the defining feature. As Bobbitt (2002: 211) noted

> Whereas the nation-state with its mass free public education, universal franchise, and social security policies, promised to guarantee the welfare of the nation, the market-state promises instead to maximise the opportunity of the people and, thus, tends to privatise many state activities and to make voting and representative government less influential and more responsive to the market.

The marketplace is lauded for its opportunity giving powers. Privatisation is welcomed, even in education. And the role for the welfare state changes from protective to the body responsible for monitoring and controlling 'good behaviour' (Ainley, 2004). It takes on an opportunity distributing function rather than its previous role to redistribute wealth; under this new discourse, the most dynamic are rewarded (European Trade Union Institute, 2001). In the 1980s the state became a 'holding company' which subcontracted services. Rather than simply delivering services itself, the market-state system began to look at its functions anew through the mechanism of contracting out often to the lowest bidder. In this way responsibility was decentralised but power was centralised. Government maintained control of the direction for policy, but required local organisations to work on its behalf; if these organisations were private, so be it. Organisations were free to respond as they saw fit, but within mandates set by central government. The state's role became minimal, driven mostly by the provision of incentives and control.

In the market economy risk replaces need when defining services; that is to say, the provision of services is not based on universal notions but rather follows a business orientation whereby provision is determined by whether or not services can operate efficiently. Notably, the middle classes are better positioned to deploy economic capital to buy educational advantage. This idea of the market is pursued further in Chapter 5.

New Labour

Neoliberalism and, to a lesser degree neoconservatism, has certainly held sway in political decision-making over the last 30 years. Whilst different governments have favoured a harder or weaker neoliberal line it is clear that internationally, neoliberalism seems to be in the ascendency. Indeed, today this economic consensus mandates that global competitiveness be seen as the driving force for national policy-making with favourable pro-choice governance mechanisms being put in place (Kelly, 2009). The aim of government now is to create conditions for facilitating innovation and investment, to keep wages and taxes as low as possible and to develop competitive modes of governance (Kelly, 2009: 54). Whilst the state is rolled back, new modes of governance and regulation come into effect to ensure that the individual acts in accordance with the doctrine of the neoliberal agenda. For education this has meant the state 'passing the ball' (Kelly, 2009) to the school in order to solve problems. The school and individual teachers have become the focus of control; contractual strategies, such as performance management, are deployed that position both school and teacher as responsible for overall performance of the system (Bonal, 2003). In truth, in England, the state performs a political pirouette: on the one hand it leaves to the school leader the means to organise and run the establishment, but it mandates how this should occur through control measures such as inspection and curriculum. If the state is required to take a more 'hands-on' approach, it is in a remedial function, a problem-solving role always as the result of an emergency. Hence is seen the status of 'special measures', or 'requires improvement' following an Ofsted inspection, coupled to 'notices to improve', all of which are statements that the school has not managed to adhere to that which the state defines as acceptable. Once the emergency has gone, the state retreats because the market will allocate and distribute resources much better than any bureaucracy (Bonal, 2003).

It is not just political parties on the right of the political spectrum that have embraced this way of thinking. The election to power of New Labour in 1997 might have been seen as the end of neoliberal policy-making in public services in the UK. Instead, however, New Labour held on steadfastly to some of the doctrines of the New Right. Whilst it is disingenuous to say that they simply continued with Conservative policies, it is not unfair to state that their political leanings were squarely behind markets and associated principles. New Labour, under Tony Blair as Prime Minister, followed 'Third Way' thinking, the architect of which could be said to have been sociologist Anthony Giddens. The Third Way is an essentially centrist approach and although it purports to be non-ideological it is necessarily so, drawing together, as it does, democratic socialism and liberalism for its vitality (Bates et al., 2011).

The Third Way

As with New Right thinking, the Third Way is an amalgam of ideas: three alternative versions of the Third Way can be identified (Gamble and Kelly, cited in Power and Whitty, 1999). Whichever approach is used, the Third Way was seen as something new:

- a middle way between capitalism and socialism;
- a revised social democratic approach offering a clear alternative to neoliberalism;
- the creation of a new and heterodox (outside of mainstream thinking) alignment of political ideas.

For New Labour, the third version is that which was followed. This facilitated the adoption of elements of Conservative thinking such as a national curriculum and inspection. Ball (2001) cites three ways in which New Labour appeared to take policy from the Conservative Party:

- choice and competition: the commodification and consumerisation of education;
- autonomy and performativity: the managerialisation and commercialisation of education;
- centralisation and prescription: the imposition of centrally determined assessments, schemes of work and classroom methods.

Bates et al. (2011: 54) note that with regard to education such thinking led to:

- the operation of market forces via competition between schools for pupils;
- the continuation of parental choice;
- the maintenance of a national curriculum and a focus on the 'basics';
- increased accountability;
- a focus on standards through assessment and testing;
- naming, shaming and closing schools;
- a focus on the use of information and communications technology (ICT).

However, the new heterodox also meant the adoption of new ways, some not traditionally associated with New Right thinking, to run in parallel with the above (Bates et al., 2011: 54):

- higher levels of public spending on education;
- more emphasis on social justice and inclusion;
- greater emphasis on partnerships and collaboration;
- greater emphasis on early years education and care;
- reduced class sizes;
- the expansion of further and higher education;
- privatisation;
- the use of paraprofessionals (teaching assistants) in the classroom.

Reay (2008: 640) notes that 'in many ways Blair has trod a well-worn path, following the steps of Old Tory policies, as much as he has forged a "new" Third Way in educational policy.' Indeed, in initial New Labour policies

> it is possible to detect the promotion of renewed state involvement and investment, a confined role for markets, reference to egalitarian principles and some indication that the welfare state should provide support for education, at least from the cradle if not to the grave.
>
> (Power and Whitty, 1999: 537)

Paterson (2003) notes that New Labour, in its educational policies across Britain, adopted three ideologies:

- New Labourism: stemming from the New Right of the 1980s and nineteenth-century Liberalism;
- Developmentalism: designed to promote the nation-state as one actor in a cut throat international, world economy;

■ New social democracy: which sees unregulated capitalism as an inadequate mechanism by which to run the country. A role for the public sector is foregrounded along with power and wealth redistribution and the creation of opportunity.

New Labour and the left/right dichotomy

The involvement of the state marked a transition from New Right thinking and demonstrated some of the left-leaning tendencies of New Labour. The state, under New Labour, sought to intervene more directly in education and policies were designed to benefit the many, not just the few. Notably, Blair's Third Way adopted a 'what works' approach; a creative partnership between neoliberalism and social democracy, although this is challenged by Power and Whitty (1999) who maintain that New Labour was more likely to do what was easy and what was popular.

For many, New Labour was more right-leaning than left. In England and in relation to schools policy, it certainly seems that the middle way was skewed heavily towards the New Right.

> in terms of the balance between old left and new right, there can be little doubt that the 'middle way' is skewed heavily to the new right. The prevalence of new right policies certainly invalidates any claims that New Labour's third way matches Gamble and Kelly's . . . 'revised social democratic approach offering a clear alternative to the neoliberal project'.
>
> (Power and Whitty, 1999: 541)

And Paterson (2003: 173) claims

> It seems reasonable to take Blair at his ideological word: his Liberal instincts incline him to competitive individualism, real partnership between public and private, and using the state only where necessary but – unlike the New Right – certainly where necessary.

But the third way is not a uniquely British institution. Indeed, many countries adopted Third Way policies and politics throughout the late 1990s and early twenty-first century. This new agenda has been felt most powerfully across parts of Western Europe, the USA and Australasia. It is a global phenomenon.

ACTIVITY 1.2

While New Labour is now beginning to build on its more targeted efforts to tackle disadvantage by focusing additional resources on pupils who need greater support, this is within the context of broader policies on school improvements, diversification of schools and parental choice that have been based on a misrecognition of the impact of structural factors on learning and on the operation of the education market.

(WHITTY, 2008: 166)

How did New Labour's twin approach of markets and social democracy work? How might the project be held together?

The 2010 general election

On Thursday 6 May 2010 a general election was held. Turnout was 65.1 per cent. Labour won 258 seats, the Conservatives 306, the Liberal Democrats 57 and others 28. The pre-election forecast of no overall winner came true. Following the result there was a period of intense political lobbying and discussion. The Liberal Democrats held the balance of power, but only by siding with the Conservatives would they be able to make a coalition which had a majority in parliament. Discussions between the Conservatives and the Liberal Democrats ensued, as did brief discussion between the Liberal Democrats and Labour. The outcome was more or less inevitable; politically the Liberals Democrats have more in common with the Tories and the maths added up.

On 12 May the newly formed coalition of Conservatives and Liberal Democrats published its manifesto for government. This manifesto stated its intention regarding education forcibly:

> The Government believes that we need to reform our school system to tackle educational inequality, which has widened in recent years, and to give greater powers to parents and pupils to choose a good school. We want to ensure high standards of discipline in the classroom, robust standards and the highest quality teaching. We also believe that the state should help parents, community groups and others come together to improve the education system by starting new schools.
>
> (Cabinet Office, 2010: 28)

Teachers and teaching

In keeping with the election manifestos of both parties, Coalition support was pledged for Teach First. Additionally, Teach Now was proposed to build on the work of the Graduate Teacher Programme. The government also pledged to seek to attract more top science and maths graduates to be teachers and existing national pay and conditions rules were to be reformed to give schools greater freedoms. Finally, anonymity was promised for teachers accused by pupils.

Teaching and learning

A major plank of the Coalition's manifesto for government was the freeing up of schools to do what is necessary for the children in their care. In this vein, schools were to be given greater freedom over the curriculum. This was particularly the case for academies and free schools; they would have to provide for a broad and balanced curriculum that included maths, English and science but which, to all other intents and purposes, could be decided by the school. There was no requirement to follow the National Curriculum.

A pupil premium was to be established that would provide extra resources for disadvantaged pupils as defined by free school meals (FSM). Schools were to be given extra support to tackle bullying and heads and teachers were to assume greater powers to ensure appropriate and successful discipline in schools. Finally, there was to be a drive to improve the quality of vocational education.

Inspection and accountability

At the heart of the Coalition's reforms was a desire to see that all schools are held properly to account. Ofsted's remit was to be narrowed, focusing on four key areas: teaching and learning; standards; behaviour; and leadership. Whilst external assessment at Key Stage Two was to stay, a review of these tests was to occur along with an increase in flexibility in the exams system as a whole. League tables would also be reformed so that schools could focus on, and demonstrate, the progress of children of all abilities; the 'gaming' behaviour so roundly condemned later on in the 2010 White Paper was to end.

What is notable from the above is the sway the Tories held in determining policy. Indeed, their Big Society agenda is writ large in the Coalition agreement. The Big Society is premised on the idea that big government is inadequate as a means to get things done. Rather than continue with state run mechanisms, this ideology has its roots in local, community action and democracy. Rather than provide everything from the centre, the Big Society seeks to address local concerns with local solutions. Once again it is an amalgam of neoliberalism and neoconservatism: free up the market to provide solutions by taking power away from politicians and giving it to the people, whilst ensuring that order and discipline occur. Whilst the Big Society has its supporters many have found it vacuous and wanting. The then Archbishop of Canterbury, Dr Rowan Williams, described it as 'designed to conceal a deeply damaging withdrawal of the state from its responsibilities to the most vulnerable' (Helm and Coman, 2012).

Putting this into practice

When reading education policy since 2010, it should be remembered that the UK is embroiled in a huge financial and economic crisis. Partly as a result of over-borrowing during the Labour years and partly due to the collapse of parts of the financial sector, Britain is faced with mounting debts and a need to reduce its fiscal deficit. Indeed, this was part of a global drive to bring national economies into line with much of Europe facing financial hardship: many countries required a European Union bailout to meet their obligations. Within this context education was to face cuts in its settlement. Although the schools budget was frozen, the overall education budget was cut; it was projected that there would be a reversal of 13.4 per cent of spending based on the Labour period in the period 2011 to 2015 (Chowdry and Sibieta, 2011).

The first action undertaken by the Secretary of State for Education was to rename the Department for Children, Schools and Families (DCSF) the Department for Education (DfE). This signalled a much tighter focus on the core business of teaching and learning; in particular a view of education that was traditionally oriented and based upon knowledge and discipline was foregrounded.

The importance of teaching

In November 2010 the government produced its first education White Paper *The Importance of Teaching* (DfE, 2010a). As the title suggests, this document held that teaching and teachers should be at the heart of change and development in the education system. The idea was to be radical so as to ensure that standards were raised in particular for those groups traditionally under-achieving. Three aspects were exemplified in the proposals.

- That the quality of teachers is paramount. Heads and teachers were to be given increased powers to deal with poor and disruptive behaviour. Schools were to be freed from excessive bureaucracy and a new 'champion' role for local authorities was to come into effect, replacing the more traditional role of supplier of educational services. Synthetic phonics was to be introduced as the official method for teaching reading, and teachers were to be trained in these methods. Ofsted's remit was to change to concentrate on four areas: teaching and learning; pupil performance; leadership and management; and behaviour. School-based teacher training was to be expanded and new teaching schools were to be created to take on this role in place of higher education.

- As much power as possible was to be devolved to the front line. New types of schools were to be established including the aforementioned academies and free schools. Such schools were to challenge the traditional dominance of the maintained sector and offer schools real freedoms to innovate and be creative. The English Baccalaureate was introduced in the summer of 2010 which required schools to comment on the number of students gaining A* to C grades in all of English, maths, a science, a modern or ancient language and a humanity. The E-Bacc was designed to meet the accusation that schools were concentrating on vocational subjects in order to meet the targets set by previous governments (Abbott et al., 2013). In addition, the National Curriculum was to be reviewed with a focus on the core knowledge in the core subjects but with enhanced freedoms for schools. Academies and free schools were to be exempt from the new National Curriculum.

- The underachievement of the poor was to be tackled. A pupil premium was to be introduced that targeted disadvantaged pupils. Schools would be given a sum of money for every pupil eligible for an FSM which they would be free to spend as they see fit. This was designed to 'raise educational standards among the poorest members of society and to reduce the attainment gap between rich and poor (Abbott et al., 2013: 183). Performance tables were to be reviewed to focus on achievement of all pupils and the use of contextual value added measures was to cease. Importantly, however, the Educational Maintenance Allowance (EMA) paid to eligible 16- to 19-years-olds in full-time further education was to be scrapped and replaced with a locally administered fund.

Oft quoted was Finland. The White Paper was clear that Finland was a country whose educational success the government wished to emulate. Yet the paper elided the fact that Finland has a comprehensive education system that was entirely unstreamed (Gillard, 2011). Private providers do not operate in Finland's schools and teachers have to attain a masters level qualification in order to be able to practice and are able to command a higher than OECD average salary.

What was clear was a strong right wing ideology. Both the Liberal Democrats and the Conservative Party favoured neoliberal and neoconservative mechanisms by which to try to improve educational success. With regard to the former, the continuation and extension of the academies model saw an increase in the use of private enterprise to run English schools. Regarding the latter, proposals to alter the National Curriculum so that it concentrated on facts harked back to a bygone era where subject knowledge held sway. Changes were to be driven by this right of centre model, directed by Education Secretary Michael Gove.

Conclusion

This chapter has discussed the role ideology plays in formulating political and educational policy. The ways in which ideology is used show that for education, politics is an inherent part of the policy-making process. However, this is not to assume that ideology alone formulates policy; rather political ideology must be read carefully, for many other features, such as pragmatism, will facilitate its development. This said, it is clear that education is an inherently political act and to ignore politics is to ignore a central part of the educational endeavour.

The politics of the post-war years centred on the rebuilding of the state and the creation of welfare mechanisms that would enable this to happen. In this regard, education was seen as too important to be left to the vagaries of the marketplace (Bottery, 2005). The welfarist settlement sought to guarantee security, inclusion, well-being and stability. Full employment, economic growth and citizen welfare were striven for.

However, by the late 1960s and 1970s this settlement was challenged by those on the right of the political spectrum and economic survival became the measure of success. 1979 saw the first woman prime minster elected to power: Margaret Thatcher. Her New Right ideologies sought to roll back the state and put economics at the heart of government. But her government agendas were an amalgam of neoconservative and neoliberal thinking and in some respects these two ideologies competed for space. In the educational arena potentially contradictory polices such as parental choice and a national curriculum were instigated, although they were justified as complementary by New Right adherents. In the end, neoliberalism was in the ascendency, however, driving, as it did, much education and social policy of the time. Efficiency and effectiveness were the watchwords and a business mentality was to be adopted across all of the public sector. In 1997 New Labour was voted into power with the slogan of 'Education, Education, Education'. Their's was a Third Way, a new amalgam of neoliberalism and social democracy which sought to do things anew. However, despite an increased role for the state and some notable policies designed to reduce social exclusion, Third Wayism was essentially a rightist ideology, particularly with regard to education.

The Coalition has continued with much of New Labour's thinking, particularly with regard to the academies programme, whilst on the other hand it has sought to distance itself from that which went before, particularly with regard to the curriculum and the ways in which teachers are rewarded. Once again, neoliberalism seems to take centre stage, but the Coalition has a pressing need to return to bygone days in the form of a curriculum replete with subjects and facts and notions of teaching that emulate drill and skill, such as synthetic phonics.

Key points

- Ideology is a difficult term to pin down; it has acquired a variety of meanings over a considerable history.

- Here, ideology is taken to mean a set of ideas and beliefs about the world held by a group of people.

- Political positions can be said to be ideological.

- Politically speaking, ideologies can be broadly said to be left or right, although this is a rather simplistic categorisation. Political parties change their position over time.

- Policy, however, derives from a number of different sources: educational, pragmatic, through negotiation, etc. Policy is not always a direct result of political ideology.

- Following the Second World War, the welfarist settlement drove the development of social policy, and values such as equity, care and social justice came to the fore. The state was seen to be a moderator of the marketplace.

- Some services, such as education, were to be provided by the state; they were seen as too important to be left to markets.

- New Right politics of the 1980s were very much in tune with individualism, private property, personal responsibility and family values.

- New Right thinking was an amalgam of neoconservative and neoliberal thinking. Neoconservatives believe in morality, law and order, tradition and hierarchy. Neoliberals, on the other hand, believe in the power of the market. Efficiency and minimal interference by government are seen to be the best way to structure civil and economic society.

- New Right thinking places the emphasis on the individual to ensure that they meet their own needs.

- The abolition of state involvement alongside a commitment to free trade marks the neo-liberal line. The state merely exists to facilitate individual choice.

- Under neoliberalism the individual is recast from social being to consumer.

- In educational terms, neoliberalism holds that schools should compete with schools and that parents should be positioned as consumers. Local education authorities are not needed, for the market will out, providing a rationale for the organisation of schools and schooling.

- Neoliberalism elevates 'middle class ideals' as those to emulate.

- The New Right was an amalgam of two competing forces: neoliberalism and neoconservatism.

- Educationally, the New Right advocated the rise of the middle class consumer parent. Educational failings were seen to be the fault of the 'victim'.

- For Ainley (2004) this was manifest in the discourse of the market state.

- In contemporary educational systems schools become responsible for solving problems and effecting educational improvement.

- New Labour offered a Third Way approach to solving educational problems.

- This meant the adoption of neoliberal ideals coupled to a reformed and redefined role for the state.

Further reading

Giddens, A. (1998) *The Third Way: The Renewal of Social Democracy*, London: Wiley. Anthony Giddens' book which introduced the ideas of the Third Way.

Harvey, D. (2005) *A Brief History of Neoliberalism*, Oxford: Oxford University Press. This book provides an excellent introduction to the principles and history of neoliberalism.

Paterson, L. (2003) 'The three educational ideologies of the British Labour Party, 1997–2001', *Oxford Review of Education*, **29**(2), 165–186. This article charts the development of New Labour's Third Way vision in education during Blair's first term in office.

2

Education policy and policy-making

Purpose of this chapter

After reading this chapter you should understand:

- that education is one facet of social policy;
- that there are differing definitions for policy but all share common features;
- that government can use different instruments and levels of involvement to action policy;
- the distinction between analysis *of* and analysis *for* policy;
- how context is vital when analysing policy.

Education policy and education studies

Education policy as an academic area of study has found its niche in the last 30 or so years. An appreciation of the need to analyse the work of government and the ways and means by which policy and legislation interact to influence the educational agenda is now considered to be de-rigueur on any education studies course. Analysis *of* policy is an academic endeavour in its own right, as is analysis *for* policy. Much that passes for undergraduate study is of the former type: an appreciation of how and why policy both reflects and influences policy. This chapter sets out to consider the nature of policy and policy-making both as practical and theoretical matters.

Education and social policy

Before considering education, it is worth spending a brief time discussing social policy. This has many meanings but simply put, social policy refers to the mechanisms by which government (predominately) provides for people in a society. Such provision takes the form of welfare (the provision of mechanisms by which individuals and groups, such as families, can be provided for) and social protection (for example, through the provision of local antisocial laws and mechanisms). Because education seeks to better the education of individuals and groups in society and because it desires to effect social change, it is a subset of social policy, along with health, housing and social security amongst others.

What is policy?

There is not a self-evident answer to this (Heclo, 1972; Rizvi and Lingard, 2010). Often policy is thought of as a thing: a statement written down (Trowler, 2003) and usually thought of in relation to government. Dye (1992: 4) provides the most succinct of all definitions when he says that 'policy is whatever governments choose to do or not to do'. Here, policies are believed to be the pronouncements of the government of the day with regard to aspects of social and public life. Certainly, government action has a great part to play and in this regard any policy analysis would have to consider the roles played by governments and political organisations. But other organisations create policy as well and this should be remembered. For example, it is clear that in the UK broadly, and England more specifically, public–private partnerships are becoming more apparent. These are situations where government will work with private organisations to deliver on policy matters. It may be, for example, that a private consortium will build a new school and then lease it to the local authority. For this reason, if no other, policy analysis can go further than government.

This is a product view of policy but is insufficient, however; it is far too limited. We need to think carefully about what policy might be in relation to action, and this is a difficult task. We might construe policy as being the actions taken in relation to some specific standpoint. For example, a current policy proposal is to allow ex-service men and women without degrees to train to be teachers in two years rather than three or four. The standpoint taken here is that such individuals have much to offer in the way of skills and discipline. Whilst actions do play a part in determining policy, they are not what constitute it in its entirety. Actions stem from policy as well as being creative of the policy itself; that is, actions demonstrate a particular policy stance whilst at the same time determining, in part, what the policy will be. In the previous example, the action to allow ex-troops to train in this way determines what actions to take and the actions themselves determine the stance about such individuals. This is complicated, but it is sufficient to note that actions are, therefore, part of the policy cycle and should be considered in any analysis. There is, then, an inextricable link between action and policy. Trowler (2003: 96) discusses this dynamic, process view as stemming from three sources:

■ conflict among those who make policy as well as those who put it into practice;
■ policy statements are open to an array of interpretations;
■ policy 'on the ground' is extremely complex.

It must be remembered, though, that not all actions are demonstrative of, or will influence, policy. Sometimes things happen that sit outside of the policy-making process. So, for example, if a government wishes to identify required levels of attainment at age

16 and it is not a part of the policy that entry for vocational examinations increases then the fact that this increase may occur could be due to something outside of the original process such as a perception that vocational exams offer a better chance of attaining the levels required by government.

For this reason we need a definition of policy that recognises the interrelationship between the two, but which is not beholden to activity. Heclo (1972: 84) does this: for him, the term policy 'is usually considered to apply to something "bigger" than particular decisions, but "smaller" than general social movements'. His work, citing other authors, displays important issues pertaining to any discussion of what policy is. Policy:

- consists of related activities and their consequences;
- is a form of more generalised decision-making;
- consists of decisions and the interrelations between decisions;
- has purpose (so implying goals, means, purpose, target and declared intent).

As Jenkins writes, policy 'is a set of interrelated decisions . . . concerning the selection of goals and the means of achieving them within a specified situation' (Jenkins, 1978: 15). In other words, policy is the ways and means by which intentions are translated into action. Care must be taken here though: just because policy implies a set of actions this does not imply that such actions will ultimately occur or, if they do happen, that they will elicit the response they desired. Clearly, policies exist that have not secured the outcomes planned for and have led to unintended consequences. A notable example is the way in which certain schools, under New Labour, entered students for certain GCSEs in order to secure higher grade point averages. Smith (1976: 13) therefore notes that policy is a 'deliberate choice of action or inaction, rather than the effects of interrelating forces'. This is important; Smith signals that policy may consist of resistance to change; a desire to maintain the status quo. In this sense action is defined by inactivity: the lack of change as a preferred outcome.

For Rizvi and Lingard (2010: 4) policy expresses

> patterns of decisions in the context of other decisions taken by political actors on behalf of state institutions from positions of authority. Public bodies are thus normative, express-ing both ends and means designed to steer the actions and behaviour of people. Finally, policy refers to things that can in principle be achieved, to matters over which authority can be exercised.

Clearly, then, policy is difficult to pin down. Whilst it may be possible to identify some com-mon themes in the literature, it is by no means clear. Policy is, however, goal directed. It is purposive and is undertaken to attempt to meet some end. In this way, we can discern some features common to most definitions of policy. Policy is about intention (what is desired) and effect (what occurs). It is certainly action-oriented (with the caveat that action might well be defined by inactivity) and it is a system of organised decision-making. A series of disconnected actions would not, therefore, constitute policy. Here there is a need to consider how action comes to the fore; for how someone decides to proceed must depend upon how they view that particular situation or issue. It is notable that values must therefore play a part in the defi-nition and enactment of policy. Even a policy of inactivity will stem from a series of decisions that will have been, at some point, guided by a particular value or ideological system, although the mechanisms and value sets by which this occurs might well differ from case to case. It is the web of decisions and decision-making within the policy process that denotes such values. Historically, politics and policy-making were separate and the latter was seen to be authorised and specialised; a hierarchical and instrumental process (Moutsios, 2010); it was seen to be:

- goal oriented;
- instrumentally rationalist;
- technical;
- neutral.

As Moutsios (2010: 124) notes,

> In this sense, education policy-making should be considered a hierarchical, expert-driven and goal-oriented process of decision-making which is based on a taken-for-granted or implicit political opinion about the purpose, the content and the pedagogic mode of learning.

Policy instruments

Accepting, then, that policy relates to a determined series of actions influenced by a particular set of values or an overarching ideology necessitates an examination of how policy is put into practice. Policy can manifest at a number of levels from the school to the nation state. For example, all schools will have written documents that attempt to guide action within the establishment in areas such as teaching and learning, anti-bullying, sex and relationships education, working with parents and so on. Similarly, at a local level, whilst the work of local authorities is currently under intense scrutiny and reorganisation, policies for such things as special educational needs provision and school transport do exist. But whilst we cannot forget this local context, or indeed the private sphere and its influence on policy (see above), we are, in this book, concerned, mainly, with policy at a national level and in this regard we can consider the ways in which government influences social policy matters, including education.

What is evident is that government does not have to carry through all of the policy process itself. Simply put, activity can occur somewhere on a continuum of high to low state involvement. Government can rely on other organisations such as the private or the voluntary sector to undertake the policy implementation. Low levels of state involvement can be said to have traditionally been the province of centre right governments such as those headed by the Conservative Party, although this has by no means always been the case. The current coalition government through its theory of 'The Big Society' (Norman, 2010) currently desires to use instruments such as community groups and the private and voluntary sector to carry through its social policy.

Conversely, governments that have deployed a greater control of state intervention have traditionally been on the left of the political spectrum. Here state instruments such as direct legislation or control of workers or the direct provision of services and resources has occurred. Once again, though, this has not always been the case. This is evident in the work of New Labour between 1997 and 2007. Under the leadership of Tony Blair private enterprise was often seen as being the most efficient way to ensure policy delivery. But New Labour was often contradictory in its approach, favouring on the one hand the direct control of state education through target setting and highly prescriptive strategies whilst on the other using the private sector to monitor results and marshal support.

ACTIVITY 2.1

- Choose a national education policy. *For example, you might choose the National Literacy Strategy as brought in by New Labour. Policies can be found by reading various books and articles on education policy as well as by searching the DfE website.*

- Which government initiated this policy? *This might be relatively straightforward as the date will indicate which government brought it in. However, it is also the case that one government may have thought of or piloted this, but another government may have enacted it. The National Literacy Strategy of 1998 is a case in point. This was piloted by the Conservative government of John Major, but introduced wholesale by Tony Blair's New Labour.*

- Identify how the policy has been implemented.

  a   Who did the training so that the policy might be implemented? *It might be that training was not a part of the policy, or it might be that the policy had a large training component. An example is the Literacy Strategy mentioned above. Initially, training was done by regional advisers who cascaded information to schools. However, LEAs also had a role to play and employed consultants to 'spread the word'. Teachers in school were also deployed as leading teachers to work with teachers in other schools.*

  b   Who did the monitoring? *In the case of the Literacy Strategy, monitoring was undertaken by the schools themselves and by the local consultants. However, part of the strategy was the setting of local and school-based targets for achieving level 4 on the standard assessment tests (SATs) (this is discussed later in Chapters 4 and 8). These targets certainly concentrated the minds of teachers and other school staff.*

  c   Who employed those undertaking this work? *In the case of the Literacy Strategy, schools and LEAs, although the Department for Education and Employment/ Department for Education and Skills (DfEE/DfES) employed regional advisers to monitor the uptake and progress of the policy.*

- Did the government of the day use high or low levels of state involvement or a mixture? *What is interesting about literacy is that it was never statutory to use the strategy. However, because of the ways in which state apparatus was used, and the mechanisms attached to the policy were deployed, effectively schools acted as though it were.*

It is the case that a variety of instruments and organisations can be used to effect policy, from taxation to direct action on the part of specific groups. This is important when considering policy and its effects for if we are to identify the mechanisms by which policy has become *enacted* (Ball et al., 2012) there is a need to recognise the role played by others than the government. The ways in which other groups make and shape policy explicitly calls into question the policies themselves and the discourses that surround them.

Levels of policy analysis

Previously, a distinction has been made between analysis *of* policy and analysis *for* policy. This is important, for the two carry different connotations. Analysis *of* policy implies the reading and interpretation of various policies and policy instruments. It is the study of content, outputs and processes. Someone who wanted to perform an analysis of the 2011 Higher Education Bill (DBIS, 2011) would concern themselves with identifying aspects of what it had to say, to whom it was speaking, what the intended outputs were and the processes by which the policy would be realised in practice. There might also be a reading in relation to other social policy missives such as the White Paper *The Importance of Teaching* (DfE, 2010a). Someone undertaking an analysis of the policy may well even try to determine the different interpretations that could be made and how these might pan out in the world of higher education. This latter activity might be called policy forecasting.

Analysis *for* policy is different, however. It may not be divorced from analysis of policy, but it has a different agenda. Analysis for policy implies consideration of different actions and values position so that policy might be influenced and made. It consists of activities such as evaluation or impact studies to determine the efficacy or otherwise of a certain series of decisions. In this way information is provided that is used *for* policy-making. The emphasis here is on gleaning enough quality information so that decisions about policy direction might be made and maintained. Part of such analyses, then, is a consideration of agenda setting as well as the production of policy texts (Rizvi and Lingard, 2010).

Those studying for education or related degrees will more than likely not engage in analysis for policy. Analysis of policy is relatively easier to undertake whereas to influence policy, even at a local level is more costly, time-consuming and difficult. This is not to say that such work never occurs; rather it acknowledges the ways in which degree courses are organised and run. Teacher education and training students may well have opportunities to influence policy in their partner school, but such opportunities are less likely for those engaged in more theoretical study unless through their research or direct work placement; it is the analysis *of* policy that is most likely to exercise such students.

Policy creation

Before policy can be enacted it needs to be created. There are many theories of policy creation, some more simple than others. Ultimately, though, they rely on some form of issue to be identified and possible solutions to be proposed and adopted/dismissed. It is important to remember that inaction or the decision not to take action can be the result of policy implementation just as much as activity or change. It is not necessary for something to have occurred for a policy to be enacted; as stated above; the policy can, just as easily, be to take no action or deliberately stop action from occurring. A good example might be the work of the Rose Review (DCSF, 2008) into the primary curriculum. Although New Labour desired to implement the recommendations of the review, the policy of the incoming coalition government was to halt this. They, instead, instigated their own review.

In this section we will further consider the stagist approach along with 'social constructionist theory' as means to conceive of the policy creation cycle.

Whilst political issues are an important part of policy creation, it is necessary to remember that there can be contradictions in educational policy-making and that these contradictions need to be ironed out in some way, shape or form:

- centralisation versus decentralisation contradiction;
- enterprise versus traditionalism contradiction;
- idealistic versus pragmatic contradiction;
- the widening participation versus increasing the financial burden of education contradiction.

'Stagist' approaches to policy creation

Stagist approaches assume that the policy-creation cycle follows a set pattern even if the actions and outcomes at each level are not always determinable. The simplest way to consider policy creation here is to think of it as a problem-solving event. An issue is identified, decisions are taken about what should be done and solutions are offered and enacted. This simple process is termed a 'stagist' approach because the work occurs in stages that can be defined as discrete events. Jenkins (1978) provides a simple process for the creation and enactment of policy:

- *Initiation*. Here decisions are taken which mean that action (or inaction) needs to be taken. This forms the basis for the policy-making cycle.
- *Information* is gathered that enables further reflection and debate. Such information can be from a variety of sources, but key is the belief that what is gathered is both pertinent to the policy process and accurate.
- *Consideration* is then given to the information. Here, individuals and groups will take stock of that gathered and check for accuracy and worth and for possible ways forward.
- *Decisions* will then be taken as to what course of action (or inaction) is required and how best to proceed.
- The actions are then *implemented* in a variety of ways consistent with the decisions taken before.
- It is at this stage that the work undertaken to date will be considered and *evaluated*. Such evaluations may be conducted externally to the process or by those implementing the actions. It is common for any evaluation to be external, however. The results of such evaluations are often used to re-inform the policy process.
- *Termination*. It is not always the case that policies continue. Some have a definite lifespan and cease after a set period. Sometimes the policy has a built in timeframe, whilst on other occasions termination occurs following the election of a new government. It may be that a policy has not worked and is therefore stopped.

Jenkins' work demonstrates a neat series of steps which, when followed, lead, hopefully, to a neat outcome: appropriate decisions are taken based on appropriate evidence and appropriate actions are put in place (Table 2.1). Indeed, this stagist approach is similar to the work of Hogwood and Gunn (1984: 13–19) who described policy as a 'label for a field of activity', 'an expression of general purpose', 'decisions of government', 'formal authorisation', 'a programme' and both 'output and outcome'. Whilst essentially the same process as that of Jenkins, their stagist approach is somewhat more elaborate.

TABLE 2.1 A stagist approach to policy creation

• Deciding to decide	***Initiation***
• Deciding how to decide	
• Issue definition	
• Forecasting	
• Setting objectives and priorities	
• Options analysis	***Creation***
• Implementation, monitoring, control	
• Evaluation and review	***Implementation and development***
• Maintenance, succession, termination	

Source: after Hogwood and Gunn (1984).

This process can be delineated into three main areas of work: initiation; creation; and implementation and development, with clear parallels with Jenkins. What is of note here is the way in which Hogwood and Gunn discuss the decision-making process. It is clear that for them decision-making is a time-laden process that involves not only deciding to decide, but also defining issues, forecasting and setting priorities and objectives. This is a much richer interpretation than Jenkins and gives a rounder picture of the ways in which decisions relating to policy are made. Certainly, in the world of policy creation, possibilities are often forecasted so that politicians and policy-makers have a better idea of likely outcome.

In a similar vein, Rein (1983) discusses three basic steps for national policy-making:

- problem or issue setting;
- mobilising government action;
- achieving settlement to appease different values.

Technicist-empiricist policy creation and analysis

What these two versions allude to is some form of rational decision-making process whereby issues are identified, the most appropriate solution chosen and implemented and the outcomes monitored and evaluated (Bates et al., 2011); in essence, what this approach seeks to do is produce a definitive position for policy from a set of truths known by those involved in the policy creation. That is to say, certain individuals decide on the situation in hand and follow the policy process to its logical conclusion. It follows, therefore, that policy analysis, in this vein, would seek to also produce something definitive; something that demonstrates an underlying truth that can be captured by the policy and the policy process. Any analysis, then, would seek to identify the *real* meanings behind the policy, its creation and execution; a search for *the* truth. This is the position of the traditional policy sciences as they sought to

> derive so called 'objective', value-free methods for the writing and reading of policy, [in an] . . . attempt to give technical and scientific sophistication to the policy process in order to buttress its intellectual legitimacy.
>
> (Olssen et al., 2004: 2)

This approach sought to ensure that no vested interests could be said to have clouded the agenda; the decisions arrived at were distanced from the thoughts of the individuals involved. Termed a technocratic approach, this method assigns various reasons for each of the stages for the policy-making process and, accordingly, similar reasons for the analysis of policy that ensues. Also, participants would find themselves designated particular roles within the process, roles that reflected objectively identified jobs with associated requirements. It is also the case that the type of information used is more often than not statistical in nature, the assumption being that numbers give objectivity. So, for example, the numbers of pupils achieving a certain grade in a test, as an example of average performance for a certain age, would be identified and such results would be used to describe whether or not an issue existed. This, in turn, would lead policy-makers to identify whether or not a new policy was needed, or whether an alteration in existing policy is necessary. Of course, the decision may be made that no change at all is required.

But it is the dispassionate nature of such decision-making that comes to the fore here. By using positivist measures, bias can be said to have been removed. It is 'facts' that are described and accepted and that form the basis for the production of policy imperatives. More importantly, any ensuing policy is assumed to have captured the 'truth' of the matter: the problem has been solved and the communication of this 'truth' and the articulation of a range of possible responses provide the means by which activity might be designed. It is also the case that activity is often couched in terms of local mediation; that is, local contexts provide the backdrop against which initiatives and actions are formed and performed.

Such technocratic policy mechanisms identify the need for local action within the frame of wider policy matters. These then direct responses as legitimate or otherwise, through the identification of 'truth'. What results are usable scripts whereby policy-makers and policy analysts might pass judgement and local individuals might provide possible local mediation of the policy messages. Thus they demonstrate a true understanding of information, ideas and intentions (Olssen et al., 2004). The key here is the use of positivist methodological measures: statistical analysis forms the cornerstone of the process for numbers 'reveal truth':

> When such mechanisms are presented as the logical conclusion of positivist methodological endeavours, the status afforded such data through its dispassionate collection and analysis would imply a set of 'truths', adherence to which would provide a means for understanding and action.
>
> (Adams, 2011a: 59)

Two assumptions give this view value. First, it is assumed that the methods used are objective in their intent and deployment. That is to say, the situation they describe reflects the 'reality on the ground'. Second, it is assumed that these reflections are accurately reflected in the policy in question; it is believed that the policy missive is reflective of that which the author intended to say.

However, whilst writing about an essentially stagist approach, Trowler (2003) notes how policy goes through a two part process: policy encoding, whereby a policy statement is created from competing interpretations and interests; and policy decoding, the selective interpretation or mediation of policy missive into the local space. Between these two lies the transmission of policy whereby individuals 'in the middle' reclassify and recast the policy so possibly interfering with the original signal. For him, the issue here is one of interpretation; there is no 'objective' reading of the policy document. This is important and further extends the debate about ideology and values and their place in the policy-making process. It is for this reason that we can consider social constructionism.

> **ACTIVITY 2.2**
>
> Use the same government policy as for Activity 2.1.
>
> ■ Was the policy consulted about prior to implementation? If so, how was this consultation undertaken? For example, who was consulted?
> ■ What objectives does the policy have? How does it intend to meet these objectives?
> ■ Has this policy a stagist approach to policy implementation?

Social constructionist policy analysis

Whilst the above might appeal to those wishing to make policy at a variety of levels it is overly simplistic. To assume a chain that clearly identifies reality (as described through positivist methodology) and binds it to action is flawed. It is not that evidence is not gathered or that decisions are not taken, rather it is the basis upon which these occur that needs to be questioned. How, for example, do decisions get made; upon what basis are they decided? Similarly, who decides on the evidence to gather and why was this chosen? It is important that we ask such questions for they reveal a lot about intent and meaning behind the veneer of policy and policy-making and thus the buttressing of the legitimacy of policy.

With this in mind, social constructionism can be deployed. Social constructionist theorising is not one field of enquiry; rather it labels a number of similar endeavours whereby researchers try to uncover and examine the methods and activities that make up society. Social constructionist theorising would seek to ask and answer questions about aims and intent and the wider structuring of decision-making that makes up the social world. For example, and to return to the exam grade discussion above, social constructionists would ask questions about the origins of the grade point used for discussion. So, rather than identify a grade as being the desired one and acting on it, a social constructivist analysis of the policy would try to determine why it was that this grade was chosen to represent average performance. Further, it would seek to ask questions as to why performance on that exam had been chosen as the exemplar for pupil achievement. Indeed, it might even question why exam performance was to be used as the basis for judgement in the first place. In so doing, a social constructionist critique would begin to identify issues wider than just the policy itself. It might, for example, question the decisions taken at the heart of government to evaluate the worth of education via statistical measures.

At the heart of this approach are the ideas of problematisation and argumentation. The former occurs when a problem is defined. Rather than seeing a problem as existing prior to someone identifying it, problematisation starts from the view that all problems are socially constructed; that is, they all have their basis in the ways and means by which we live our social lives. For example, the problem that not enough children have reached a certain level on a certain test is only a problem because it has been defined that this test, measuring these things, in these ways, is to be the barometer of academic success and that this certain level is the desired, average age-related score. This, coupled with the statistical fact that 'not enough young people are reaching a stated level' (itself a constructed problem), then creates the 'problem' for the policy to solve. The process of problematisation takes hold and defines what is to be considered. Clearly, though, problems are not constructed separately from historical, cultural and social issues. Problems must thus be seen as socially constructed responses to historical-social-cultural specificity: our ways of viewing the world are encumbered by our history our society and our culture. Thus problematisation is so encumbered as well. Policy is thus 'context rich' in a social constructionist vein.

Problematisation goes hand-in-hand with argumentation. Once the problem has been constructed, a response then has to be manufactured. Whilst this might well be the result of time spent in consideration and evidence gathering, clearly, following on from the previous points, the ways in which we are encumbered will play a part in the decisions we take. Thus, to argue for one course of action is to present as definitive a particular storyline, a particular way of reading and responding to the world. To return to our testing issue: the response to the constructed problem might well be to impose a prescriptive programme of lessons that seeks to ensure that the required proportion of pupils at the required age are taught certain material, knowledge of which should glean the required results. But in a democracy this response has to be won by argument. It might be the plank of a political party's manifesto which, once they are elected, can be actioned. In any eventuality, argumentation defines policy as a process whereby shared or accepted understandings are promoted. What is signalled to be 'fact' becomes so following a particular line of argument that seeks to promote one course of thinking over another.

Policy as discourse

Within the social constructionist line policy is often described as discourse. Discourses are

> about what can be said, and thought, but also about who can speak, when, where and with what authority. Discourses embody the meaning and use of propositions and words. Thus certain possibilities for thought are constructed.
>
> (Ball, 2006, p. 48)

Policy as discourse is by no means an agreed field; there are a number of differing interpretations of what might be meant (cf. Bacchi, 2000). But it is possible to discern a number of similar features. What policy as discourse does is to note the sort of discussions outlined above; the interplay between policy creation and response.

Writing in this vein, Kenneth Gergen (1995), a well-known social constructionist writer, highlights the ways in which language is the key to meaning-making. His work helps us to think about the ways in which the language used to determine policy actually constructs the very policies it seeks to describe. So, in creating a policy about literacy, the policy itself defines what literacy is. This is very powerful for it moves our thinking away from ideas that policy results from a series of dispassionate and unbiased observations and decisions towards a position that actively acknowledges that policy has a performative function, that is, policy is a performance of a series of conversations rather than a static entity. It signals that policy is neither a true representation of reality nor an accurate reflection of intent. This means that policy is not simply understood and applied in context, it is actively performed. But the performance does not start with the putting into practice of the policy; it starts with problematisation. This means that when we think of policy we must think of the production of the 'text', the ways in which policy is consumed and the delineation of social practices, such as 'professional', 'teacher' and so on.

In the problematisation and argumentation process outlined above, the role for history, culture, society, etc. was highlighted. Policy as discourse acknowledges this; it identifies how prevailing social, cultural and political ways of viewing the world impact on the policy process. For example, viewing educational success by the realisation of certain levels in a national test says as much about prevailing societal and political values as it does educational ones. The ways in which certain behaviours are seen to be successful reflects how we view the world. The fact that we judge educational success in terms of grades on a test reflects society's views about the relationship between tests, education and success. Particularly, discourses are '. . . practices that systematically form the objects of which they speak' (Foucault, 1977: 49). Discourses do not just represent reality, they help to create it and in so doing they deny us the language we need to be able to think about it and describe alternatives (Trowler, 2003). In a sense they trap us in their own creation.

For example, politically, great stall has been set by children and young people acquiring certain credentials through the schooling system. But this, as we shall see in later chapters, reflects socio-political ways of viewing the world, ways that are wrapped up with certain views for education, wider services and the ways and means by which such success should be gleaned. The techno-empiricist line would not question such assumptions; rather it takes for granted that such measures and ways of being and acting are unproblematic for they simply reflect what is true. In this case, the discourse of standards seeks to deny us a language to challenge the assumptions inherent within the discourse itself. Importantly, the social constructionist line, taking policy as discourse as its basis, requires us to challenge this. It makes us think about the ways in which we have been positioned to think of education in certain ways. It notes the mechanisms by which policy performs certain functions. As Adams (2011a: 60) states, policy, then, 'should not be seen as an accurate portrayal of some pre-existing status but is, rather, a social construction given legitimacy through the permission it gives to speak'.

Such a position not only challenges us to think about how policy is made, but also how we read policy and how professionals interact with texts, discourses and role definitions. What is clear is that we cannot simply assume that 'truth' has been captured for there is no truth independent of the meanings attached to certain things. Thus, when examining professional decision-making there is a need to understand that action is embedded in certain ways of seeing the world, ways of seeing that stem from culture, politics, economics, social standing, etc. Policy as discourse requires us to examine the uses and effects of policy in relation to these influences, the ways in which this is deployed professionally and the social conditions which have created the language used in the policy itself. In short, it requires us to think of policy as social construction.

This brings us back to the process of problematisation. The different ways in which we can view the world not only give us mechanisms by which we might understand 'reality', they also determine the very 'problems' policy seeks to address. In this way, certain situations are deemed noteworthy and in need of action. But situations do not exist separately from those thinking of them. We cannot say, for example, that 70 per cent of 11-year-olds getting level 4 on a SAT test is, objectively speaking, insufficient, any more than we can say that raspberry jam is better than other conserves. It is a matter of opinion and position. What we can say, however, is that given the ways we have of viewing education currently, 70 per cent is too low and something needs to be done. But this is a political and social statement; it makes reference to beliefs and ideas about what is a 'good education', indeed, what an 'education' is. We must consider wider discourses if we are to understand policy. And it is the process of argumentation which constructs 'solutions' as 'acceptable'. When educationalists or politicians talk of solutions to problems, they are talking about acceptability: this way of acting fits with my beliefs regarding the 'problem' and thus is the 'right' one. Again, there is a need to understand the wider discourses and ideologies that go together to make up such responses, we need to understand the arguments put forward to help 'solve' the constructed problems.

Policy as discourse, then, establishes three key principles. First, it signals that 'problems' do not pre-exist human thought, but rather that they are determined by specific ways of seeing the world. Second, these lenses are also the means by which 'solutions' captured as policy pronouncements, might be constructed. Thirdly, policy as discourse constrains the scope of policy: the discourses available to use present a viable set of alternatives.

ACTIVITY 2.3

Use the same policy as for Activities 2.1 and 2.2.

■ What discourses does the policy deploy? For example, it might make certain statements about teaching and learning or professionalism.

■ What 'problems' does the policy identify (problematisation)?

■ What solutions does it offer (argumentation)?

Policy as text

For Ball (2006) policy can be thought of as discourse and text; for him, policies have a two-fold existence. In his theory, Ball notes how policies are statements born of struggle and compromise between the different individuals, groups and interests involved in the process of policy-making. The theory also notes how at the point of decoding policy, varying interpretations will be placed on the text. Here, teachers and officials in school will interpret within the context of their own geography and culture. Thus we have some form of disruption to the intention: that intended by the policy may well not get enacted or may well get enacted in a novel manner. However, degrees of difference are not seen in all situations. Ball talks about some texts being more 'readerly', that is, interpretation can be more readily put on them, and more 'writerly', that is the scope for individual interpretation is reduced. Trowler (2003: 131) notes that this view 'stresses the importance of social agency, of struggle and compromise, and the importance of understanding how policy is "read"'.

Policy as discourse and policy as text together note the way in which policy is much more than a specific document; they note how policy is both a product and process wherein texts are produced, modifications are made, and the issues therein are implemented into practice (Rizvi and Lingard, 2010). It is important to note that policy texts can take the form of speeches, press releases and blogs; discursive mechanisms by which policy pronouncements are displayed.

Policy and values

What should be clear in the above discussions is the role that values play in determining policy. The positions governments adopt when defining policy texts are themselves statements of worth; government decides on that which it feels is appropriate and defines policy accordingly. Policy is an attempt to direct action and attitudes and as such appeals to individuals or not; policy attempts to have effect in the broader social, cultural and political domains (Rizvi and Lingard, 2010). At one level policy attributes or withholds funding, based on decisions taken regarding the worth of an activity or direction of travel.

Notably, though, policies differ in their clarity, complexity and commitment (Rein, 1983). Thus, the likelihood of implementation differs between policies and between times. Some policies are symbolic and have little or no funding attached (Rizvi and Lingard, 2010). Such policies may not be intended for implementation, or in fact they may set the discourse furthering the ends of other policies and directives. It can also be the case that policies are implemented from other previous policies and are thus incremental in their origins and implementation. Here it may be the case that the development of particular policy lines follows the election patterns of political parties; one government might implement a particular policy only to have this developed or discarded by the next government who wishes to stress how different they are from the previous administration (Rizvi and Lingard, 2010). Finally, rational policies are those which are pointedly prescriptive: they go through a number of distinct phases of development and implementation (Rizvi and Lingard, 2010).

Conclusion

Education policy is, then, not simply a matter of decision, transmission and act. The process of making policy is far more involved. Whilst it might seem convenient to think of policy creation as a simple technical-empiricist matter, it is clear that when values and ideologies are factored in, the process becomes rather more complicated. Wider social, political, cultural and historical issues become part of the very fabric of policy creation and are seen to be embedded within the processes there involved. Policy as a social construction acknowledges the inherently political nature of human existence and how this influences the policy-making process. This is important, for the rest of this book takes as its starting point the idea that policy is not something simply created on high and mediated into the local space. Rather it assumes that complicated forces intertwine to create a rich tapestry of possibilities that are resisted, taken up, moderated and implemented according to social taste. When reading the remainder of the book it is important, then, to remember that the interpretations given here are exactly that; they are no more 'truthful' than any others you might which to conceive of. Evidence will be provided for the various standpoints presented, but at this level there is a need for discourse to be examined fully so that policy might continue to be further examined and debated. When reading the remainder of the book it is important to identify differing discourses for the way in which they impact on prevailing policy. The reader's own interpretations, if evidenced, are just as important as the ones presented here.

Key points

- Defining policy is not an easy task. We can, however, note that action is part and parcel of the policy-making process. Action can be defined by a decision to act or not to act.

- Government can use a variety of instruments to influence and implement policy. Policy can be actioned by state apparatus or be more devolved from it, for example, to the private sector.

- Analysis for policy concerns itself with identifying how and why policy might be created and implemented. Analysis of policy is an analytical endeavour undertaken to understand how and why policy might have been so created and deployed.

- Stagist approaches to policy creation assume that the policy creation/implementation cycle is linear in orientation and can be said to follow a distinct pattern.

- Technicist-empiricist orientations follow from this and assume that the creation and implementation of policy can be easily identified. In this view, the decisions taken by policy creators stem from objective evidence free from any type of bias and the implementers of policy action in an unproblematic straightforward manner.

- Social constructionist theory questions the value-free nature of educational decision-making. Its view is that the policy-making process is imbued with social, cultural, historical and political meaning. It would seek to question, therefore, the decisions taken as to the basis for action.

- Policy as discourse and policy as text are forms of social constructionist theory which see education policy as stemming from the performative function of language. Discourses construct and are constructed by the very language used to try to problematise a situation. Similarly, the processes of argumentation construct solutions as 'acceptable' and in so doing are constructed by and construct the discourses marshalled in their support.

Further reading

Ball, S.J. (2006) *Education Policy and Social Class*, London: Routledge (Chapter 3). This chapter gives the reader a good insight into what Ball describes as policy as discourse and policy as text.

Rizvi, F. and Lingard, B. (2010) *Globalizing Education Policy*, London: Routledge (Chapter 1). This chapter offers the reader theoretical insights into defining policy.

Trowler, P. (2003) *Education Policy*, London: Routledge (Chapters 3 and 4). Both of these chapters offer some illuminating insights into the policy-making and policy implementation process.

The phases of education

3

Secondary schools

Purpose of this chapter

At the end of this chapter you should understand:

- how secondary schools were organised following the Second World War and the tripartite system;
- the process of comprehensivisation that occurred in the 1960s and 1970s;
- Conservative changes to secondary schooling introduced between 1979 and 1997;
- New Labour changes to secondary education that occurred between 1997 and 2010;
- some of the similarities and differences between the Conservatives and New labour policies for secondary schools;
- extended schools and Every Child Matters.

The post-war settlement

Prior to the 1944 Education (Butler) Act, 90 per cent of young people left school at 14 following attendance at all-age elementary schools. Despite the fact that this system had achieved much, it remained that, by the end of the Second World War, the desire to see increased access to education had given way to disillusionment. Many were simply denied any form of education beyond the basics and education persisted as a means of class control and a mechanism for the creation, legitimisation and justification for class-based positional advantage (Tomlinson, 2005: 13–14).

> Despite the education successes and advances that could be recorded, a major theme in the literature is that any expectations that more access to education would lead to a more equal society rapidly gave way to disillusionment. Education persisted as a means by which inequalities were created, legitimized and justified, and privileged groups continued to use the divisions and distinctions of schooling to confirm and reproduce their own position.
>
> (Tomlinson, 2005: 13–14)

Following the Butler Act primary schools were created for children up to the age of 11, to be followed by secondary education until the age of 15. However, this post-war system grew out of a democratic consensus which rejected the concept of one local school for all pupils. Whilst the 1944 Education Act emerged out of agreement between state, church and education, the new system introduced the 11-plus as the mechanism for determining who was to attend which school following primary education. This was a mechanism to separate children, at age 11, on the basis of age, ability and aptitude into grammar, secondary modern and technical schools. The exams were not designed to be seen in terms of 'success' or 'failure'; rather they were used to bracket children into groups according to three types of mind: the academic, the technical and the practical, as accepted by the Norwood Report (Norwood Committee, 1943). In reality, though, mainly grammar and secondary moderns were created; only about 6 per cent of the population ever went to technical schools. The system was not equitable and by 1946 some 80 per cent of pupils were educated in secondary modern schools (Tomlinson, 2005). Whilst grammar schools prepared pupils for professional and white collar jobs, secondary modern schools prepared pupils for factory and secretarial work. In effect the new system was designed to, and did, reinforce a class-based society. As Simon (1991: 115) notes 'Even under a Labour government elected with a massive majority the mediation of class relations was still seen as a major function of the education system.'

Such changes, whilst in many ways ground-breaking, did not challenge the orthodoxy that had existed in education for centuries. Such thinking proposed that certain types of people benefitted from certain types of education. In the main, education, for most of the population, was a preparation for the world of work. Whilst there were challenges to the idea of grammar schools from the mid-1950s onwards, it is certainly the case that the idea of education as preparation for work has never retreated and can be seen today. In a modern sense, this is played out through the auspices of markets in education, traditionalism and the extension of choice.

The post-war system modelled the ways in which those in positions of authority and control achieved and maintained their lot in life. Although the schools were universal and free, 'the division into . . . different "types" of student with different "types of mind", was clearly modelled on a class-divided version of education, albeit a more porous one than before' (Ball, 2008: 66).

ACTIVITY 3.1

The 11-plus was based on notions of intellectual ability. What might contemporary notions of intelligence today have to say about sectioning children according to such a test?

Towards comprehensivisation

As Ball (2008) notes, signs that the tripartite system was not in total command showed in areas such as London where, by 1947, 64 comprehensive schools were planned. In the main, however, it was weak and reluctant central direction which gave rise to tripartism and small attempts at comprehensivisation. As early as the 1950s research suggested that working class children left school earlier than those from the middle class, even when attending the same schools. Class-based divisions were obvious between the intake of grammar and secondary modern schools, but were also marked within these schools themselves. Indeed, grammar schools remained predominantly middle class establishments, except in areas where the working class intake was proportionately higher, such as in mid-Wales (Ball, 2008).

Shifts in thinking regarding selective and non-selective education did appear early on; the emergence of planning for comprehensive schools in London demonstrates this. Additionally, from as early as 1954 David Eccles, Conservative Minister for Education, approved the establishment of comprehensive schools in new towns or where there would be no competition to the existing grammar/secondary modern order. However, cut against this was the belief that grammar schools gave parental choice and that it was the role of secondary modern schools to develop specialist status (Tomlinson, 2005).

As the 1960s developed, though, there was a broad Labour/Conservative consensus that comprehensive schools should be developed. Starting in 1964 there was a drive for a more egalitarian system and in 1965 Anthony Crosland, the Labour Minister for Education requested, through circular 10/65 that local education authorities (LEAs) submit plans to reorganise along comprehensive lines. This request was repealed in 1970, and only became statutory in the 1976 Education Act. Notably, though, the largest growth in comprehensive schools occurred between 1970 and 1974, under a Conservative administration ideologically opposed to them.

However, as Tomlinson (2005) notes, right wing commentators from the 1960s onwards continued to bemoan so called 'progressive education' and comprehensivisation as a dumbing down of the education system and a period of liberal anarchy. The national media largely took the side of the right wingers and many articles appeared maintaining that standards had fallen since the introduction of non-selective systems. These attacks led to cracks appearing in the fragile consensus that non-selective education was the way forward and advocates of selection gained considerable headway. In 1970, Margaret Thatcher, the Conservative Education Minister, issued circular 10/70 removing the request of circular 10/65 and grammar schools continued to be presented as the only schools that could maintain high standards.

By the 1970s there was a general decline in the support for the comprehensive system. Later that decade saw a growth in the doctrines of the New Right amongst the Conservative Party. This rejected high taxation and public spending instead promoting the idea that the welfare state was nothing more than a drain on private enterprise. Neoliberalism became the order of the day with its antagonism to the welfare state. 'Market proxies' (Ball, 2008: 77) were introduced with their mandate for choice and business-like manner. The Conservatives continued to attack non-selective education, and choice and standards became the new mantras, something, they maintained, only a selective system could offer.

ACTIVITY 3.2

Why might a comprehensive system based on the idea of a local school for local children be fairer to all children of all ages?

The Conservative legacy

Part of the drive for a market-based solution to educational issues and problems is the intro-duction of choice into the system. It was the 1980s dominance of public choice theories which encouraged such market-based reform, introduced to reduce alleged inefficiency and ineffectiveness (see Chapter 5). The result was an increase in outcome-based approaches and personal choice. However, choice was, in small ways, already a feature of education, even in the welfarist era. Whilst the 1944 Butler Act established the principle of universal and free secondary education for all, this was not delivered with parity of esteem. The tripartite system was, then, a poor exercise in choice, but nevertheless, choice was marshalled as a defence of the system. Indeed, as late as the 1970s the Conservative Party still maintained that a selective system gave parents choice over their child's education (Tomlinson, 2005).

The election of Margaret Thatcher's Conservative Party to political power in 1979 marked a new era for public services broadly and education more specifically. The underlying rationale for education change throughout the 1980s and 1990s was a mixture of nineteenth-century liberal individualism and a traditional conservative appeal to order and moral authoritarianism. This translated into a market-based ideology where consumer choice was pre-eminent. Cen-tral funding was to replace local authority control and education was seen as a commodity, with parents free to choose. Good education was to be a positional good to be competitively sought and provided:

> The core focus of Conservative educational policy under Thatcher was an emphasis on the use of markets and free enterprise to produce and then distribute, with a minimum of regulation, the goods and services wanted by consumers.
>
> (Tomlinson, 2005: 31–32)

The 1980s: the era of the Education Act

In the 1980 Education Act, Mark Carlisle, Conservative Secretary of State for Education, declared that comprehensive education was no longer national policy. The Conservatives were to pursue the diversification and selection of education where possible. This did not mean dis-mantling the non-selective system that existed in most local authorities, but was, rather, made up of a number of policy changes designed to usher in a new form of state education. In order to support children from less-well-off backgrounds, the assisted places scheme was introduced. This required LEAs to provide support for able pupils to attend private, fee-paying schools. The link between ability and selection was marked out quite openly in such policy: those pupils who demonstrated aptitude would benefit from the more academic environment of the fee-paying sector who were more able to deal with ability than the comprehensive school.

For the first time, parents were also allowed to express a preference for their child's school. This was a marked change from the system of local catchment that had been in operation since 1944. Opening up the system was seen as a way to drive up standards: parental choice increased covert selection between comprehensive schools and began the sharp social divide between 'popular' and less popular schools. The idea was that good schools would persist and poor schools would close. Some commentators went even further and called for the introduction of education vouchers whereby parents would be given the price of state education to spend in whatever school they saw fit including the private sector. This, it was believed, would create a market system, further driving up standards of education. However, the idea was resisted by educationalists and was dropped. In a further call to differentiate between schools, the right of local authorities to refuse pupils from other geographical areas was also curtailed, further opening up schools to a free flow of pupils not necessarily from their local catchment. Finally, to extend further the rights of schools to determine their own affairs, the constitution of school governing bodies was also altered so that teachers and parents had a place at the table.

But it was the 1988 Education Reform Act which produced the most far-reaching set of changes since the advent of the welfare state. Running to 238 sections and giving the Secretary of State for Education 451 new powers, the Act saw the introduction of a number of market-type mechanisms designed to impact on all schools, not just the secondary sector:

- A national curriculum which detailed the subjects and content to be taught to all pupils of statutory school age.

- Open enrolment for schools whereby any parent would be able to express a preference for any school and that admissions be open and transparent, taking into account parental preference.

- Local management of schools (LMS) whereby payment to schools were determined by school roll (Glennerster, 1991). LMS sought to deliver to head teachers and governing bodies control of the school budget to deploy as required to meet the needs of the school. It was an attempt to empower school staff through the reduction in control of the LEA, so 'freeing up' schools to respond more effectively to local need.

- The creation of grant-maintained (GM) schools. These were state schools that received their funding directly from the government with concomitant control over the use of their budgets, by-passing local authorities. The intention was to free up schools so that they might innovate without LEA interference.

- LEAs were to start charging services to schools at cost. Problematically, under the new system disadvantaged schools suffered the most.

- The creation of city technology colleges (CTCs). With direct funding from business and the government, such colleges were to teach the National Curriculum but specialise in science and technology-based subjects.

Diversification and differentiation

The Conservatives believed that there was far too much uniformity in the state system despite the fact that a variety of different types of schools has existed since 1944 (the system of primary and secondary schooling was not the only one to exist across the UK, in some areas, middle schools were created in the 1970s, for example). At the heart of these changes lay the belief that diversity acts as a basis for the realisation of competition for a simplistic market only works if there is a variety of providers (Ball, 2008). Added to this was the orientation that desired to see schools behave like schools and not community hubs; the enthusiasm for community schools slowly dissipated throughout the 1980s and 1990s as Ofsted and standards began to bite (Bangs et al., 2011). Whilst schools did continue to work with their local communities, many felt constrained in the ability to do so.

The Conservatives desired to see more differentiation in the system and wished to pass control for school processes to schools themselves. The creation of GM schools was a mechanism to realise this ambition. Many feared that such schools would become selective in their intake and this, coupled with larger amounts of direct funding than local authority schools, would mean that they held prestigious places in the local schooling system. The aim was for all schools to become GM but by 1996 only 1090 had adopted this status, 60 per cent of which were secondary. The conservatives also introduced CTCs and specialist schools. CTCs are independent schools paid for by the state and private business which teach predominantly technology-related subjects. However to establish such schools business sponsorship was required, something which proved difficult to achieve. Accordingly, few CTCs were created.

Between 1988 and 1996 Conservative policy aimed to consolidate a market ideology, part of which was parental choice. The egalitarian system was slowly replaced by a 'fragmented and divisive system' (Tomlinson, 2005: 49). The 1988 Education Reform Act (ERA; DES, 1988) ushered in consumer choice and individual entrepreneurship. Its major feature was open enrolment or a parental right to choice. Furthermore, LEAs could no longer fix admissions figures to keep open unpopular schools. The aim of all this was to ensure that parents were positioned as consumers with choice and power in the system.

Specialist schools were launched in 1994. Such schools work in partnership with private sector sponsors and attract additional government funding. They pursue a distinctive identity through their specialism, although they must still adhere to the National Curriculum. Initially £100,000 had to be raised by the school before the status could be considered. This was then matched by government money. This proved difficult to achieve for many schools, so the amount was reduced to £50,000 with available funds to help those schools struggling to attract sponsorship.

There was a contradiction in policy, however: whilst consumer choice in the arena of school admissions was heralded, central control of things such as the curriculum and funding increased. By 1985 government policy had removed the historic partnership between education, local authorities and teachers replacing it instead with government edict and centralisation. GM schools were promoted as an alternative: free of local authority control they were believed to be able to be responsive to local parental wishes and funded directly from government. It was argued that they provided diversity within the system.

Social class and schooling under the Conservatives

An outcome of all this was the continued stratification of schooling according to social class. Choice proved to be a crude mechanism for social selection (Tomlinson, 2005). Those who were destined for manual work received a different form of education from those whose future lay with the professions or management (Tomlinson, 2005). Whilst the organisation of the tripartite system was not evidenced in most places across England, a few areas held onto their grammar school, 11-plus system for sorting pupils (currently, 15 local authorities still maintain some form of selection in this guise). By 1987 distinctions were already in existence between schools that were private, grammar or in more affluent areas and other schools. Those on the right presented this as the fault of teachers: if different geographical areas have differing results then the work of staff in the schools must be to blame. Issues such as social class and poverty were ignored. But it was the way in which parents were able to select the education of choice for their children which marked the continuation of class-divided notions. Those with the wherewithal to make such selections were better positioned in the market economy that was school admissions. This privileged the middle classes who had the cultural and social capital to capitalise on the mechanisms that sorted pupils into differing schools. That is to say that the middle classes possessed attributes such as education and language and the social ties and economic methods by which they were able to understand the education system and hence play the system. Consequently, some schools became 'richer' and others 'poorer'.

> But the creation of a market in education, driven by the self-interest of knowledgeable parents and the competitive strategies of schools which had been forced, with varying degrees of reluctance, to market their schools to attract desirable customers, was ensuring a first and second class division in state schooling.
>
> (Tomlinson, 2005: 78)

ACTIVITY 3.3

Which of the following is the most important Conservative introduction and why?

- a   Grant maintained schools
- b   The assisted places scheme
- c   The National Curriculum
- d   Specialist schools

The rise of New Labour

Following the Conservative years New Labour perceived that there was a need for both intellectual and financial investment into education (Abbott et al., 2013) and expectations across the profession were high. In their election manifesto New Labour signalled the importance they placed on education: 'Education will be our number one priority; and we will increase the share of national income spent on education as we decrease it on the bills of economic and social failure' (Labour Party, 1997: 5).

Among its promises, the party sought, in government, to: develop and extend the education of the under 7s; raise standards; increase spending; and improve technology use in schools. Blair's governments 'had one primary and incontestable aim: that is: the achievement of high quality education for all children and young people' (Bangs et al., 2011: 13). However, in many ways New Labour in its first session continued with the Conservative mantra of markets and centralisation, although it is unfair to caricature the two parties as being of entirely the same ilk. There were a number of key differences between New Labour education policy and that of the Conservatives, but two stand out: the heavy involvement of the prime minister in educational matters and an increase in funding (Abbott et al., 2013). But the party was keen to send two very clear messages to the teaching profession: the government was on the side of the users of education, not the producers; and, the Labour Party was not the same as the one that had been in power before, they would not just be in favour of what teachers did (Bangs et al., 2011).

Post-1997 New Labour felt that the only way to keep the middle classes on board with state education was to give them what they would get if they were to go private. Consequently, the state could be said to have gradually withdrawn as the 'provider' of education in place of a role as funder, commissioner and monitor of the system (Ball, 2008). In short, there was a neoliberal revolt against public services which sought to restructure schools around a market model.

> In the market sense, therefore, schools act as the *providers* of educational services which are *consumed* by the *customers* – the parents and their children – and have to *compete* with one another to secure the funding to enable them to survive. It is suggested that such competitive *market forces* will make schools more *customer orientated* and will force schools to innovate in order to raise the standard and quality of their provision or else fail.
>
> (Bates et al., 2011: 82 emphasis in original)

In the run up to the 1997 general election, Labour had proposed three types of schools: community, aided and foundation. These could be easily mapped onto aided schools for faith-based institutions and foundation schools for GM schools. However, New Labour accepted the Conservative lines of choice and competition and diversity of schools continued to be promoted (West and Pennell, 2002) even though they abolished the assisted places scheme (Bates et al., 2011). Indeed, the labelling of failing schools continued and shortly after election the Secretary of State for Education, David Blunkett, named and shamed the worst performing secondary schools. New Labour continued to promote the failing school policy even though the majority of schools labelled such were in poor areas or had high proportions of minority ethnic pupils with English as a second language, or pupils not wanted in other schools (Tomlinson, 2005).

Extending choice

The first White Paper, released only 67 days after their coming into office, committed the government to putting education at its heart. This said the direction was an unrelenting focus on standards with zero tolerance of underperformance. Part of this was the continuation of a diversified secondary offering; parental choice was still to be very much part of the system. In this vein the specialist schools policy continued with a new target of 800 specialist secondary schools by 2002. Additionally, the number of faith schools, expanded under Conservative rule, continued to grow. Indeed, from 1997, Tony Blair gave his personal backing to faith schools as well as 'arguing for a more prominent role for faith-based organisations in policy and public debate' (Ball, 2008: 124). Although faith schools appear to perform better in state exams and tests, their intake is often skewed in favour of middle class parents and away from pupils in receipt of free school meals. New Labour's diversification programme also contained academies and trust schools. GM schools were removed, but they remained as their own admissions body.

Additionally, LEAs continued to be marginalised. Their role changed to one of support from a distance rather than control of schools.

> The LEA's task is to challenge schools to raise standards continuously and apply pressure when they do not. The role is not one of control. Those days are gone. An effective LEA will challenge schools to improve themselves. Being ready to intervene when there are problems, but not interfere with schools that are doing well.
>
> (DfEE, 1997: 27)

Control was either centralised in the hands of the Department for Education and Employment (DfEE) or its quangos or pushed to the margins: onto schools themselves. In many ways this was a continuation of the Conservative line.

Academies

Importantly, the policy of failing schools required a new mechanism following the abolition of GM status. New Labour was quick to identify such a process: in March 2000 city academies were announced. The creation of academies encapsulated the agenda of diversification; the five year strategy of July 2004 promised 200 academies by 2010. Academies were independent semi-privatised schools set up as limited companies with charitable status, 'in effect private schools publically funded' (Tomlinson, 2005: 127). Land and buildings would be transferred to the partnership running the school and sponsors would appoint the majority of the governing body. Sponsors were seen to be key to the proposals, bringing with them not only funding either in monetary terms or in kind, but also expertise both from the educational and business sectors. Academies were to be their own admissions body, setting their own criteria for entry if they were oversubscribed. They had no LEA input and were run by central government, voluntary organisations, church or business sponsors. They were given much greater freedom in terms of curriculum, pay and conditions. A variety of sponsors entered the academies project including evangelical Christian organisations. Notably, some academies were run along corporate lines designed to prepare pupils for certain sectors of work in certain industries (Bates et al., 2011).

This programme was to prove very contentious and the results from academies were mixed. Research seemed to show that improvements in exam results were the result of a better intake and that admissions procedures had become convoluted with some schools ignoring the admissions code altogether (Tomlinson, 2005). As Tomlinson (2005: 104) states '[t]he modernized comprehensive system now sanctioned selection and differentiation, the education market encouraged schools to avoid or exclude children who were difficult to teach.' Importantly, the academies programme was more a political than educational statement and critics maintained that they:

- permit various groups to have too great an influence over the running of state education;
- sit outside local democratic oversight;
- undermine the independent role of school governors;
- transfer land and buildings from the state and into private hands;
- take resources and pupils from other local schools;
- increase the number of excluded pupils in the system;
- operate 'selection by stealth' and as such are not 'local schools';
- do not offer a better education, they merely improve their intake;
- are often imposed against local wishes;
- in some areas are resurrecting the old two-tier education system of grammar and secondary moderns (Bates et al., 2011: 91).

In sum, Ball (2008: 184) notes that the academies programme 'stands as a condensate of New Labour education policies, an experiment in and symbol of education policy beyond the welfare state and an example and indicator of more general shifts taking place in governance and regulatory structures.'

Diversity

The 1990s saw the rise of school effectiveness research which maintained that poverty is no excuse for educational failure; this led to the creation of a blame and shame culture. As the twentieth century drew to a close it became obvious that the needs of the middle classes were taking precedence over the needs of the many and emphasis was placed on the deficiencies of the excluded so that they might be blamed for their situation.

Whilst during New Labour's first term the emphasis for government had been on primary schools, during their second term New Labour's focus shifted more in favour of the secondary sector. They desired to see gains made including an increase in higher education participation rates and greater success at GCSE. A target of 20 per cent of all pupils achieving five or more A* to C grades at GCSE by 2004 was set, with the extension of this to 25 per cent by 2006 (Abbott et al., 2013).

Importantly, New Labour sought to extend choice and diversity in the system and by 2006, 2000 specialist schools were planned. The most contentious part of the 2004 Five Year Strategic Plan (DfES, 2004) was the drive to create such schools in place of the traditional comprehensive. The then education secretary, Charles Clarke, maintained that specialist schools offered a choice between strong independent schools for parents (Tomlinson, 2005). The specialist schools policy continued to expand due to on-going popularity (Abbott et al., 2013) and by 2007/8 88 per cent of all secondary schools were specialist. These schools could admit up to 10 per cent of their intake by aptitude in the relevant subject. Further, most secondary schools, it was proposed, would be able, by a simple vote, to become foundation schools, thereby taking on the ownership of their land, employ their staff directly and be their own admissions body (Tomlinson, 2005). What was at stake was the very existence of the comprehensive school. But much of this was down to a certain reading of what such schools are like and for. As Fiona Millar, ex-No. 10 advisor and education campaigner and journalist states:

> There was a real divide within number ten, between people they would see as old Labour . . . and the sort of thrusting young Middle-England people, who allegedly knew what parents wanted . . . Some of them had just made their minds up that Comprehensive schools were a disaster, without thinking what the term Comprehensive actually meant . . . it's become a phrase that was used to brand something else, which was failing inner city schools, basically, made up of very tough kids.
>
> (cited in Bangs et al., 2011: 14)

Indeed, the 2004 five year plan signalled this and the continuing marketisation agenda of New Labour, underpinned as it was by five principles (Tomlinson, 2005), all of which leant towards the provision of choice, privatisation and diversification:

■ greater personalisation and choice;
■ opening up services to new providers;

- freedom and independence for head teachers and managers;
- a commitment to staff development;
- partnership working.

The policy of city academies continued. Most were located in areas of socio-economic disadvantage whilst many, under new leadership and sponsorship, replaced existing schools. The terms and conditions of employment for teachers were flexible and the school could select up to 10 per cent of their intake based on pupil aptitude in the school's specialist status. Abbott et al. (2013) note that the Specialist Schools and Academies Trust (SSAT), originally established in 1987 to promote CTCs, continued to support and promote on-going Labour policy in these areas. As a quango it increased government expenditure to £50 million by 2007. The increase in power and influence of the SSAT (a non-elected body) sits in contrast to the declining powers of democratically accountable LEAs. Indeed, in the 2005 Education Act the funding of maintained schools was removed from LEAs and passed to central government. In the 2005 White Paper *Higher Standards, Better Schools for All: More choice for parents and pupils* (DfES, 2005), trust schools were proposed. These were independent, non-fee-paying state schools. They had wide-ranging powers including the ability to set their own admissions criteria, employ their own staff and appoint the board of governors. The proposals were railed against by Labour MPs with 46 voting against and the bill only passed through parliament with the assistance of the Conservative Party. As Abbott et al. (2013: 162) note, a recurring feature of the period 2001 to 2007 was 'the drive to fragment the comprehensive system and to develop greater choice and diversity'.

Although between 2001 and 2007 there was increased spending on education, much of this new money was allocated according to a 'bidding culture' created by the DfEE and the Department for Education and Skills (DfES; Abbott et al., 2013) whereby schools had to bid for extra funds for specific ear-marked purposes. In this way the flow of money was controlled and spending was targeted at key government agendas.

Education and work

One aspect of New Labour which deserves mention is the way they viewed education as key to international competition. As Abbott et al. (2013) note, New Labour developed a simple argument that saw the development of the knowledge economy as the key driving force for economic prosperity. The 2003 White Paper *21st Century Skills: Realising our potential* (DfES, 2003a) detailed the so deemed obvious links between skills and the economy. Education's role in this was to be played out through the auspices of improved standards in schools which in turn would lead to a flexible and skilled workforce. A major plank of New Labour's policy was also, though, a reduction in poverty and social exclusion. This naturally leads to an increase in measures of a more vocational orientation (Pring, 2005). In and of itself this is not a bad thing, but it does mean that a system geared primarily towards academic credentialising requires change. The 2002 Green Paper *14–19: Extending opportunities, rising standards* (DfES, 2002) raised the prospect of a new set of qualifications of a vocational nature to be taken from the age of 14.

Additionally, from 2003, all 15/16-year-olds were to be provided with the equivalent of five days enterprise activity. Enterprise was noted as those further skills required in the 'skills revolution' and the fight for economic prosperity. As a prime aim of education is increasingly seen to be about economic achievement both for the individual and for the wider community, so 'enterprise' becomes the new educational virtue.

(Pring, 2005: 74)

Under New Labour there were an increasing number of vocational courses offered in school sixth forms and an increasing number of academic subjects offered in the incorporated further education (FE) colleges. In September 2008 students were able to enrol on new 14 to 19 specialist diplomas. These were vocational qualifications that involved time spent with an employer to develop the theoretical work done in the classroom. Although a sizeable number of students started these courses they were never particularly popular. Additionally, this was set against the fact that provision for post-14 education was increasingly undertaken in a vast array of providers from academies, through sixth forms, to tertiary colleges. To overcome the problems this entails, the New Labour government proposed collaboration as the new way of working. As Pring (2005: 75) notes, the New Labour government

> insisted upon the need for the educational system to produce the kind of skills, knowledge and qualities which serve the economy in a very competitive global market. 'Inclusion', 'relevance' and 'standards' have been the watchwords, and policies and funding have been applied to ensure that these aims are achieved.

Problematically, this economic argument misses the point, however, that a host of other issues also play a part in the development both of schools and the economy, for example, economic policy. For as Bangs et al. (2011: 30) note

> It was Basil Bernstein who famously wrote, four decades ago that schools 'cannot compensate for society' (Bernstein, 1977). They cannot repair the ruins of social policy of environments unfit for children and families and however resilient children may be, resilience is . . . not an inexhaustible commodity.

With regard to such matters and early on in their first term in office, Education Action Zones (EAZs) were created as a cooperative venture between LEAs, business and schools. EAZs were designed to offer novel and innovative solutions to educational problems in disadvantaged areas. Some EAZs eventually merged into the wider Excellence in Cities initiative which was designed to raise standards in inner city schools wherein six broad areas were identified to help raise standards such areas:

- extra beacon and specialist schools;
- a focus on gifted and talented pupils;
- support units for disruptive pupils;
- learning centres with advanced information technology (IT) provision;
- smaller EAZs;
- the provision of learning mentors.

But throughout this period, as Pring (2005) states, such economic-related policies failed to foreground the ultimate role for education; they failed to give any clear statement of aim or purpose over and above a contribution to the economy. Moreover, in the documents produced and the practical activities envisaged or put into place there was no mention of

> the kinds of qualities and values which make young people into better human beings, no vision of the kind of learning which one should expect of an educated person in the present economic, social and environmental context. The policy is trapped in a language which militates against the broader moral dimension of education – the language of skills and targets, of performance indicators and audits, of academic studies and vocational pathways, of economic relevance and social usefulness.
>
> (Pring, 2005: 82–83)

Education and the whole child

New Labour, in the middle term of its time in office, began to place emphasis on health and well-being; alongside an obsession with standards and league tables ran a concern for maximising children's citizenship and social and educational inclusion. Notably, from 2003 New Labour began to discuss the individual child, and personalisation came to the fore in government rhetoric. The left of centre policy think-tank Demos led a call to move away from centrally imposed, test-driven educational policy towards individualised learning. This was taken up by Schools Standards Minister David Miliband and termed personalised learning. However, even by 2009, critics still maintained that the erosion of teachers' responsibilities was continuing through the imposition of centrally determined, prescriptive curriculum packages.

Through the late 1990s and early 2000s a number of high-profile events such as the murders of James Bulger and Stephen Lawrence, the abuse and subsequent death of Victoria Climbié and the murders of Holly Wells and Jessica Chapman caused widespread public revulsion and gave government a sense of urgency in tackling child welfare. But it was the death of Victoria Climbié at the hands of her guardians that sparked the inquiry which led to the publication in 2003 of the Green Paper *Every Child Matters* (ECM; DfES, 2003b). The Laming report, an independent statutory inquiry led by Lord Laming, concluded that the death of Victoria Climbie was due, in no small part, to communication failure between the various agencies, such as the NHS and social services, involved with Victoria at the time of her death.

ECM put children at the heart of government policy and sought to ensure that services were organised around their need (DfES, 2003b). It was far-reaching, calling as it did for the restructuring of LEAs and social services departments and the requirement that all agencies involved in the protection of children's welfare work together more closely and harmoniously (Roche and Tucker, 2007). ECM identified five outcomes for children that all children's services were supposed to achieve:

- being healthy;
- staying safe;
- enjoying and achieving;
- making a positive contribution;
- achieving economic well-being.

A new Children Act in 2004 saw the proposals contained in ECM enacted. The legislation was designed to usher in a new era of interagency working, joined up thinking and public sector reform. At its heart this legislation seeks to place the child at the forefront of service delivery whilst changing the organizational ethos of those services traditionally bound by role and sector definition.

(Adams and Tucker, 2007: 210)

But it was hard to see how the plan could be put into practice (Abbott et al., 2013). Whilst the aims were laudable, it was soon clear that the various roles for each agency were difficult to pin down. Where, for example, did education's role start and end? It was also the case that different professionals have different values and ways of working. This does not suggest that any group's values are more worthy than the others; rather it signals that the different ways in which the groups involved in achieving the aims of ECM worked made for potential overlap or confusion. And the workload for teachers was large as well. Bangs et al. (2011) suggest that teachers broadly welcomed the emphasis of ECM, but that the accompanying accountability procedures were the source of much frustration. They also cite research which indicates that some parents felt that the role of the school had expanded to encompass areas traditionally the province of parents.

An aspect of the ECM and Children Plan agenda which deserves merit is the introduction of the extended schools scheme whereby schools were expected to work with and in their local community, offering extended opening hours and developing new areas of work such as parenting classes or the integration of health care into the premises. Drawing on the aptly titled 'community schools' in Scotland such schools were modelled on the USA's full service school concept which gave parents and the community a 'one door' entry to educational and social services (Bangs et al., 2011: 36). By 2005 the government had spent £160 million on the extended schools scheme, and had promised a further £680 million by 2008 (Abbott et al., 2013). This programme promoted more responsiveness to the needs of local communities. However, as Cunningham (2012: 7) states 'the introduction of "academies" contradicted the principle of local accountability by reducing community representation on governing bodies, which could henceforward be dominated by independent sponsors'. ECM, then, was an example of how policy can become contradictory.

It was clear, however, that this second Labour administration was never going to backtrack on its target-driven culture (Bangs et al., 2011). Despite this orientation towards social inclusion the legislation introduced through ECM and related actions did not replace any school responsibilities, rather they added to them. Importantly, some have argued that in the main the education policies of New Labour up to 2007 unequally favoured the middle classes; the policies of selection and choice marked out for the middle class the means by which to elevate their position in the educational landscape.

The New Labour governments produced an education system consistently favouring the middle classes, despite a constant rhetoric promising opportunity for the many not the few. They appeared pleased to collude with 'middle England' and policies of choice, selection, exclusion, and attention to the academic and the gifted and talented, resulted in the separation of vocational education and the denigration of schools largely attended by the poor. By the early twenty-first century disinterested observers could be forgiven for wondering whether it was a New Labour objective to eject troublesome lower class children and make schools safer for the middle classes.

(Tomlinson, 2005: 165–166)

Certainly the politics of standards and a lack of tolerance of 'educational failure' mark out the New Labour project under Blair. As Tomlinson notes, whilst private education only benefits those with the means to pay, competition and choice policies benefit disproportionately those with the ability to choose: the middle classes. An education marketplace was introduced whereby the middle classes were more favoured. Funding and administering education along such lines introduced new 'modes of class disadvantage' (Tomlinson, 2005: 174).

ACTIVITY 3.4

ECM supposedly offered a new way of running education.

    a   In what ways was it new?

    b   In what ways was it a continuation of the old?

Use Chapter 4 to help you with this.

Brown's legacy

Following Gordon Brown's elevation to prime minister in 2007, a greater emphasis was placed on cooperation between schools rather than the competition which had marked Blair's tenure (Abbott et al., 2013). The 2007 Children's plan reflected this, based, as it was, on the idea that every child can succeed with the support of an integrated approach to children's services.

> And by investing in all those who work with children, and by building capacity to work across professional boundaries we can ensure that joining up services is not just about providing a safety net for the vulnerable – it is about unlocking the potential of every child.
>
> (DCSF, 2007: 18)

The emphasis was on 'outcomes across the breadth of school performance: pupil attainment, progress and well-being; a school's success in reducing the impact of disadvantage; and parents' and pupils views of the school and the support they are receiving' (DCSF, 2009a: 3). This was established, in part, so as to create political distance between Brown's Labour and the Conservatives. The former, it was argued, had a vision for a school system-based solution whereas the latter only had school-based ambitions. Ambitious targets for 2010 were set in the areas of child health, education and poverty levels. In 2007 this was supported by the radical renaming of the government department to the Department for Children, Schools and Families (DCSF) to reflect a wider role for education and its links with other areas of government and local provision. Ed Balls became the Secretary of State for Children, Schools and Families although he was often referred to as the Children's Secretary. Higher education was hived off into a new department called the Department of Innovation, Universities and Skills (DIUS) under John Denham. As Gillard (2011) maintains, there was some logic to these moves; DCSF brought together all policy relating to young people: youth justice, child poverty and children's health were all shared responsibilities with other relevant government departments.

The 2009 White Paper advocated integrated working through the creation of 'multi-agency teams in schools bringing together a wide range of children's services professionals' (DCSF, 2009b: 9). With echoes in ECM, this was another play in the drive to ensure that joined-up government occurred at the school level. It sought to ensure that the various services designed around the child all worked in tandem for the best interests of all children. The work that teachers did in schools also reflected this emphasis as well. In 2007 the secondary curriculum review developed a series of cross-curricular links which directed education policy towards helping to solve a number of social, cultural and lifestyle issues in addition to maintaining high standards.

To reflect the importance of a properly qualified workforce, it was proposed that teaching should become a masters level profession. To reflect the importance of education, the statutory age until which children should be involved in education or training was set to increase to 17 by 2013 and 18 by 2015. However, a concentration on raising standards was also part and parcel of the drive to improve education. In 2008, 638 secondary schools with results below 30 per cent A* to C grade at GCSE were targeted. £400 million was provided to effect improvement with £200 million going into converting 70 of these schools into academies.

The Coalition

School organisation was to prove a major area of reform under the Coalition's agreement. The system was to be reformed to ensure new providers can enter the state school system in response to parental demand. In particular, parents, teachers, charities and local communities were to be given the chance to set up new free schools; schools funded by the state but out of the control of the local authority. New technical academies were to be opened and more faith schools would be encouraged. The Coalition also wanted to halt the 'unnecessary' closure of special schools, and remove the bias towards inclusion whereby pupils with special educational needs (SEN) are educated, mainly, in mainstream schools.

But it was the Coalition's policy on academies which was to prove most controversial. Although the government wished to ensure that all new academies follow an inclusive admissions policy, the extension of the academies programme from that established by New Labour provided for a radical departure from the historical organisation of schools set out by the 1944 Education Act. All schools deemed outstanding by Ofsted were to be pre-approved for academy status; those schools in an Ofsted category were to be given a finite period of time to improve or they would be converted.

In many ways the Coalition has continued with the policies of New Labour. In this regard they have both a neoliberal and neoconservative agenda. The ways in which the school system has been skewed towards academies and free schools marks a clear neoliberal line. Such patterns of governance exemplify parental and local choice over the needs of central government for the definition of curriculum matters and pay and conditions. For academies and free schools are exempt from having to teach to the National Curriculum and both sets of schools can employ staff on their own terms. But the way in which subjects have been targeted as being of importance as well as a return to more traditional modes of examination for GCSE signal the neoconservative elements within Gove's educational policy. In 2013 the government announced new measures for examinations at 16. Continuous assessment would be replaced by end of course exams and the new syllabuses would require more facts and knowledge. The skills-based agenda of the New Labour era was to be replaced with measures designed to raise standards. Clearly, the Secretary of State wishes to roll back the years to ensure that rigour is once again part and parcel of the education system.

Conclusion

It seems that the history of state secondary schools has been turbulent since the advent of truly state education in 1944. The initial organisation of the system into three separate, but supposedly equal elements, grammar, technical and secondary modern, was nothing if not an exercise in advantage for the middle class. Certainly some working class pupils did gain admission to grammar schools, but in the main the middle classes populated these, with the remaining 80 per cent of the population making up numbers predominantly in the secondary modern sector. The country's brief flirtation with comprehensivisation from the 1960s to the 1980s tells a tale of an education system determined to break the cycle of class advantage and ensure that all children have the same opportunities. But this was to be relatively short-lived for the 1980s saw the advent of new types of school divorced from local democracy, and the election of a Labour government to power in 1997 did not change this. New forms of schooling were imagined and realised, taking the secondary education sector into unchartered waters. Specialist schools and academies became a byword for educational development, seen, as they were, as the means by which educational improvement and driving up standards might be gleaned. But these schools were not without their detractors; many felt and continue to feel that they offer the middle classes yet more leverage to elevate their children into a better education and better employment. Whether such favour is set to continue with the advent of the Coalition is dealt with in the final chapter.

Key points

- Prior to 1944 secondary education was mainly for the middle and upper classes; the working class were often precluded from schooling after the age of 14.

- The 1944 Butler Act established a primary/secondary divide for children up to the ages of 11 and 15 respectively.

- Attendance at secondary school was decided on the basis of the 11-plus; a test which determined whether pupils were to attend grammar, technical or secondary modern school.

- Although comprehensive schools were planned for, it was the 1960s which saw the advent of comprehensive schools.

- The 1980s and 1990s saw successive Conservative administrations create and maintain a market for education, driven by parental choice and school diversification.

- The 1988 Education Reform Act saw the most comprehensive set of educational changes since 1944, including a national curriculum, LMS and open enrolment.

- The quality of education was deemed to be a professional matter; issues such as social class were ignored as mediators of academic success.

- New Labour continued the diversification programme started under the Conservatives.

- A new breed of schools, academies, was created as part of the failing schools agenda.

- The success of academies was contested by those who felt that they had skewed their work towards more favourable groups.

- The world of work formed a major plank of New Labour education policy: upskilling for the workplace was a recurrent theme.

- Every Child Matters was introduced to meet children's wider needs and involved substantial reorganisation and interagency working.

- Brown's legacy operated on a system of school co-operation rather than competition.

- The Coalition has continued with the theme of diversification and choice alongside a desire to return to more 'traditional' forms of schooling and exams.

Further reading

Ball, S.J., Maguire, M. and Braun, A. (2012) *How Secondary Schools Do Policy: Policy enactments in secondary schools*, London: Routledge. The whole book offers an interesting insight into how secondary schools cope with facets of education policy; how policies are enacted in schools and the roles for the actors therein.

Bates, J., Lewis, S. and Pickard, A. (2011) *Education Policy, Practice and the Professional*, London: Continuum (chapter 5). This chapter provides a good overview of matters relating to school organisation, both primary and secondary from 1870 until the present day.

Tomlinson, S. (2005) *Education in a Post-welfare Society* (2nd edn.), Maidenhead: Open University Press (Chapters 1 to 5). These offer an excellent in-depth overview of changes to the education system from 1944 to 2005, based in an appreciation of the welfarist settlement and the post-welfare era.

4

Primary matters

Purpose of this chapter

After reading this chapter you should have:

- an understanding of the ways in which primary education altered between 1944 and the 1960s;
- an understanding of changes in attitudes towards primary education from the 1960s to the 1970s;
- an understanding of the ways in which the 1988 Education Reform Act (ERA) altered primary education;
- knowledge of the ways in which New Labour instigated change in the primary sector, in particular through:
  - o coercion and pressure;
  - o defining high-quality teaching;
  - o the curriculum;
  - o knowledge of the recent role performance and standards have had on primary education.

A brief history

Before looking at the state of primary education up to and including New Labour's terms in office, it is worthwhile spending time considering some of the ways in which primary education has altered over time. Following the introduction of the 1862 Revised Code, a system of payment by results was established for the nation's elementary schools. This code stipulated what was to be taught and how much progress pupils would have to make each year. The code brought about payment by results and a narrowing both of the elementary school curriculum and pedagogic practice. Teachers' fate financially, indeed professionally, was determined by centrally identified curricula and the progress their pupils made. This continued until 1897 and the repeal of the code. What is of note is the culture in which teachers had to operate. The regime ensured that teachers complied with central mandate rather than exercise individual judgement or creativity.

Elementary schools continued until the end of the Second World War after which they were gradually phased out. Prior to this, however, the Hadow Report of 1926 had recommended the division of the elementary phase into two distinct parts: infant and junior. This could be achieved either by running an all-age 5 to 11 primary school, or an infant school from 5 to 7 and a junior school from 7 to 11.

Whilst the modern primary may well differ in many respects to its 1940s counterpart, it has its basis in the welfarist settlement. Following the Second World War the assumption was that civil servants were more effective than private enterprise in providing public services. Whilst both private and state require an ethical basis upon which to operate, the former seeks to provide profit to shareholders and owners, whilst the latter seeks public good. The belief was that those working in the public sector should have high levels of education to be sure that the ethical basis for action was met.

Initially, the way in which primary schools were organised was akin to their status as the formative training ground for the newly developed secondary system. At the end of their time in primary schools, pupils sat the 11-plus, an exam designed to identify the 'type of mind' an individual child possessed. If they were academically minded, then a place would be offered at the grammar school. If they were technically minded then a place at one of the few technical schools might be forthcoming. The remaining 80 per cent of the population attended secondary modern schools, designed to prepare young people for the world of work in industry or retail. This system of schooling required the primary school to be a proving ground; a means to ensure that children were placed into the right secondary schools.

This was to change, from the 1960s, however. Following the Labour government's circular 10/65 calling for comprehensive secondary education to be considered at the local education authority (LEA) level, primary schools became freer to innovate, freed as they were from the shackles of the 11-plus. Subsequently, in the 1960s and 1970s the belief was that primary age children need their own curriculum and pedagogy. In 1967 the Central Advisory Council for Education (CACE) produced the Plowden Report. This generated much media coverage and helped to raise the consciousness of the population as a whole to the needs of primary aged children, their curriculum and pedagogy (Cunningham, 2012). At the heart of its recommendations lay a belief in child-centred notions of education; a belief that the primary age child is in a unique stage of development that requires a particular education. Elevated status was granted to topic-based work; a means of ensuring that knowledge was presented to pupils in a real world manner and not as individual subjects divorced from the reality of the child. The report extolled the virtues of independence for teachers in determining the curriculum, a principle which was apparent in the work of the Schools Council for Curriculum and Examinations. At the heart of Plowden was an attempt to realise a new pedagogy for the primary sector.

This was new and supposedly ushered in a period of progressivism and child-centredness. Primary education, post-Plowden, is often seen as a golden age full of child centred practice and progressivism. In practice, research suggests that this was not the case and that literacy and numeracy were emphasised and lessons were often targeted at the middle ability. In addition, serious inconsistencies between schools were demonstrated in terms of breadth, balance, quality and management.

Importantly, the economic situation of the 1970s challenged such ideals as primary schools were increasingly called upon to meet the needs of the economy. Throughout the late 1960s and 1970s progressive education was challenged by the political right. The publication of a series of papers criticising state education, and in particular primary pedagogy, were published. These 'Black Papers' signalled a strong move by the right wing to denigrate that which they maintained was occurring in state education in an effort to win public support for more 'traditional' methods and organisation. In part these were driven by neoliberal ideologies, but they also pandered to neoconservative thinking through their deployment of tradition as an argument. The first Conservative Secretary of State for Education in 1979, Keith Joseph, abolished CACE in an effort to win back control from what was perceived to be far left-leaning organisations controlling the educational landscape. The political right wing felt that CACE stood for progressivism and an expanding role for the state in education, things which flew in the face of Conservative aspirations regarding the development of the education system. As Garratt and Forrester (2012: 76) note, 'it was becoming apparent that the role of schools was to prepare pupils for the workplace and, due to the unpredictability of society, their learning for life.'

The Conservative legacy

The period from 1979 to 1997 was marked mainly by the passing into legislation of the Education Reform Act (ERA; DES, 1988). The introduction of the Act with its far-reaching and wide-ranging statutes, articulated six key, New Right elements (Ball, 2008: 80):

- the establishment of a 'national' curriculum which described the content to be taught to all children between the ages of 5 and 16;

- suspicion of teachers and their politics and hence the need for control and accountability mechanisms;

- a move to 'teacher-proof' evaluation most notably manifest in the form of national public examinations to be taken at age 7, 11, 14 and 16;

- parental choice within a marketplace;

- the devolving of school budgets and responsibility from LEAs directly to schools;

- an increase in the responsibilities and powers of head teachers and governors.

More importantly, for the changes within the ERA itself, the neoconservative introduction of a national curriculum was seen to be a necessary precursor to the introduction of an educational marketplace. This, it was felt, would enable parents to choose from a level playing field whilst ensuring that certain standards were realised among schools as a whole. But the concept of a national curriculum is Janus-faced, looking as it does towards central, bureaucratic control for its direction but also to consumer (in this case parental) choice as the means by which local accountability can be enforced (Lawton, 1994). Clearly some things were seen to be worth learning (namely 'traditional' subjects) whilst others were dangerous and to be discouraged ('progressivism' and 'child centredness'). Particularly, the ERA, through its inception of a national curriculum, shifted the focus for pedagogy away from much maligned progressive ideals towards discussions dominated by a belief in the need to instruct young people into the discipline of life and accepted forms of knowledge in a controlled manner. It should be noted, though, that the first National Curriculum orders as published in 1988 were somewhat of a disappointment; they lacked the wider influences desired by the Neoconservatives and instead promoted 'a collection of traditional subjects not too dissimilar to those studied in schools fifty years earlier' (Best, 2003: 17).

The 1992 Education (Schools) Act established Ofsted as a body designed to carry out independent inspections of schools. Ofsted was not universally welcomed and the teaching profession found the inspection process to be laborious, time consuming and extremely stressful. There were also many who questioned the validity of the reports, and their accuracy and objectivity were often called into question. Importantly, there was an attempt to give power to those who had no background working in schools through the addition of a lay-inspector. Such individuals were not seen as a positive move however. More importantly, the head of Ofsted from 1994 was Chris Woodhead. Throughout his tenure he seemed to be on a collision course with the teaching profession. He was often outspoken and used his office to promulgate his views on the impoverishment of 'progressive' education and the need for 'traditional' values and ways of teaching.

Whilst the Conservatives ventured into new areas, it was the case that their administrations held no overarching aims to prescribe or proscribe teaching methods over and above a desire to see a return to whole class teaching. But this was an inspirational measure not realised through particularly prescriptive measures. In point of fact, whilst the ERA (DES, 1988) secured statutory intervention in the curriculum, ministers stated that they would not tell teachers how to teach. So, for example, Ofsted, although concerned with the quality of teaching, did not countenance desired lesson formats over-and-above comments about 'whole class teaching'. As Dadds (2001: 44) notes,

> In Britain, successive Secretaries of State for Education have claimed that the pedagogical choices made for delivery of the National Curriculum should be left to the professional judgement of teachers.

The report by Alexander, Rose and Woodhead (1992) – commonly known as the 'Three Wise Men' – did appear to criticise child-centred teaching and called for a return to more formal methods of education. However, they also showed that despite popular media images, non–child-centred, subject-based work was still very much in evidence in primary schools; Plowden was not as well realised as the popular press would have people believe. The effect of this report and subsequent government rhetoric was a steady increase in the use of whole class teaching and grouping by ability in primary schools and Ofsted's concentration on these and the basics. Concomitantly, during the Conservative era, primary teacher preparation changed from being child-centred to society-centred with the emphasis on subject specialisation.

Pedagogy → New idea+argument

In many ways pedagogy has been the battleground for primary education since the inception of Plowden. The debates have often been portrayed as polarised between left and right politically and in many ways this is borne out by the ways in which particular political parties have used ideology as the means to drive through change. The above brief introduction notes the fact that little was explicitly done by government to control pedagogy through the years following the Second World War. However, this was to change with the election of New Labour to power in 1997. It was they who introduced non-statutory guidance for literacy and numeracy which pointedly controlled primary pedagogy through a variety of mechanisms, most notably the standards agenda. Indeed, the standards agenda was at variance with the traditional child-centred focus for primary education (Cunningham, 21012). Allied to pedagogical changes was a ratcheting up of the stakes for testing at age 11, the end of Key Stage Two, and the introduction of increasingly rigorous inspections with increasingly draconian measures put in place for those schools which failed to meet the grade. As Cunningham (2012: 7) writes,

> In respect of national accountability, school inspection was exploited by the incoming Secretary of State in 1997 as a means of 'naming and shaming' 'failing schools'. Whether or not this policy contributed to improving standards remains debatable and politically contentious.

In contrast, opposition to this testing and inspection regime has been widespread and vociferous.

New Labour

In 1997 the Labour Party, now called New Labour, swept to victory. Whilst it might have been expected that much of the discourse of the New Right would be dismissed, it was soon very clear that this was not to be the case. Although it is disingenuous to state that New Labour simply continued with the policies of old, it is the case that much of the marketplace rhetoric and practice built up over the previous 18 years was, in one form or another, adopted and deployed. Whilst New Labour adopted neoliberal privatisation and centralising tendencies from the Conservatives, there are fundamental differences between the New Right and the Third Way of New Labour. Importantly, whilst neoliberalism rests on a rather rigid belief in markets and the private sector coupled with an almost zealous disregard for the public sector, New Labour's approach utilised 'a "flexible repertoire" of state roles and responses' (Ball, 2008: 88). Put more simply, New Labour's mantra was more akin to the non-ideological adage of 'what works'. This was particularly notable where pedagogy was concerned. Brehony (2005: 41) notes this but also signals the politics inherent in the way in which New Labour adopted this position:

> One prominent element of New Labour's policies towards primary schools, whether or not they were intended to appeal to the electorate, has been their claim to have policies based on research. Conceived as an antidote to ideology, the mantra 'what works' is itself ideological because it ignores the asymmetries of power and its operation and it rests on the firm conviction that 'what works' can be identified with some degree of precision, whereas most social science research tends to produce not a single answer but several . . . At worst, this has led to the selective appropriation of evidence and rejection of that which did not suit New Labour's political purposes . . .

At the start of the New Labour era there was an unrelenting focus on the basics. The lack of overt government input regarding pedagogy seen under the Conservatives was to change starting with the introduction, in September 1998, of a highly prescriptive National Literacy Strategy (NLS) (DfEE, 1998c) and associated literacy hour. This was soon followed in 1999 by an equally prescriptive National Numeracy Strategy (NNS; DfEE, 1999). The

Stifled creativity
teach + student

NLS and NNS were contentious: evidence for their structure was controversial. Notably, both were non-statutory, although they did contain statements as to how the strategies should be implemented. Concern was very soon expressed concerning the time taken up by the strategies and their focus on narrow aspects of the curriculum. The approach taken to the management of teachers was overly dirigiste, and would, it was believed, do little to release the creativity and innovation which the knowledge-based economy would require (Brehony, 2005).

Questions must be asked, then, concerning the ways in which that promoted under their auspices became so prevalent in schools to the point where other pedagogic forms became, at one time, marginalised to the point of extinction. In answer, three mechanisms were used: coercion and pressure; defining high-quality teaching; and curriculum.

Coercion and pressure

Upon publication, the literacy and numeracy hours were pointedly clear: schools needed to consider how they were to adopt the prescribed teaching methods or demonstrate that they achieved high standards in these two areas through their own methods. As Dadds (2001: 45) notes, the way in which the 'guidance' was produced was specific to the point of being formulaic. From 1997 whole class teaching and ability setting were encouraged by New Labour and Ofsted (Brehony, 2005; Cunningham, 2012). Targets were set, standards were to be 'driven up', failure was to be given 'zero-tolerance', and practice was to become 'evidence-based'. However, the evidence used was selected to meet particular political ends which fitted

with the aims of the New Labour administration. Lessons were split into three parts (whole class teaching, small-group work, whole class teaching), teaching methods were described at the level of word and sentence work and phonic analysis, and teacher-defined objectives were held up to be the way in which better learning and teaching might occur. It was doubtful whether any school or teacher had the time, or inclination, to produce something as comprehensive as this. The NLS and NNS were designed to be 'teacher proof' (Brehony, 2005) and any alternatives to the structure of the literacy and numeracy strategies had to be justified to Ofsted. The assumption was that the official pedagogic line was right and that all other pedagogies were inferior.

This prescription alone was not enough to coerce professionals into adopting that proclaimed as right and proper. Part of both strategies was the creation of an army of literacy and numeracy consultants, mostly attached to local authorities whose job it was to support and monitor the implementation of literacy and numeracy. Schools were effectively pitted against each other in a game of 'sharing good practice' whereupon those officially deemed to have 'got it right' were paraded as beacons of 'best practice'. This strategy was taken further with the instigation of leading teachers of numeracy and literacy; teachers who were seen to be exemplars of this 'best practice' who could parachute into other schools and help 'struggling' professionals by sharing their expertise. Mostly attached to LEAs, these consultants and leading teachers formed a surveillance technology, all powerful in its ability to hold schools to account through the mechanisms of panoptic self-surveillance and calls to professional good will.

It was through calls on professionalism also that such pedagogic formulation came to fruition. The language of high expectations and excellence came to be seen as a mantra for a rejection of failure but also a clarion call to the professional heart of teachers. For it is difficult to argue against such a mantra; should not all staff wish to see the very best for their pupils? Further weight was added to this discourse by Barber (2001) when he advocated that whilst the Thatcher era had driven teachers and teaching from *uninformed professional judgement* towards *uninformed prescription*, the literacy and numeracy strategies and associated legislation had altered this state of affairs and ushered in an era of *informed prescription*. The argument here is that teachers previously operated 'professionally unsighted' but that New Labour had removed the blindfold and demonstrated what good teaching and learning look like. Many strong head teachers and their staff did resist such calls to informed prescription, however, arguing that they had good standards in their school and good teaching practices to match. Clearly, though, not every head or professional felt they could act in such a manner and in many respects this led to a loss of confidence in some staff (Dadds, 2001). Higgins (1998) also reminds us that many teachers, tired of being blamed for the ills of education, countenanced this external prescription as a means to absolve responsibility should things go wrong. Some argue that teachers unquestioningly complied with central mandate and government direction and diktat to ensure a sense of 'doing it right' rather than 'doing the right thing' (Webb et al., 2004).

The advice associated with the strategies (schemes of work), although presented as 'guidance' were widely adopted; this adoption by the profession of the proposed teaching methods and content could be said to mirror the sort of action stemming from statutory requirements. For many teachers the standards agenda set a performative line that permeated every facet of primary education. Webb et al. (2004: 98) cite one head who sums the situation thus: 'We are about figures, we are about statistics, we are about targets but we are not about the heart of education – children and what is actually needed for them.'

In many ways it was a blame culture that drove the development of pedagogy in such a prescriptive manner. Throughout the 1980s and 1990s teachers had suffered from a culture of derision. Often cited as incompetent, letting down pupils and parents, this discourse presented teachers as a group, not to be professionally trusted, but rather to be scrutinised, observed, monitored and controlled. New Labour took matters further, however. Although their language was somewhat more balanced than that of the Conservative administration, the discourse became much more focused on a specific form of standards and accountability.

Shortly after taking power New Labour initiated a high-stakes assessment regime. The then Secretary of State for Education, David Blunkett, announced stringent targets for 11-year-olds at the end of key stage standard assessment tests (SATs) in the areas of literacy and numeracy, to be achieved through the aforementioned strategies. He even went as far as to announce that should these targets not be realised he would resign. These targets were filtered through LEAs: targets for the LEA were set and these were duly passed on to schools, which, in turn, were required to set targets for individual pupils. It soon became the norm that the teacher would set certain requirements of pupils, in terms of achievement levels, which would, in turn, necessitate certain actions. In effect, pupils became required to give an account of themselves through the technology of the testing regime. In the main, three mechanisms for improving performance were adopted: excessive coaching in how to pass exams; booster classes; and cheating. In reality, the latter was extremely rare and was in no way approved by anyone in the profession. However, it is notable that some teachers and head teachers did feel under such pressure that they did engage in illegal activities (Swaine, 2009).

Early improvements ensued, but this was attributed, in part, to the Hawthorne effect, the situation whereby results improve because people are being observed. By 2001 the rate of improvement had slowed and the goal of continuous improvement seemed illusive. Issues wider than the school were blamed for this; nevertheless, the high stakes regime continued. Schools also reported that Ofsted inspections seemed determined by a school's results, rather than wider outcomes.

Often, interim, optional SATs were used to measure progress against the defined requirements and mechanisms such as 'top up' and 'booster' classes were put in place to militate against the chance that targets would be missed; these were advocated in the drive to improve the quality of education as measured by the numbers of pupils achieving level four in each of English and maths. These were found to be head teachers' preferred methods for raising attainment (Gray et al., 2003). Once again it was the discourse of high expectations that was deployed to support this endeavour.

Ofsted was deployed in this task as well. The inspectorate determined whether or not schools were making appropriate progress against national targets in core subjects and in many ways such measures became limiting factors in determining a school's grading. Teachers initially felt powerless in the face of Ofsted, but gradually staff, especially heads, began to feel able to challenge the process (Webb et al., 2004). As a counterpoint, heads welcomed an increase in classroom surveillance as they felt it enhanced their professionalism. Teachers were undecided, however: some felt that it stifled creativity and reduced risk-taking with the onus on getting it right for the observer (Webb et al., 2004); others saw the strategies as empowering because they shared good practice (Cunningham, 2012). Whatever the view, many agreed that the onus had moved away from learning onto performing.

> In England . . . national policy was aimed at standardising teaching, reinforced by local authority advice filtered down from government guidance, generating mechanisms to assess pupils, promoting and monitoring didactic skills-based teaching, instead of empowering pupils.
>
> (Cunningham, 2012: 70)

Whilst the notion of 'high expectations' is one which is difficult to ignore or disagree with, it is clear that the very definition of expectation and the context in which this occurs must be considered. The expectations of some (those who were likely to achieve the government targets of level 4) embolden a certain education orientation: the conferment of worth through testing. What is elided is the potential of all to succeed. And it must be remembered that expectations lead to behaviours with concomitant effects on the learner. In turn these lead to achievement which further confers expectation. Whereas the uninformed professionalism derided by Barber (2001) probably required teachers to use wider judgements to inform them as to the 'worth' of the individual (and hence negate the idea of 'uninformed'), under the new regime of target setting, such wider judgement becomes obviated. As Flecknoe (2001: 220) states:

> The quest to raise achievement has therefore become associated with raising attainment in a narrow range of tests. Increasingly, teachers are being rewarded for teaching pupils to pass tests. This approach to education is predicated on the 'Squirrel' paradigm of education in which we provide children with an excessive number of units of knowledge (nuts), during a period of compulsory education (autumn), which they proceed to bury in their brains against the possibility that some may come in useful in later life. It is problematical but possible to audit the number of units of knowledge retained. Most, of course, are never used. Some, which would be useful, cannot be retrieved. The alternative to this paradigm is one which values the ability to learn in problematical circumstances but this would give those who seek to audit education an even more difficult job.

Thus teachers and schools were faced with a choice: adopt the strategies with the possibility of official approval, or plough an individual furrow and risk criticism. This was a dilemma and many in the professional did not have the wherewithal to undertake the task of political challenge.

> It might be possible for the profession to sell other values to the public and to the gov-
> ernment by which to be assessed. However, target setting is here to stay as a means of
> political control. The question is whether teachers and schools can subvert the process
> to include the relevant stakeholders so that it may be a tool for the raising of relevant
> achievement. This requires not only political nous, it also demands time for consultation
> with pupils and parents. It requires skilful and intuitive control of culture in the school
> among the teachers and among the pupils with the aim of influencing the culture of the
> community. This is a tall order for hard-pressed schools and for teacher unions!
>
> (Flecknoe, 2001: 227)

Through the necessities of the testing and inspection regime, made clear by certain teaching learning discourses, teachers were required to act in ways which conferred both themselves and school with certain accolades: excellent teacher; outstanding school; etc. It is this adherence to performance that so dominated education in the late 1990s and early to mid-2000s. Although the national targets were dropped in 2004 the culture of constant year-on-year improvement prevailed.

Webb et al. (2004) identified that whilst the need for greater assessment did lead teachers to better target planning and learning activities, teachers felt enormous pressure in years 2 and 6 to prepare pupils for the SATs; teachers' workload increased dramatically as a result of the strategies (Galton, 2007). Although they found that teaching to the tests was against teachers' better judgement and professionalism it was deemed necessary in order to reduce pupil stress and prepare them to do as well as possible on the tests.

New Labour's focus on literacy and numeracy and the advent of national targets led to a loss of breadth and balance in the primary curriculum; primary practice became skewed. Up to half of the week was spent on the two subjects alone, with everything else squeezed into the remaining time. Additionally, research suggested that pupils liked school less than prior to 1997 and that the more able pupils were, the more likely they were to dislike school. The standards agenda seemed to steer pupils' behaviour towards doing what they needed to in order to succeed as judged in quite narrow terms. Indeed, throughout that time, teachers reported that pupils were less willing to continue to undertake work once a desired level had been achieved and pupils themselves cited less enjoyment through learning but more enjoyment through attaining (Galton, 2007). Pollard and Triggs (2000) found pupils to be outcomes driven, sometimes at the expense of the processes of learning. The ensuing competitive environment sought to validate pupil progress through the adoption of simplistic cause–and–effect models of learning. In an effort to stay ahead of other schools and achieve higher league table status, teaching was all too often reduced to a mechanistic ritual designed to ensure that pupils are able to perform on externally driven tests. The standards agenda was pursued despite the fact that employers were vociferous in their need for creative and talented individuals and their belief that the standards agenda was not delivering this (Cunningham, 2012). Further, Ofsted often criticised teachers for failing to be questioning and reflective concerning their application of the guidance, despite the pressure they felt to conform.

Defining high-quality teaching

Such matters of coercion and pressure have their roots in the desire to govern. New
Labour's approach to education was to manage, from the centre, the work that teachers undertook. It was not enough that measures were set in place to orient work in the
desired direction; technologies for ensuring that certain lines were followed needed to
be deployed. Accordingly, national strategies coupled to stringent targets for attainment
provided a discourse whose orientation meant that professionals constantly scrutinised
that which they and others did; the perception that other schools were adopting certain
methods and achieving success led to the importation of such measures. But this desire
to govern pedagogy, manifest via central steerage, was also operationalised through the
very definitions of pedagogy held up at the time. The advice contained in the literacy and
numeracy strategies were two cases in point. But literacy and numeracy related to specific
curricular areas. What was needed was a case in point that would transcend subject and
age-range divisions and which could provide a rallying point for government in its drive
to 'improve' teaching and learning. Ways of delineating the 'good' from the 'bad' were
required; what was needed were ways of demonstrating how better teaching leads to better pupil learning, the assumption being that increased success in tests provides appropriate
evidence. As Hartley (2003: 90) noted:

> The raising of standards has become something of a clarion call. League-tables abound.
> Performance – and its measurement – has been the watchword. There has been a peda-
> gogical drift back to basics, back to whole-class, direct teaching.

Such moves to define pedagogy were attempts to ameliorate the effects of poor teaching
assumed to have existed prior to the introduction of literacy and numeracy and the realisation
of certain technical skills. Thus the initiatives themselves defined the problem to be overcome
in so much as they identified that teaching deemed 'other' to that described by official guidance was problematic; they conferred status through 'official pedagogy'. Norms were created
so as to hold up as an exemplar a certain view of pedagogy. This 'new' pedagogy aligned well
with the political demand that teachers be accountable for the quality of school development
(Wrigley, 2003). And so, from early on in New Labour's first term in office, whole class teaching and ability setting was promoted both by the government and Ofsted (Brehony, 2005).
With regard to pedagogy, pace appeared to take precedence over thinking time (Galton,

2007). Importantly, though, evidence seemed to suggest pedagogically, little had changed since the 1970s, particularly in relation to the way in which pupils and staff interacted; staff still questioned, pupils still answered. But Galton (2007: 173) was more concerned still:

> More seriously, primary classroom practice now seems more akin to stereotyped secondary school lessons, dominated by a fast pace, with restricted questioning and a tendency for teachers to control the discourse such that transmission rather than exploration dominates.

However, by 2002 there was mounting concern that the literacy and numeracy strategies were distorting the primary curriculum (Brehony, 2005). Teachers were reporting that they were unable to offer a broad and balanced curriculum and Ofsted evidence suggested that enquiry, problem-solving and practical work had suffered under the new regime. A review of the two strategies undertaken by Michael Fullan and colleagues concluded that changes in teaching practices had been marked, in particular the fact that more whole class teaching was used, attention was now paid to lesson pace, and planning was based on objectives not activities (Earl et al., 2003). However, they were less sure as to the effects on pupil learning. Most notable was the caveat they added: the use of ever-increasing national targets was skewing the activities with which schools engaged and was leading to a marked decrease in pupil and teacher motivation. Ofsted published its own reports into the strategies' successes and concluded that whilst substantial improvements in classroom practice may have occurred, overall management of the strategies in school was weak and too often teaching lacked questioning and reflection (Ofsted, 2002).

It was also clear, as noted by Michael Barber (2002, quoted in Brehony, 2005: 39) that 'the framework for continuous improvement had been less successful in tackling low performance which results not from school failure but from a combination of factors such as low community aspirations, high pupil turnover, serious poverty and/or fractured communities'. This is most notable given that for some time prior to this, government had chosen to play down the effects of socio-cultural factors as explanations for low educational outcomes. Importantly, whilst overtly politicising the process of pedagogic formation, government had sought to elide social, cultural and political issues in forming any part of the definition itself.

ACTIVITY 4.2

- In what ways is pedagogy the province of the professional?
- The national strategies tended to ignore socio-economic issues. Why might this be an issue when considering what pedagogy might look like?

Curriculum

The New Labour government inherited a curriculum that had more or less stood still since 1988. Although the Dearing Review (Dearing, 1994) had suggested loosening the curriculum to allow for more flexibility and creative use of time by primary school staff, subjects remained in force and the emphasis was still on the basics of literacy and numeracy. The introduction of the literacy and numeracy strategies in 1998 and 1999 respectively was one way in which the curriculum was altered following the election victory of 1997. The new government was also conscious, however, that things were not rosy in the curricular garden. In particular, teachers felt that too much was asked of them. There was also the belief that key areas of the curriculum were missing or did not receive wide enough attention.

Curriculum debate had occurred for some time, though. Certainly, Callaghan's speech in 1976 started the discussion. Throughout the 1980s discussions were had as to whether or not a 'core' or 'common' curriculum could be identified but it was not until 1988 and the ERA that a new National Curriculum was enforced. Immediately the curriculum was seen to be overloaded and bloated and with considerable gaps. The latter were 'plugged' by cross-curricular themes, such as health education and citizenship introduced to 'give coherence to the educational experience of the pupil' (Brandom, quoted in Adams and Calvert, 2007). But these proved too difficult to weave into the already voluminous fabric of the statutory curriculum and for the most part they were ignored.

Shortly after taking power, New Labour undertook a review of the curriculum, the outcome of which was, in many ways, unsurprising. As already mentioned and although not statutory, the focus on literacy and numeracy was to occupy the minds of all in primary schools. Although the new curriculum was the third since 1988, precious little had altered. Most notably there was still a hierarchy of subjects: English, maths and science were deemed core whilst others such as art and PE were deemed foundation only. A further group of subjects, notably personal, social and health education (PSHE) and citizenship education (CE) were given the status of non-statutory guidance only. They were seen to be important, but not important enough to warrant inclusion in official requirements. What was notable was the inclusion of a set of values for the curriculum, something that had been lacking since 1988. Crucially, the new orders required a broad and balanced curriculum whilst recognising that the school curriculum and the National Curriculum are not synonymous: the latter is but part of the former. Indeed, the National Curriculum has never signalled how the school curriculum is to be organised.

But the National Curriculum did impact greatly on the means of organisation of the primary school, if not directly, then certainly indirectly. Whilst increases in the number of subject lessons occurred, primary schools were still organising their work around themes or topics until New Labour came to power; for it was the advent of literacy and numeracy which had the greatest effect on the way in which schools organised their timetables (Watkins, 1999). Pressures to achieve in literacy and numeracy via the SATS for English and maths created a two-tier curriculum and a loss of creativity and risk-taking (Brehony, 2005).

The National Curriculum, although side-lined by literacy and numeracy, played a major role in the development of primary practice post-1997. Whilst development prior to this did occur, certainly with regard to an increase in subject-based teaching, the emphasis of New Labour was upon the ways in which the curriculum could be used to meet certain political ends.

In 2003, and in an attempt to reduce the stultifying effects of the performance culture, the Primary National Strategy (DfES, 2003c) was published. Titled *Excellence and Enjoyment* this sought to enable every primary school to 'build on their own strengths to serve the needs of their own children' (DfES, 2003c: Foreword). Although the national targets for literacy and numeracy were dropped shortly after publication (in 2004) the strategy still required schools to set themselves challenging targets so that there would be year-on-year improvement in the results for end of Key Stage Two tests. However, teacher autonomy was heavily implied:

And they [schools] themselves will take responsibility for making what they do better all the time. I want every school to drive its own improvement, to set its own challenging targets, and to work tirelessly to build on success. However good our schools are, for the sake of our children they can always be better.

(DfES, 2003c: Foreword)

Excellence and Enjoyment sought to reassure those who were concerned that hitherto the standards agenda had constrained primary practice and curriculum; it sought to reduce government prescription.

Although the strategy acknowledged concerns raised in other government quarters than the Department for Education and Skills (DfES), by thinkers such as Bentley (1998), a director at the think-tank Demos, it was, once again, founded in the drive to raise educational attainment albeit with a measure of enjoyment thrown in. As Galton (2007) notes, though, whilst the desire may well have been an increase in enjoyment, the methods of the national literacy and numeracy strategies were the favoured mode of organising teaching for the primary school. Indeed, the strategy was clear: it desired the extension of such methods to all parts of the curriculum. As Cunningham (2012: 68) notes,

> The PNS [Primary National Strategy] showed few signs of a serious desire to move away from 'standards' in favour of creativity and pupil-centred curricula. It claimed to increase teachers' autonomy on the grounds that the strategies, though strongly supported by government, were not statutory.

Alexander (2004) suggested that *Excellence and Enjoyment* still focused on what it 'knew' worked and common-sense notions of pedagogy. But he is more scathing still, pointing to dishonesty of intent on the part of the government: whilst the rhetoric may be of 'enjoyment' and 'enrichment', instrumentality of purpose characterises the project. He writes,

> Against the ostensible offer of autonomy, we have the continuing pressure of testing, targets and performance tables and the creeping hegemonisation of the curriculum by the Literacy and Numeracy Strategies, with three-part lessons, interactive whole class teaching and plenaries soon to become a template for the teaching of everything.

(Alexander, 2004: 15)

For Cunningham (2012) any connection with culture and social structure was lost. Teaching was the focus, not learning, and to mark this, new standards for teacher trainees were introduced which graded them excellent, competent or unsatisfactory.

By 2006, results had seemed to plateau. Whilst the government continued to claim massive gains in results due to the standards agenda, other research (for example, Tymms and Fitz-Gibbon, 2001; Tymms and Coe, 2003) suggested that the gains were more modest. Importantly, in 2003 Her Majesty's Chief Inspector (HMCI) David Bell announced that the literacy and numeracy strategies were skewing the curriculum. Indeed, from 2000 onwards inspection reports and research studies revealed pressures on the primary curriculum and damage to breadth and balance. Creative subjects were in decline, as were aspects of mathematical education such as problem-solving and practical work. In 2008 the Children, Schools and Families Select Committee (HCCSFC) found that testing at 11 was skewing children's' education. They advocated a root and branch reform of the system.

In 2008 the government commissioned the Rose Review, led by Sir Jim Rose. His remit was to examine how the primary National Curriculum could be brought into the twenty-first century. He examined a number of areas and made recommendations, the main one being the proposal of six areas of learning rather than traditional subjects. Shortly after publication, the government began implementation, going so far as to design schemes of work to aid teachers in the delivery of the new curriculum. However, the Rose Review was not commissioned to consider the exams and assessment system; this lay beyond its remit. Accordingly, many questioned whether the review would actually achieve anything; many felt that given that the assessment tail was wagging the curriculum dog, to ignore such a fundamental part of primary school life would neuter the review.

Parallel to this, starting in 2006 a group of academics, led by Robin Alexander of Cambridge University, began their own review of the curriculum (Alexander, 2010). Entitled the Cambridge Review and funded by the Esmee Fairbairn Foundation, this was the most comprehensive review since the Plowden Report. Undertaken between 2006 and 2009 the review generated evidence from community soundings, written submissions and produced many interim reports and briefing papers (Garratt and Forrester, 2012). Problematically, the report, from the outset, was critical of state-endorsed practice and policy. This set the review on a collision course with government who felt obliged to respond, negatively, to the many interim reports and especially the final submission. One of the main thrusts was the belief that government mandate had created a creativity vacuum whereby teachers did as they were told. There was never any intent on the part of minsters in the New Labour government to use the Cambridge Review. Minsters tried to discredit it and bolster their own Rose Review. They were keen to extol the virtues of Rose and so described the Cambridge Review as woolly and unclear. It was questionable, though, whether anyone in government actually read the Cambridge Review in its entirety.

ACTIVITY 4.3

■ In what ways is it problematic to have a narrowing of the curriculum? Why is a broad and balanced curriculum a good thing?

■ Read *Excellence and Enjoyment* (DfES, 2003c). In what ways does the discourse advance enjoyment?

■ Look at the Rose Review of the curriculum (available at http://www.educationengland.org.uk/documents/pdfs/2009-IRPC-final-report.pdf). What is the curriculum discourse it promotes?

Every Child Matters

In the latter years of its administration New Labour sought to extend Ofsted's role to encompass elements of safeguarding, welfare and health. Such moves were ushered in as a result of *Every Child Matters* (ECM) (DfES, 2003b) and a belief in the role of schools as engineers of social inclusion. Whilst Ofsted's position has never been widely lauded within the educational community, it is clear that these changes sought to acknowledge the wider role schools play. Whilst ECM did not explicitly discuss pedagogy or curriculum, part of the undercurrent of their rationale concerned achievement. Indeed, ECM did, as one of its five outcomes, cite the need for children to 'enjoy and achieve'. Through the deployment of attainment targets as a means to judge success in this matter and in the other four outcomes, the standards agenda, still very much a part of government rhetoric, became allied to the protection of children. It was no longer enough that exam scores be seen solely as indicating educational success; rather, continued improvement in educational outcomes as measured by the number of pupils achieving certain levels in the key stage two SATs became part of the drive to safeguard.

A broader view of pedagogy was implied in the ECM policy. However, this was problematic. The discourse of high expectations was that which continued to drive the development of education; the marking out of certain levels and types of achievement served as a mechanism for the evaluation of the system as a whole and in particular a determination as to the quality of pedagogy and learning. Whilst certain measures, such as safeguarding and creativity, may have been put in place to attempt to embolden wider considerations, these were themselves judged in the same way: simplistic measures designed to capture some 'essence' at the heart of the educational project. Yet, what these measures also did was fail to explore the myriad ways in which matters such as 'enjoyment' and 'achievement' might be understood. For example, whilst it is clear that attaining on tests is one way to judge, this measure misses fundamental points about learning and its relationship to personal position and growth. Formative measures that examine the learning process as opposed to just the outcome are reliable ways of making judgements about how well pupils are enjoying and achieving at school.

Yet caution should prevail, particularly with regard to primary education. The positioning of learning in primary school as matters of attainment *and* the safeguarding of children is problematic; for whilst the former articulates success by an increase in exam scores, the latter is akin to a discourse of care. Better exam scores and care need not be mutually exclusive; but *caring for* is a position which requires not the achievement of some preordained ideal, but rather goals internal to the caring relationship. Unfortunately, the expectations extolled by the standards agenda sat external to the requirements of a caring relationship for they did not emerge from the relationship itself. *Care for* requires the conceptualisation of learning as 'an essentially human element; an essentially holistic endeavour' (Adams, 2007: 231). This was potentially lost in the defined targets for ECM against which Ofsted judged progress. It might be argued that Ofsted's remit, at the time, concerned institutional arrangements and not the care agenda. However, this cannot be said to be the case, for Ofsted were concerned with the very fabric of ECM and issues such as pupil well-being.

The Coalition

Prior to the 2010 general election, the three main parties all had policies for the primary sector, and in particular teaching and learning. The Conservatives proposed to introduce synthetic phonics as the official way to teach reading and to train teachers to use this method. In addition they proposed to introduce a reading test for 6-year-olds and an overhaul of the National Curriculum for all ages. The Liberal Democrats proposed extra money to be invested to cut class sizes, pay for one-to-one tuition and introduce catch-up classes. A pupil premium for disadvantaged pupils would be introduced with schools being able to decide what they wished to do with the money; there was to be no ring-fencing. Steps were to be taken to improve discipline in schools and measures taken to confront bullying. Whilst all of these measures apply to pupils of all ages, they were expected to have a particular resonance in the primary school given the ways in which this sector of education was viewed as a proving ground for secondary education. In addition, there was to be guaranteed special educational needs (SEN) diagnostic tests for all 5-year-olds with extra improvements in SEN provision overall and extra SEN training for teachers.

Importantly, the Liberal Democrat position was that the National Curriculum was restrictive and artificially split the vocational and academic. The proposal was to replace the National Curriculum with a slimmed down Minimum Curriculum Entitlement.

Labour also promised to introduce a pupil premium to target the disadvantaged. In addition, those primary and secondary children who fall behind in the 'three Rs' were to be given one-to-one tuition. In an effort to support children to cope with and get the best from school, teacher training institutions were to be asked to provide training on pupil resilience and responsibility.

In November 2010, and shortly after taking power, the new Conservative/Liberal Democratic Coalition government published its education White Paper, *The Importance of Teaching* (DfE, 1010a). The Coalition government seemingly embarked on a notable mix of policy that can be said, in some regards, to mirror the discourse of New Labour. Certainly, the measures used to call schools and teachers to account seem to be an area of continuation. The Coalition does not differ from New Labour in matters of accountability through performance and comparison; it does, in fact, recognise the positive features of such a system.

The White Paper was clear in its undermining of the ECM position, however, instead seeking to 're-focus Ofsted inspections on their original purpose – teaching and learning' (DfE 2010a, 4) so that inspectors might 'spend more time in the classroom and focus on key issues of educational effectiveness, rather than the long list of issues they are currently required to consider' (13). Further, they were clear: national government has no role to play in deciding pedagogy. There was a desire to ensure that best-practice is shared, but nothing was said about how pedagogy can develop to meet the standards set for primary attainment.

The Coalition is also clear in that it wishes to move teaching away from theory and towards craft-based notions. Michael Gove's position is that teaching is a craft best learned by working alongside great teachers. The Coalition's concentration on accountability measures is to occur within a system which favours the craft of teaching; the elevation of day-to-day, practical matters of the classroom. And in other matters the Coalition's position seems to hark back to disappeared 'halcyon' days. The government proposes that the primary curriculum will be more centred on subjects with increased rigour and accountability. The consultation on new proposals saw a series of subject, knowledge-based curricula reminiscent of the early days of the ERA (DES, 1988) or perhaps even earlier, similar as they were to the prescriptive, content-based approach of the 1862 Revised Code. This despite the fact that one of the four key advisers contracted to oversee the development of the new curriculum described it as potentially flawed, leading to a target driven culture and a lack of a broad and balanced curriculum (Paton, 2012a). The primary sector has come in for much sustained change and has seen its fair share of overhaul. In addition to the above, floor targets of pupils gaining a level 4 in the end of Key Stage Two English and maths SATs was initially set at 60 per cent, but were raised to 65 per cent for the 2013 tests. Effectively this meant that many primary schools risked being labelled as failures (Shepherd, 2013).

The changes wrought by the Coalition have not been met with much professional support. Indeed, the National Association of Head Teachers at its annual conference in 2013 passed a vote of no confidence in the Education Secretary for his proposals and 'forced' academisation of schools (Paton, 2013). Michael Gove's response was to insist that he was 'not going to stop' demanding higher standards.

Conclusion

It would seem, then, that primary education has, at the same time, seen great changes whilst also retaining some of its character that existed in the nineteenth century. Although there have been periods when the sector was driven by policies of a more child-centred philosophy, it is clearly the case that traditionalism has never really been left behind. Targets and standards have been the watch word for at least 30 years and inspection now plays a large part in the ways in which education is oriented and organised. There is much commonality between the curriculum of a hundred years ago and that which seems to characterise the Coalition's time in office; subjects and a concentration on the basics were and continue to be, the centre of attention. In this regard little has changed and teachers still work to the same ends as before in terms of meeting targets and producing results; a harkening back to the days of the Revised Code perhaps? Research may have moved on our understanding of pedagogy from Victorian times, but it seems that much that drove our forebears is still seen as meritorious today. Questions can be asked, then, about why advancements in society have been so great yet so little has changed with regard to primary schooling.

Key points

- Primary schools predominantly emerged as a result of the Hadow Report and the 1944 Education Reform Act.
- Following the Second World War primary schools were seen as proving grounds for secondary education whereby pupils were assessed according to the 11-plus.
- Changes in the 1960s challenged the tripartite organisation of secondary schools and thus freed up primary schools to work in more creative ways. This was supported by the publication of the Plowden Report.
- The political right of the 1970s challenged so-called progressive education and the tenor of the Plowden Report.
- The 1998 Education Reform Act established a national curriculum for primary schools.
- The 1992 Education Act established Ofsted and a new inspection regime for primary and secondary schools.
- New Labour, in many ways, continued with the ideals of the Conservative Party's administrations of 1979 to 1997.
- New Labour introduced prescriptive Literacy and Numeracy Strategies in an attempt to increase the number of pupils achieving level four at the age of 11 in the SATs.
- In order to control primary practice, New Labour used the mechanisms of: coercion and pressure; defining high-quality teaching; and the curriculum.
- Although much has changed in primary education over the years, much has also stayed the same, for example the concentration on the basics and national testing and inspection to determine the fate of schools. The Coalition government has sought to return to bygone years of primary education.

Further reading

Ball, S.J. (2008) *The Education Debate*, Bristol: The Policy Press (Chapter 2). This chapter sets out changes in education organisation and structure since 1870. It is written with both primary and secondary in mind, but provides a good summary of the important changes and policies of the times.

Cunningham, P. (2012) *Politics and the Primary Teacher*, London: Routledge (Chapters 3 and 5). These chapters deal with the politics behind curriculum and pedagogy respectively.

Galton, M. (2007) *Learning and Teaching in the Primary Classroom*, London: Sage (Chapter 2). This chapter sets out the changes that have been instigated by New Labour administrations and challenges some of the assumptions behind the rhetoric and practice.

Political discourses

5

Markets

Purpose of this chapter

After reading this chapter you should understand:

■ the principles behind markets in education;

■ market-based reasons for a shift from the welfarist settlement;

■ how the Conservatives between 1979 and 1997 introduced an educational marketplace;

■ contradictions in Conservative notions of an educational market;

■ the shifts in thinking that dominated New Labour's use of the market in education;

■ the positions of the three main political parties prior to the 2010 general election;

■ why education is said to operate under a quasi-market.

As seen in previous chapters, various changes in education were enacted from the end of the Second World War (Ball, 2008). In brief, such changes amounted to:

■ the introduction and maintenance of a welfare state through the welfarist settlement between the years 1944 and 1979;

■ a break with the welfarist system and moves away from comprehensivisation between 1979 and 1997;

■ a continuation of the move to a post-welfare era and the end of a national education system, locally administered, from 1997.

With this in mind, the ways in which the education system has moved towards a market-based system for its orientation can be explored. This chapter charts such changes and outlines the features of a new system of schooling. This system is a break with the welfarist settlement and is marked by the introduction of mechanisms which provide for market oriented solutions to perceived educational problems.

The end of the welfarist settlement

As seen earlier, in the 1970s worldwide economic downturns and US and UK financial and policy changes made the economics of the welfare era unsustainable (Olssen and Peters, 2005). To offer a mechanism whereby individuals could be provided with social services, free at the point of delivery, whether taxes were paid or not was judged to be no longer justifiable. This is not to say that mainstream politicians wished to see a return to conditions prior to the introduction of the welfare state, rather they questioned whether that which had gone before could be continued. The view taken was that the economic and social situation of the 1970s meant that profligacy was ill-conceived. To ensure that the populace accepted such change, the 'Report on Governability' (Crozier et al., 1975) singled out education and the media as in need of control as, it was argued, they constrained the ability of government to make people more governable and more able to service capital. Welfare settlement economics was blamed, the global market gradually gained the upper hand and economic survival became the key measure of national and individual success. As Davies and Bansel (2007: 251) note,

> Individual survival became attached to national survival, and both were tied to the market. 'Survival' was, and is, routinely constituted in economic terms dictated by the market, and this has the double force of necessity and inevitability.

By the 1970s discussions about educational organisation and links to the world of work came to dominate. Following Ruskin and building upon the belief that the post-war period had failed to attain its goals of eradicating social inequality and redistributing wealth, the Conservative New Right agenda of the 1980s and 1990s questioned the wisdom of raising aspirations for those destined for lower-status jobs. For the Right desired to see education return to its role as . . . allocator of occupations, a defender of traditional academic values, teaching respect for authority, discipline, morality and "Englishness" and preparing a workforce for the new conditions of flexible insecure labour markets' (Tomlinson, 2005: 26).

This was to be achieved under the liberal doctrine of market competition. The New Right sought to reorient public policy along the lines of the marketplace. It was their belief that the 'restricted practices' (Tucker, 1999) of the post-war public sector period were ineffective and inefficient and had led, in part, to the left failing to meet its objectives and ideals. Justification for change was made through a preoccupation with meeting targets and producing savings: the cult of consumerism and associated beliefs in value-for-money entered the realm of the public service (Tucker, 1999). This period saw the rise of Human Capital Theory: developing human skills and abilities so that they might contribute to the development and growth of the economy. (Human Capital Theory is a portmanteau term for a variety of slightly differing interpretations all of which centre on the economic worth of an individual.)

By the 1990s British policy-makers had assigned education a major role in improving national economies: improvements therein were seen to lead to improvements in economic growth and productivity. Importantly, the knowledge and skills deemed appropriate to learn at school became those more closely attuned to the workplace and celebrated in the commercial world (Tomlinson, 2005). Economics held sway and the drive to improve education became synonymous with the drive to improve economic growth and outputs; a national efficiency drive (Ball, 2001). Indeed, in 1991 McMurtry (1991: 211) noted: 'it is difficult to avoid the conclusion that the educational process has been so persuasively subordinated to the aims and practices of business that its agents can no longer comprehend their vocation in any other terms.'

ACTIVITY 5.1

Create two lists, one which identifies the good elements of the welfarist settlement and comprehensivisation and another which points out the shortcoming in such a system.

The rise of the market

Whilst competition has always been a feature of education systems and education has always attempted to innovate, in state-run systems the belief is that these have occurred so as to conform; there has been a lack of 'disruptive' activities that might lead to systemic and economic growth (Lubienski, 2009). Throughout the Conservative era and in response to Public Choice theorists who maintained that top-down bureaucracies do not allow those who know (in this case teachers) to innovate (Lubienski, 2009), market forces have been brought to bear on education quite dramatically. In the late 1970s, the Conservatives, under Margaret Thatcher, offered a coherent rationale for government and hence education, built upon notions of competition, a free economy and deregulated markets (Tomlinson, 2005). During the 1980s, through various education acts, a variety of market-driven mechanisms were introduced. The policies of the 1980 Education Act (DES, 1980) introduced a raft of mechanisms with their basis in market principles and the 1986 Education Act (DES, 1986) took such matters even further. But it was the 1988 Education Reform Act (DES, 1988), introduced by the Conservative government, which mandated the most sweeping changes to the educational landscape.

The 1980s was the period that saw an acceleration of educational reform, in part driven by a desire to free up school entry and deregulate the educational landscape. This would, it was believed, bolster good, strong schools and leave the weak and unpopular to fail (Lubienski, 2009) by providing marginalised pupils with access to the best schools through the processes of parental choice: the resultant public sector market operated on Darwinian principles (Gewirtz and Ball, 2000). What became crucial was the control of the product as determined by key information and outputs. In particular, the introduction of a market-based approach to the organisation of school-education positioned parents as consumers who scrutinise league tables organised from the results of standardised testing. What is promoted is choice within prescription with schools organised according to industrial-age modes of delivery (Hartley, 2008). Under such New Right thinking, change went in the twin directions of increased school autonomy (for example, local management of schools, LMS) *and* increasing state control (for example, the National Curriculum): the contradictions were palpable. Choice, within the marketisation mantra, positioned the parent as a rational and informed decision-maker, able to choose from a variety of possibilities through the use of key data sets. Importantly, these changes desired the creation of consumers but not a consumer culture, for as Hartley (2008: 366) notes,

> Consumer culture celebrates variety and differences. It is the expression of an identity-seeking self who is continually in makeover-mode, in search of a stylistic edge over others, forever focused on the superficial, at ease with ephemerality.

Notably, consumer culture elides centralised mandate such as a national curriculum.

However, there was a dichotomy of organisation at work here. On the one hand schools, through LMS, were given considerable autonomy to determine spending and organisation. On the other hand, in some matters, such as a national curriculum and testing and inspection regimes, they were required to follow strict national guidelines. This occurred because the belief was that state control was necessary to provide a common base by which parents would be able to judge the worth of a school. The National Curriculum provided such a base: if every school teaches according to a set curriculum, then any differences in performance would, theoretically, be due to the school itself and not the way in which the curriculum was organised. Add to this a national testing system through the auspices of standard assessment tests (SATs) at ages 7, 11 and 14 and GCSEs at age 16, and a national inspection system, and the mechanisms for market control are realised. As Glennerster (1991: 1270) noted at the time:

> Under the UK schools market now emerging, the government will ensure that an acceptable standard of common education is provided by means of the National Curriculum, assessment tests and a national system of inspection . . . With such enhanced information on output, parents and pupils will be able to judge in an informed way between the services offered by competing schools. The most efficient will gain pupils and resources, the others will decline.

It could be argued that the principle behind such changes was the desire to shift responsibility from the centre to local organisations. Hence, the government set the scene for education through matters such as the curriculum and testing, but left the achievement of such aims to those working in and for schools locally. Whilst this may have been a part of the agenda, it is certainly true that since 1976 education has become one of the defining aspects of any government. It is likely, therefore, that the localism argument, whilst true in part, is only one aspect of what is a very complicated relationship between centre and local.

These market reforms brought about mass customisation: the creation and marketing of products with mass appeal (Hartley, 2008). Parents were able to choose from what was on offer, tailored to meet the perceived needs and desires of certain groups. Schools were positioned as businesses, parents as consumers; market advantage was either given or taken away.

In the main, Conservative orientation for policy-making was endogenous; policy was enacted that attempted to make the public sector act in a business-like way and was achieved by (Ball, 2008):

- linking funding to recruitment, consumer choice and institutional budgetary and managerial autonomy;
- encouraging entrepreneurship;
- improved marketing and promotion strategies;
- use of performance indicators.

ACTIVITY 5.2

■ Using the information above and that contained in Chapter 3, make two lists: of the good and bad points of Conservative changes to education.

■ Compare this list with the one made for Activity 5.1.

Markets develop

So it can be argued that, during the 1980s and 1990s, schools started to operate as mini-businesses, competing for pupils. The quasi-market entailed a shift from participative and professional modes of operation to those of a more technical and managerial orientation. The market discipline shifted the discourse for school organisation from 'Welfarism' to 'New Managerialism' and posited that gaze should shift from the learner to the institution.

Welfarism was bound up with 'Bureau-Professionalism': the mechanisms by which professionals might exercise professional judgement in the discharge of their duties. It was a rule-bound and hierarchical approach to organisation which ensured a neutral welfare state. Conversely, New Managerialism is about unquestioningly promoting aims which lie external to the organisation and

> views bureaucratic control systems as unwieldy, counterproductive and repressive of the 'enterprising spirit' of all employees. Its notion of the route to competitive success is to loosen formal systems of control . . . And to stress instead the value of motivating people to produce 'quality' and strive for 'excellence' themselves. Managers become leaders, rather than controllers, providing the visions and inspirations which generate a collective or corporate commitment to 'being the best'.
>
> (Newman and Clarke, 1995: 15)

Gewirtz and Ball note the key features of New Managerialism:

■ a customer-oriented ethos;

■ decision-making is instrumentalist and driven by efficiency, cost-effectiveness and the search for a competitive edge;

■ there is an emphasis on individual relations which has been achieved mostly through the marginalisation of trade unions and new management techniques such as total quality management (TQM) and human resources management (HRM);

■ relationships are authoritarian;

■ competition is key to the success or otherwise of the organisation and individuals therein;

■ managers are generically socialised, i.e. within the field and values of 'management studies'.

New Labour and the market

The move that defined the shift from 'Old Labour' to 'New Labour' is often cited as the moment when clause 4 was removed from the British Labour Party's constitution. This clause was somewhat ambiguous in its terminology, but, since 1918, had been taken to mean nation-alisation or common ownership of industry. The removal of this clause by Tony Blair fol-lowing a successful vote at the party's 1995 conference marks the moment that New Labour embraced the principles of socialism but via different mechanisms for its achievement than had hitherto been adopted. In summary, New Labour's position was most definitely of the post-welfare kind. The party swiftly moved, once elected, to ensure a much reduced role for government than had been desired under Old Labour. A new central role for markets was envisaged along with greater individual choice and reduced trade union and public sec-tor influence. New Labour was essentially an entrepreneurial government (Osborne and Gaebler, 1993) in that it sought to promote competition between providers whilst empower-ing citizens. Control was to be pushed away from bureaucracies towards the community in an attempt to decentralise authority so that problems might be prevented rather than cured. The welfarist era notion of clients as service users was to be replaced by 'the customer' who was to be provided with choice. Performance was to be measured by outcomes and indicators. At the heart of this new agenda was the marketplace. Much of this smacked of Conservative thinking:

- choice and competition as the basis for the provision of public services;
- education as a market commodity;
- state regulation and control over issues such as the curriculum;
- institutional management as akin to the private sector;
- customer rights; and
- raising standards.

It should be remembered, though, that New Labour did not wish to, as Blair stated in a 2008 Fabian Society Pamphlet entitled *Socialism*, 'run a Tory economy with a bit of social com-passion'. Rather he desired to see left-leaning notions of social justice, cohesion, equality of opportunity, inclusion and community. Whilst selection and competition became defining features, New Labour did desire to mitigate the worst excesses of the market and exclusion. As Savage and Atkinson (2001) note, there was an attempt to combine economic dynamism and social justice through the auspices of social inclusion and equal opportunity. Whilst the neoliberal line maintains that individualism is the motivator of human action, Blair's govern-ment sought to redefine the basis for action as stemming from moral endeavour as the driver of individual conduct. For New Labour the difference between it and the neoliberals was in its stress on inclusivity and community and its commitment to higher spending levels. Based on Giddens' (1998) notion of the Third Way and Etzioni's (1995) belief in Communitarian-ism, Blair's New Labour sought to redefine the ways in which the market could be brought to bear on public services. Underpinning this belief was a rather utilitarian view of education:

> Underpinning New Labour policies are the beliefs that education enables individuals to obtain employment and stable income sources in a competitive global market, that edu-cation is crucial to overcoming the low-skill equilibrium of the British economy.
>
> (Kendall and Holloway, 2001: 154)

However, from the outset New Labour engendered a shift in market function towards more collaboration as seen in the White Paper, *Excellence in Schools* (DfEE, 1997). Here, and subsequently, competition and collaboration were equally championed. This was an ideology more akin to European social democracy (Kelly, 2009) in that it desired to see free markets, whilst acknowledging the state as mitigation for the social consequences of such a market. Neoliberalism believes that democracy flourishes best in a competitive market economy. It cites as exemplars for the formation of society minimal state involvement and individual freedom rather than the social collective.

In its 1997 election manifesto (Labour Party, 1997), New Labour promised that education would be its number one priority and that spending levels would increase. 'Education, education, education' was the mantra. Until 2007–2008 education spending did increase. Whilst neoliberal mechanisms such as league tables and linking of funding to pupil numbers remained, mechanisms such as Excellence in Cities, which required a more collegial and community-based approach to educational organisation and provision, were introduced. Schools were required to work together to raise standards, even though they were, via Ofsted and league tables, competing with each other for market share. The creation of specialist schools, for example, was tied to the ways in which such organisations worked with other schools in the locality to promote their specialism. The same was true of beacon schools. The discourse was one of cooperation to raise standards within a culture of competition and target setting. Foskett (2004) identified this as the 'post-marketisation' era. In contrast to the Conservatives, New Labour policy was exogenous, that is 'allowing for the possibility of new providers from outside the state sector to deliver public services of various kinds' (Ball, 2008: 119). A business-like agenda was thrust onto schools and was part of an agenda of modernisation by privatisation (Ainley, 2004).

Targets and performance

New Labour desired to move the country towards an informational and service economy (Ball, 2008). There was a focus on the use of targets and performance measures as a means to direct the work of institutions with funding increasingly ring fenced for stated aims and programmes along with funding for private firms to undertake contracted out roles. New Labour's view was very much a pragmatic one. Electorally, education became a buzz-word with attendant policies towards choice and standards. And Labour's academies programme is a case in point. Conceived as a way to uplift the educational offerings in 'failing' inner city schools, private providers were enticed into running the schools thereby shifting state money into private hands, albeit on a not-for-profit basis.

An analytical model of such public market frameworks acknowledges that market elements such as choice and diversity are necessarily embedded in wider frameworks, such as the social milieu. This differs from the free market in that it acknowledges the need for public interest, such as, for example, through the needs of the community as a whole, rather than the individual consumer. The model also acknowledges that a multiplicity of factors condition and direct the operations and effects of market-like systems and which give a market its character and direction. New Labour was at pains to acknowledge and work within local context; but at the same time it was devoted in its attempts to identify and weed out poor performance.

But Power and Whitty (1999) maintain that the state did not get involved soon enough following the Conservative era for even though New Labour promoted social capital and citizenship their adoption of the neoliberal policies of choice, selection and an increased role for the private sector engendered an era of 'performativity' (see Chapter 8):

- centralised decision-making;
- assessment against external indicators;
- punitive measures such as naming and shaming.

Opponents to this discourse maintained that such an agenda prioritised results over children; outcomes became more important than processes.

Gordon Brown's tenure as prime minister from 2007 to 2010 was also marked by high levels of public spending, although the exact amounts were disputed in the press due to cumulative counting rather than actual amounts. What was clear, however, was the zeal with which Blair's reforms of the comprehensive system were taken up. Brown was keen to ensure that schools received their money direct and made such payments in the budgets of 2006–2007 and 2007–2008. Market-based principles for the organisation and funding of education, started under Blair, were continued.

What emerged from New Labour was a mixture of old left-leaning styles such as notions of the citizen, coupled with neoliberal styles of consumerism. As Brehony (2005: 30) identifies, the New Labour government

> has adapted the fundamental neoliberal programme to suit its conditions of governance – that of a social democratic government trying to govern in a neoliberal direction while maintaining its traditional working-class and public-sector middle-class support with all the compromises and confusions that entail.

Emphasis was placed on the notion of 'the citizen'. But this is problematic. The personalisation of services coupled with a consumer mentality for delivery accentuates individualism. But the discourses of citizenship promote collective effort and the binding of individuals together. Attempts were made to bind the two; to create a hybrid identity that, on the one hand, understood the need for collective effort and action, but, on the other, desired meritocracy and the rise or fall of the individual due to individual effort and gain. As Hartley (2008: 368) explains, though,

> the concepts of citizen and consumer cannot simply be hyphenated so as to form a new coherent hybrid. Their ideals are quite different: state and market; public and private; political and economic; collective and individual; de-commodification and commodification; rights and exchange.

New Labour's ideals were, then, somewhat confused. In part they wished to extend individual rights such as the right to choose, but on the other hand they desired the extension of public services so that all might gain.

ACTIVITY 5.3

- In what ways was New Labour similar to the Conservatives with regard to market-based principles?
- In what ways did it differ? Use Chapters 1, 3 and 4 to help you.

Market conditions

Advocates of free market theories maintain that market forces unleash increasing efficiency and rising standards within schools. The results are institutions that are more responsive to parents, have better standards and which meet need and preferences more fully. As Jongbloed (2003: 111) notes, however,

> Markets bring together buyers and sellers of goods and services, capital, labour and so on. 'Market' is a shorthand expression for the process by which individuals' (or households') decisions and consumptions of alternative goods, firms' decisions about what to produce, and workers' decisions about how much and for whom to work are all reconciled by the adjustment of prices.

Thus, through the notion of 'freedoms', eight conditions for a market can be defined (Jongbloed, 2003). Four 'freedoms' for providers:

- *Freedom of entry into the marketplace.* Until very recently there have not been mechanisms for new state-run schools to open, although this has now altered with the Coalition's introduction of Free Schools.
- *Freedom to specify the product.* Schools in the state sector have to follow strict guidelines for the curriculum and are subject to a testing and inspection regime which curtails freedom to innovate.
- *Freedom to use available resources.* All schools have a certain degree of flexibility, enshrined in the Education Reform Act (DES, 1988) to use and deploy resources as they see fit. Guidance is provided by central government and local authorities, but essentially it is up to the head teacher and governing body to decide the place and form for resource deployment. Such freedoms have been further extended through the creation of academies and free schools.
- *Freedom to determine prices.* All schools are given a certain amount of money per pupil. Although this differs from location to location, the amount given is determined by a centrally operated funding formula; there is limited scope for schools to raise extra capital through charging parents. Indeed, any charges for educationally related activities can only be justified if they are asked for on a voluntary basis.

And four 'freedoms' for consumers:

- *Freedom to choose the provider.* Although parents and students do have the right to express a preference for school, there is no guarantee that places will be available. Certainly, in the secondary sector, schools admissions and choice mechanisms are a notable area of concern for parents, teachers and the government. The idea of choice in education, as discussed more fully in Chapter 6, is a contested concept.
- *Freedom to choose the product.* As stated above, state schools operate within tightly defined parameters for matters such as curriculum, testing and inspection. Indeed, as discussed in Chapter 4, pedagogy has come in for a certain amount of government control as well.
- *Adequate information on prices and the quality of resources.* All schools are required to publish details of their testing results and information about the school, annually. This information

must be presented to parents and the wider community in an effort to hold schools to account for how they spend tax-payers' money.

- *Direct and cost-covering prices paid.* In the state system, the costs of education are borne by the tax-payer but children receive an education regardless of whether their parents pay tax. Usually, extra costs to the consumer are not associated with markets, although increased 'donations' for extra-curricular activities and trips often occurs (Lubienski, 2009).

The quasi-market

With this in mind, it is not clear that school-based education does operate as a true market. Although choice, diversity, efficiency, effectiveness and value-for-money formed the keystone to such moves, made possible by funding, curriculum and testing mechanisms and the then ever-increasing control of teaching practice and teacher training, on many of the eight conditions Jongbloed describes, education can be found wanting. Whilst in three conditions recent changes to education policy may have furthered the move towards a true market, this is still some way off. It is for this reason that commentators often describe education as a quasi-market. Whilst some of the following has changed since New Labour, during the Conservative era of 1979 to 1997:

- money was not given to the private sector for the provision of educational or allied services;
- there was no free entry for new providers of state education; new city technology colleges (CTCs) were built under government planning;
- the introduction of a common national curriculum curtailed real parental choice;
- national salary scales were maintained; local pay bargaining was not on offer.

As with true markets, quasi-markets are influenced by the New Right, in particular neoliberalism, and seek to apply market principles to the provision of public services (Croxford and Raffe, 2007). Quasi-markets are free to the user and providers may not run the services on a for-profit basis. Typical features of the quasi-market in education are (Croxford and Raffe, 2007):

- parental choice;
- publication of information to inform such choice;
- funding linked to pupil enrolment;
- local management of schools;
- a reduction in local authority power;
- the encouragement of diversification.

One view is that what quasi-markets entail is intense competition between schools and the removal of the local, comprehensive ethos. Some argue that quasi-markets give positional advantage back to the middle classes in a better way than selection did previously and that this leads to social closure, i.e. the middle class are able to close out certain parts of the system for themselves:

This change in the rules of engagement is giving the middle classes the opportunity to capitalise on their superior market power in the competition for credentials within a market-driven system of education.

(Brown, 1995: 46)

This social closure occurs through a number of mechanisms:

- The middle classes have more effective market strategies; they are able to both understand and play the market-based system to their children's advantage.
- Parents' choices create or accentuate a hierarchy of schools; again this is associated with social class. Some schools are seen to be 'more desirable' than others and hence attract more 'custom'.
- Schools then respond in ways which reinforce this hierarchy, for instance, 'better' schools operate mechanisms which encourage middle class families; this confirms and exacerbates the cycle.
- As a consequence, within-school class inequalities in attainment increase; the divisions that exists, performance-wise, in terms of the differential between the social classes becomes more acute.
- This leads to an increase in social segregation which leads to further class based inequalities in attainment.
- This contextualised effect then becomes stronger.
- Finally, the culmination is a reduction in the capacity of the system to progressively change.

However, advocates of the quasi-market cite competition and diversity as the main positive features (Lubienski, 2009) and argue that it improves efficiency by maintaining 'E' competition: as the government ensures the basics through the provision of a national curriculum, national testing to determine the quality of education on offer, and Ofsted inspections to measure the quality of schools as institutions, schools can be compared like with like (Glennerster, 1991). There is a general belief that market mechanisms bring better options for choice and diversity:

the logic reformers and theorists have articulated clearly indicates that policies such as decentralisation of authority, deregulation, consumer choice, and/or competition between providers produce incentives that will drive innovations.

(Lubienski, 2009: 16)

Further, the assumption is that quasi-markets transcend context. Part of this is the belief that choice is crucial, whether between providers or by simply funding all forms of schools with state aid. The rhetoric maintains that the principles of quasi-markets lead to innovation which can then create something new in terms of process, product, organisation or marketing, for example through the deployment of uncertified staff to cover for teachers. Such instances occur in part because of a need to provide suitable experiences for children, e.g. cover for physical education in primary schools, but also in a drive to extend the range of skills on offer in the organisation. This innovation occurs, according to advocates, through the mechanisms of, in particular, choice and competition as part of a new

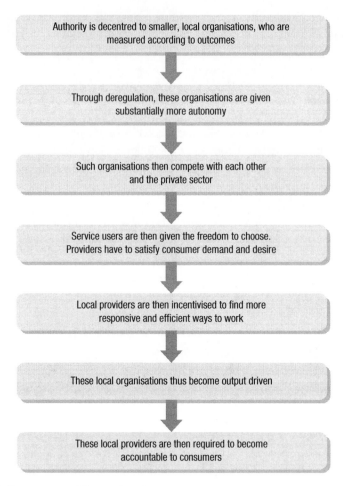

FIGURE 5.1 The processes of the quasi-market

public management. New public management (NPM) is a feature of neoliberalism in that it: desires to see organisational flexibility; and, decries the monolithic state-run organisation instead positing that flexibility both in terms of provision and contractual arrangements gives rise to greater efficiencies and effectiveness (Olssen and Peters, 2005). NPM in the late twentieth century was the product of an increase in bureaucratic, state-run efforts to control education and the advent of the market. In this discourse objectives become clearly defined and provision is oriented to be outcomes driven, rather than procedurally focused. Notions of contract replace the welfarist norms of the 'common good' and 'public interest'. Economy, efficiency and effectiveness enter the lexicon through the idea of markets and tendering and the state is shrunk so as to allow for privatisation and the market (Pollit, 1990). As institutions seek to extend their portfolio they increase their marketability. It is neoliberalism which has encouraged a shift in accountability measures towards market processes and quantification. There has been a shift from bureaucratic-professional accountability (regulation in terms of process and based on expertise) to consumer-managerial accountability (based on price, performance contracts, externally set targets and objectives)

(Olssen and Peters, 2005). Figure 5.1 shows how these discourses become defining features of the quasi-market organisation (after Lubienski, 2009).

Such processes are not without their potential problems, however, and innovation is not cost-neutral (Lubienski, 2009). The capacity schools have for the pace of change is different from institution to institution and stated intentions and outcomes play a large part in detailing the ways in which innovation can occur. Importantly, what may be innovative in one context may well be part of existing custom and practice in another. It is clear, then, that innovation cannot be simply mandated by the move to quasi-market mechanisms. Change may or may not be supported by market principles; to assume that they automatically support innovation is at best unwise.

For many, quasi-markets are unhelpful and should be replaced and not all researchers agree about the impact of reform. Some argue that the introduction of a quasi-market has brought benefits whilst others argue that it has led to a decrease in collegiality and equality (Power and Frandji, 2010). Others (e.g. Croxford and Raffe, 2007) maintain that quasi-markets reduce further social inequalities and segregation; the belief is that choice assists those with less ability to pay to get their children into the better schools. However, in any market, providers seek to attract the most cost-efficient customers. For example, in education, those pupils with complex social, emotional or educational needs potentially carry with them a limited amount of currency for they require increased intervention at increased cost. Indeed, the difference in marketing strategies between schools in high and low socio-economic areas is noted in the literature: the former group tend to engage in activities which promote middle class aspirations and values, whilst those in lower socio-economic status (SES) areas tend to market themselves to everyone. Glennerster (1991: 1270–1271) notes this and compares the situation to what was occurring at the time in the health care system.

> It is crucially important for any health care provider to exclude high cost, high risk, patients . . . It is thus not surprising to find that an enormous amount of attention is paid . . . to ensure that a minimum number of these high cost patients are attracted. Schools are in a similar position . . . what went on in the school only explained about 5% of the variance in pupil achievements. These are . . . relatively small compared to the 64% of variance explained by initial attainment and social background. Any school entrepreneur acting rationally would seek to exclude pupils who would drag down the overall performance score of the school . . .

Glennerster's concern was that individual schools would seek to maximise their position in the educational marketplace by defining their core business in terms of those features that are measurable: tests scores and Ofsted inspections, and will pay limited attention to matters outside of this purview. This cuts against the fact that the largest gains in educational attainment, certainly up until the 1990s were made in the 1960s and 1970s under a system of locally administered comprehensive schools with no market features (Tomlinson, 2005):

> an internal market will, other things being equal, produce a selective system of education, selective according to the attributes that determine school performance most strongly, that is inherited ability and social class. Does this matter? There is still dispute about the research evidence but, on balance, it would seem that the introduction of non-selective schooling in Britain in the 1960s and 1970s did raise the educational outcomes of the schooling system especially for the average and below average child . . .
>
> (Glennerster, 1991: 1271)

However, it is important to note that certain sources of variation do occur in any quasi-market system. Just because markets exist does not mean to say that they all operate similarly or, indeed, to the same effect. At least three sources of variation contribute to the strength of any market regime:

- The market model: quasi-markets can be run anywhere on a continuum from a fully planned system (where local schools plan for intake based on set criteria and along comprehensive lines) to a complete free market (where school admissions, for example, is down to complete free choice with no local planning). The more market-based features that are introduced the stronger the market orientation.

- Market conditions: local arrangements such as the number of schools from which to choose, population size, travel arrangements, etc. all impact on the strength of the market. For example, the more schools from which to choose, the stronger the market.

- Educational cultures: the values and beliefs of participants in the system, e.g. parents, teachers, are brought to bear on the ways in which a market-based system is run. If market culture is resisted in a wide body of the populace, then such principles may not be in the ascendency.

But it is not clear that innovation and change have necessarily occurred as part of the quasi-market culture. For example, whilst alternative schools such as Steiner-Waldorf have seen an increase and many schools have adopted specific foci or curricular ends, particularly through schemes such as specialist schools status, in order to position themselves in the marketplace, it remains difficult to identify pedagogic innovation as a result of quasi-markets; the trend in schools has generally been towards more 'traditional' types of pedagogy (Lubienski, 2009). The market can, in some instances, actually constrain experimentation. It can have the effect of standardising options: panoptic self-surveillance may increase, whereby schools act as they think they should, based on what they perceive other schools are doing. Further, consumer choice may also lead to increasing standardisation. Whilst market theorists tend to believe that parents are rational choosers, in many instances a traditional educational fare is desired; parents are often more interested in the basics than innovation (Lubienski, 2009). The fact that schools are judged on exam scores can have further traditionalising effects. It is also the case that globally, more marketised state-run education systems do not necessarily show improved outcomes. As Lubienski (2009: 37) notes,

> It appears that quasi-market mechanisms of consumer choice and competition between largely autonomous providers may be more successful in promoting structural changes through policy, diversification of provision, and marketing and organisational innovations than in inducing produce and process innovations in classroom practice.

ACTIVITY 5.4

- Do you think that a quasi-market for education is a good or a bad thing?
- What features help you to make this decision?

A continuation of the market

In the early to mid-part of 2010 the country prepared itself for a general election. Labour's terms in office had been uninterrupted since 1997 even though there had been a change of prime minister in 2007. Despite the downturn in the fortunes of Labour and the growing recession and financial crisis, it was surprising that no one party seemed to hold enough support to gain 326 seats in the House of Commons that would secure an outright victory. Indeed, all opinion polls seemed to suggest that the time had come for the Liberal Democrats to hold the balance of power in what was to be a hung parliament. Whatever the outcome, though, education was one of the major battlegrounds for votes, with all three parties signalling a raft of measures they would take if they were voted into power. What was notable, though, was the role markets would play in the manifestos of all three of the main political parties.

The Conservative Party manifesto (Conservative Party, 2010)

According to the Conservatives, Britain was slipping down the international education league tables with troublesome behaviour a growing problem in schools. It was their view that the growing gap between the richest and poorest was unsustainable; for these reasons something had to be done for the sake of the next generation.

School organisation

Based on a Swedish model, the Conservatives proposed to introduce free schools. These would have smaller classes and higher standards of discipline. In addition, all schools were to be able to become academies with outstanding schools pre-approved. There was also an explicit move away from the principles of educational inclusion with the promise to end the so-called 'ideologically driven' closure of special schools and the bias towards inclusion of children with special educational needs (SEN) in mainstream education. They also proposed a pupil premium to help the most disadvantaged.

Inspection and accountability

School league tables were to be reformed so that schools demonstrate they are stretching the most able and raising the attainment of the less able, with contextual value-added data removed. Ofsted was to concentrate on the core business of teaching and learning, behaviour, standards and leadership. Additionally, any school that is in special measures for more than one year will be taken over by an academy provider. To ensure parental access to good schools:

- parents were to be able to save local schools;
- legislation would make sure that academies have certain freedoms to innovate;
- failing schools were to be inspected more often and the best schools inspected less frequently.

The Liberal Democrat Party manifesto (Liberal Democrats, 2010)

The focus for the Liberal Democrats was funding and ensuring every child had a fair chance:

> We will give every child the fair start they deserve by providing cash to reduce class sizes and increase one-to-one tuition. This is the best way to ensure, over the long term, that every child has opportunities, no matter their background, their home town or their parent's bank balance.
>
> (Liberal Democrats, 2010: 10)

School organisation

The Liberal Democrats promised a good local school for every locale. Schools were to be encouraged to be genuinely innovative and this included removing schools from local authority control, but maintaining the local authority's responsibility to manage overall strategic priorities, including intervening when performance is weak. They also planned to allow the establishment of faith-based schools. Help was also to be given to schools to enable them to become more energy efficient.

Inspection and accountability

The Liberal Democrats promised to establish a fully independent body to oversee the examinations system, inspection and accountability and the detail of the curriculum. They desired to see an increase in teacher assessments at Key Stage Two with national testing scaled back. League tables were to be reformed so as to remove the incentive to concentrate on those pupils on the C/D borderline. More controversially, the party desired to remove the politics from education and promised to introduce an education freedom act banning politicians from the day-to-day running of schools.

The Labour Party manifesto (Labour Party, 2010)

The Labour Party also centred its ambitions on an understanding of the importance of teachers:

> No school can be better than the quality of its teachers. We have the best generation of teachers ever, supported by teaching assistants and the wider workforce.
>
> (Labour Party, 2010: 3:3)

School organisation

Labour rejected a return to the 11-plus or a free-for-all admission system and was committed to a fair admissions system. To complement vocational learning, University Technical Colleges and Studio Schools were to be established and new providers were to be encouraged to take over pupil referral units.

Inspection and accountability

In a drive for customer satisfaction, Labour promoted the idea that if parents are dissatisfied with local schools then local authorities will have to do one of three things:

- take over poor schools; or
- expand good schools; or
- offer entirely new provision.

Additionally, if parents were unhappy with an existing leadership team, then Labour proposed to allow ballots to bring in a new team from a list of accredited providers. Finally, school report cards, which advised on standards, parental satisfaction, behaviour and bullying and the progress of all pupils, were to be introduced.

ACTIVITY 5.5

- In what ways are the policies of the three parties similar?
- In what ways are they dissimilar?
- Make a list of the similarities and differences to compare based on the topics introduced in preceding chapters in this book.

What was clear for all three parties was the market-based approach. There was a clear consistency of support for measures such as private involvement and mechanisms for measuring effectiveness and value for money. Indeed, this was a line that was adopted by the coalition government when they took power. The diversification of the school system and the ways in which private finance was to enter the educational arena all indicated singularly market-driven ideologies. What is notable is that some on the left of the political spectrum can see no ideological opposition to private finance being used to run schools for profit (Hasan, 2012). This marks a changing line from that previously adopted whereby although money from investors was welcome, the schools themselves could not be run for profit. But not everyone is of like mind. For some, the rise of the educational, profit-making entrepreneur is not to be welcomed. In fact, if the opinions polls are to be believed, 'fewer than one in four voters think free schools will improve education standards and less than a third of voters are in favour of allowing private companies to manage such schools' (Hasan, 2012).

It is clear that the mechanisms employed by the coalition through Secretary of State for Education Michael Gove are part of the new agenda for the reform of the education system. It is a thoroughly neoliberal project in many ways, driven as it is by a belief in the small government, small state argument and a position that sees private enterprise as an inherently good thing. Such matters are discussed further in Chapters 6 to 8.

Conclusion

The introduction of markets in education has been heralded by Labour, the Liberal Democrats and the Conservatives as the means by which to engender increased attainment and improved educational outcomes. This is an all-pervasive technology which seeks to drive schools and other educational institutions to operate according to consumer choice within the auspices of efficiency, effectiveness and accountability. Such changes were instigated by the Conservatives but were continued, albeit with a slight shift in emphasis, by New Labour.

Based in neoliberal ideals and ideology these changes recast the educational landscape. The principles of the marketplace were brought to bear, namely (Newman and Jahdi, 2009):

- an increased profile for marketing in institutions;
- viewing parents and students as consumers;
- a focus on consumer need;
- the measurement of consumer satisfaction.

This all implies a shift towards a customer-centred approach.

In fact what they achieved was the introduction of a quasi-market, a half-way house between the old methods of the welfarist settlement and a true market picture. With its lack of operator profit and a strong sense of central control, the quasi-market sought to position education as a personal, individual right, rather than a public good. Indeed, the basis for market principles, neoliberalism and individualism, promote life as a 'project' in which 'the self is the subject of continuous economic capitalisation' (Pick and Taylor, 2009: 78).

This individualism calls for decisions to be made concerning what school to attend and the means to be taken to achieve such ends. Responsibility is cast back onto parents so that they might ensure the correct positioning of their offspring in the educational marketplace. Duly, schools have a need to promote themselves in ways which appeal to their core clientele; this may mean adopting certain ways of operating or indeed, may involve positioning themselves in the market as different, but successful. The marketplace that is education requires, then, schools and parents to adopt the mechanisms of advantage.

Key points

- Financial and policy changes in the 1970s made the economics of the welfare era unsustainable.
- The New Right of the 1970s came to believe that the 'restrictive practices' of the welfare era were inefficient and ineffective.
- Work and school became closely aligned.
- Thatcher offered a rational for government built upon competition, a free economy and deregulated markets.
- Policies were enacted which saw a drive towards deregulating the educational landscape.
- These saw an increase in school autonomy *and* central control in an effort to bolster the good and close out the poor.
- The approaches taken were decidedly akin to New Managerialism and the promotion of aims external to those of the institution.
- New Labour adopted a post-welfare orientation for their work whereby control was pushed away from bureaucracies towards the community.
- Blair's government sought to engender a more collaborative culture, but within the confines of market mechanisms and thinking.
- This rather confused thinking continued under Gordon Brown.

- Free market theorists maintain that markets in education mean schools that are more responsive to customers and have better standards.

- Education is more akin to a quasi-market than a true market.

- Quasi-markets favour the middle classes through the cultural capital they have within the education system.

- The quasi-market has its basis in the ideas and ideals of new public management.

- But market-based systems have not produced the greatest gains in educational achievement; this happened during the 1960s and 1970s during the era of comprehensivisation for all.

- The Conservative Party in their pre-election manifesto pledged to move teacher training into schools alongside a raft of other measures designed to increase and improve the status of teachers.

- They pledged to increase school autonomy through the creation of free schools and academies.

- Ofsted's remit was to change to focus on a smaller number of areas than previously.

- The Liberal Democrats focused their pre-election pledges on fair funding and ensuring every child has a fair chance.

- They also proposed to increase the numbers of teachers trained on the job.

- They proposed to remove the politics from education.

- The Labour Party concentrated on improving the quality of teachers. To this end they pledged more teachers and teaching assistants.

- All three parties had similar pledges but differed enough for there to be some clear water between them.

Further reading

Glennerster, H. (1991) 'Quasi-markets for education?', *The Economic Journal*, **101**(408), 1268–12761. Provides an overview of education and markets, landing on the term quasi-market to describe education's relationship with and to markets.

Lubienski, C. (2009) *Do Quasi-Markets Foster Innovation in Education?: A comparative perspective*, OECD Education Working Papers, No. 25, OECD Publishing. A report from across the EU on the relationship between educational markets and educational innovation.

Power, S. and Frandji, D. (2010) 'Education markets, the new politics of recognition and the increasing fatalism towards inequality', *Journal of Education Policy*, **25**(3), 385–396. This paper offers a powerful critique of education markets, in particular the link between marketisation, performance data and educational inequalities.

6

Choice and diversity

Purpose of this chapter

After reading this chapter you should understand:

- the nature of choice in education and how it is aligned with market-based ideals;
- Conservative educational reform and its intended and unintended outcomes regarding choice and diversity;
- how New Labour continued with the mantra of educational choice;
- the ways in which choice is aligned with social class;
- the mechanisms by which parents and others choose schools for their children;
- the relationship between performance and choice.

Choice and the markets

> A good part of getting on in life is doing well at school, and doing well at school is helped by attending a good school. Since not all schools are good schools, places at good schools need to be allocated. These two assumptions – that schools matter and differ – mean that education markets have to solve an important assignment problem.
>
> (Burgess and Briggs, 2006: 1)

In the late 1980s and early 1990s many countries enacted mechanisms to enable school choice in an effort to move control from provider to consumer. Initial moves were designed to reduce producer capture and enhance customer choice; competition was key. As Hirsch (2002: 4) notes, 'More specifically, a "neoliberal" revolt against existing public services was seeking to restructure them around a market model in which "consumers" chose which service to use just like when buying commercial products.'

Creating choice requires informing parents of their options and giving them the information required to make a choice from those options. This can be difficult and costly, however; parents often end up with unequal choice about the choice mechanisms themselves and from what they can choose (Waslander et al., 2010). Despite this, choice mechanisms have become interwoven into education policy in a number of countries for two reasons: first, in order to meet the aspirations of those who would wish to have choice, i.e. parents, and second, to wrest control away from professionals and give non-professionals a say in the educational process (Hirsch, 2002). In turn choice has become part of the rhetoric of successive general elections in Britain.

Simplistically, school choice rests on two types of education (Oría et al., 2007):

- individualised and competitive; and
- somewhat precariously, resting on notions of community, social diversity and sociality.

In current English education policy these two versions are in imbalance and the personal standpoint is systematically privileged. Market mechanisms have been introduced which enhance parental choice, encourage inter-school competition, abolish catchment areas, create voucher-type programmes and set up independent schools within the state funded sector. Many of these features have been present in English education policy since the end of the 1970s wherein, it is suggested (Dronkers et al., 2010) the middle classes lost confidence in the comprehensive system. Certainly, since 1988 a major thrust of educational policy has been towards a competitive market environment (Bagley, 2006). Market-based techniques and measures have held sway in the drive to improve education, and educational outcomes are cited as combining the ethical value of free choice with efficiency in the allocation of resources (Bowe et al., 1992). Choice advocates claim that schools will become more efficient and will raise standards and be more responsive to parents. In the main, it is the diversification of the education system through changes to school structures, choice mechanisms and selection that seems to have concentrated the minds of politicians on both the left and the right. Schools compete for pupils, even though choice itself is limited by a variety of systemic factors and even parental situation (Ward and Eden, 2009). Indeed, it has been the case that those of all political persuasions now seem to argue for choice discourses as the means to produce a world class education system.

Why choice?

A key assumption in the designation of choice-based systems is that of purposive action (Bowe et al., 1992: 26); that is, individuals act in an active, informed and selective way to achieve certain goals. Hence, key data sets, such as league tables of test results, are created to objectively and subjectively allow individuals to choose; *producer* information is provided. At the heart of such endeavours is the belief that the mechanisms of the private sector are better than those in the public services, and, hence, importing the mechanisms from the former to the latter seems like common sense.

> Why does enhancing choice seem so attractive to policy makers? There is an appeal to a simple economic argument. Consumer choice creates competitive pressure which acts as a major drive for efficiency in the private sector. Private firms cut costs and improve their goods and services in order to attract customers. It seems easy to transfer this logic to the provision of public services such as education. Giving parents the ability to choose applies competitive pressure to schools and, analogously with private markets, they will raise their game to attract pupils.
>
> (Burgess et al., 2007: 129)

In education, choice, diversity and selection have been mainly a response to middle class aspirations and the secularisation of public life. Moreover, school choice, as a manifestation of market-based solutions, has now become a mechanism for the colonisation of education by the middle classes and the means by which to alter stagnant educational systems and processes: 'markets have been created by education policies that purposefully encourage competition among schools and parental choice to improve the performance of the education system presented as "fossilized" by uniformity and bureaucracy' (Dronkers et al, 2010: 100).

The usual mechanism for exercising choice is that parents identify a group of schools from which to choose. However, how schools end up on this list differs between socio-economic groups; it seems that rational decision-making does not always take place in all parts of the choice process (Waslander et al., 2010). Gorard and Fitz (1998) note the ways in which discussions for and against choice and diversity can be grouped. The reasons for introducing choice mechanisms into education can be categorised in three ways:

- arguments about liberty: choice is a freedom and as we live in a free society we should be able to exercise that choice;
- economic beliefs: linking funding to choice and diversity drives up educational standards;
- the belief in equality: choice extends to all the position previously held only by the privileged.

In a neoliberal sense choice is enabled so as to drive up standards; it is not a means to an end in itself (Ward and Eden, 2009). But the question then becomes one of how to measure standards; what measures could be taken as an indicator that educational achievement is rising? Post-compulsory participation rates might be one option, but such measures depend on a range of factors (Gorard and Taylor, 2002). In England, efficiency measures and exam scores are thus generally cited as proxies for improving education.

Conversely, the arguments against choice can also be grouped threefold (Gorard and Fitz, 1998):

- Central control brought cohesion to the system. Organising education according to local mechanisms which ensure that local needs are met across a geographical area ensures that all have access to education.
- Education is not marketable as other products are. Education cannot be bought and sold in the same way as televisions, for example.
- Choosing requires the 'right' cultural and social capital. Some are in a more advantageous position than others to make choices and follow them through.

Critics claim that choice tacitly acknowledges that some children and young people will have a better education than others as not everyone will get their first choice, and that choice undermines the national system of schooling (Bates et al., 2011). As Moser (2006: 2) notes,

> While market discourses suggest that the mechanism of parental choice is a force for equality because it offers choice for all, the reality is that school choice is dependent upon the amount and type of resources parents have at their disposal . . . [which] include economic and cultural capital.

Others cite the fact that assessment can be unreliable for a variety of factors such as different tests each year, differing syllabi among exam bodies and the ways in which differing groups fare in exams (Gorard and Taylor, 2002). It should be noted, though, that choice mechanisms have not created a true market in education. What currently exists in the UK is both neigh-bourhood schooling (attending the local school) and choice-based (choosing to travel further afield) (Burgess et al., 2007).

ACTIVITY 6.1

- Choice seems to be a political reality in that it provides much of the education rhetoric for political parties. Why might this be the case?
- What might political parties have to gain by adopting choice-based mechanisms as a means to organise the education system?
- What might they have to lose by so organising education?

The Conservative legacy

Three key ideas underlay Conservative policy in the 1980s and 1990s (Trowler, 2003):

- a desire to remove producer capture (running schools for teachers' benefits);
- a desire to see schools become less insular;
- a challenge to a perceived culture of low expectations.

As discussed in Chapter 5, the Tories desired to see the extension of marketplace principles into education; education became a quasi-market as part of a competitive agenda (West and Pennell, 2002). In particular they extolled the idea that good schools would thrive and drive out the bad and would hence, and out of necessity, become responsive to consumer demand. Eight mechanisms were put in place to achieve these ends (Trowler, 2003):

- The number of seats parents had on governing bodies was increased.
- Parents were given the ability to state a preference of school. Schools were thus obliged to take pupils that fitted with their admissions criteria up to their school-roll; catchment areas for schools became less important.
- Schools had to make public information about the establishment, including test results;
- Ofsted was created so that a system of rigorous school inspections could take place. Parents had open meetings with the inspectors and information on the inspection result was to be made publically available.
- Unsuccessful applicants for school places could go to independent appeal.
- Different types of schools were created to offer diversity within the new system.
- Funding became dependent, predominantly, on the numbers of pupils on roll.
- Parents could vote as to whether their child's school could opt out of local education authority (LEA) control and become grant maintained.

Parental choice has thus been the cornerstone of market ideology and a central plank of edu-cation policy-making for over 20 years (Bates et al., 2011). It is important to note, though, that some form of parental choice has always been available via the ability of parents to opt for home schooling, a privately funded education for their children or a range of different state schools, such as those of a religious denomination or a particular ethos, such as Steiner schools. However, in all of these, parents face constraints in their ability to choose. To send children to a private school requires considerable surplus income and, in many cases, a certain level of pupil ability. Home schooling is available only to those who have the time to stay at home with their children, and faith-based schools, who generally act as their own admissions body, usually prioritise pupils from homes who follow the particular religious denomination. For most children and young people prior to the 1980s, school place was allocated according to catchment and worked along the lines of local schools for local children.

Choice is often legitimised by the idea that it is good for parents, and that children and parents desire it (Bates et al., 2011). As a mechanism of schooling, choice was extended by the Conservative government. They believed that such market-based solutions would drive up standards and weed out the least successful schools. In 1980 the Conservatives introduced a number of initiatives. These included the toleration of private education through the introduction of the assisted places scheme whereby able pupils from the state sector received funding to attend private schools. In effect, admissions became competitive with money following the pupil. In essence what was introduced under the Conservatives was a quasi-voucher system whereby funds were earmarked but paid directly to the provider rather than paid via the purchasers, i.e. parents. Throughout the 1980s and 1990s choice, diversity and selection continued to be constant themes in educational debate and policy. Policies were systematically introduced which enabled parents to state a preference for the school of their choice.

The mechanisms of choice, as educational policy, gained momentum throughout the late 1980s and continued throughout the 1990s. But it was the 1988 Education Reform Act which extended the process forcibly. Here was seen the introduction of open enrolment and different statuses for schools. In essence what the act did was introduce the principles and mechanisms for market-based solutions in education with choice as the keystone.

Subsequent policies and educational acts throughout the 1990s intensified the choice phenomenon and moved education towards a highly marketised system. Conservative policies of the time pandered to a particular ideological and political belief that the market was the best way to solve educational 'problems'. For example, the 1992 Education White Paper *Choice and Diversity* (DfE, 1992b) promoted the idea that good schools would and should attract students whilst poor schools would and should perish (Tomlinson, 2005).

By 1993 forms of selection were operating at the school level and informal selection mechanisms seemed to be on the increase. However, by 1992 only 422 out of some 24,000 schools had voted to become grant maintained (GM) (Tomlinson, 2005). The majority were opposed to the establishment of GM schools and yet more selection; something radical was needed. Further changes were introduced in the 1993 Education Act. In order to revive the flagging GM project the category of 'failing school' was created within the auspices of the Ofsted inspection. The idea was that such schools would be given a limited period of time to 'turn around'; if sufficient improvement was not evidenced in this timeframe, then these schools would be taken over and converted to GM status. Changes were made to make it easier for GM ballots to be held and clusters of schools could apply to go GM. Importantly, what was notable in the literature was the way in which parents felt marginalised in grant maintained schools.

After 1993 the numbers of GM schools did increase, slowly, but accompanying this was an increase in covert and overt selection within such schools. Schools became choosier, often making the admissions process difficult to navigate, so favouring middle-class parents; disadvantaged parents found it more difficult to operate in the climate of marketisation (Trowler, 2003). Exclusions also increased markedly in the 1990s as schools sought to manage their intake more obviously towards the compliant and more able (Trowler, 2003). Those with cultural capital were placed at a distinct advantage in mediating the new marketplace. Ofsted became an important tool in driving the choice agenda. The best and worst schools were identified and this led to calls for more GM status and reduced LEA control. This led to an emphasis on testing and outputs which in turn led to labelling at an early age, often reinforcing stereotypes based on ethnicity or social class. Importantly, those schools that achieved less favourably in national tests became disadvantaged and in turn often achieved poorly in Ofsted inspections. The final Tory White Paper proposed increasing selection in all schools: it was proposed that GM schools be able to select up to 50 per cent of their intake, specialist schools 30 per cent and local authority (LA) schools 20 per cent.

All of this was supplemented by extensive literature for parents to better enable them to make an 'informed choice'. In 1991 and 1994 parents received a 'Parents Charter' noting that they were able to choose a school for their child. But the only schools mentioned were GM schools, city technology colleges (CTCs), independent schools and the assisted places scheme; LEA schools were later referred to as council schools (Tomlinson, 2005: 55). In a further effort to give parents more information and hence choice, in 1992 exam results were published. These were soon presented as local league tables by the press.

Some evidence of success for these changes was found. Schools certainly became much more adept at marketing themselves according to what parents wanted and their day-to-day operations became more 'customer friendly', including dealing with discipline more swiftly and providing extra-curricular activities. McPherson and Raab (1988) found that whilst schools in less popular areas became undersubscribed, schools in affluent areas became oversubscribed; for the latter policy had elevated their status and standing in the community.

However, the system was not without its problems. In reality, choice mechanisms do little more than permit the stating of a preference for a particular school or schools, and many parents soon came to realise this. Further the belief that all parents wanted and would benefit from choice was not borne out by the limited research that has, to date, been undertaken (Coldron, 2007). In actuality, most parents, if they did not opt for private education or selective schools, simply wanted a good local school (Tomlinson, 2005). As Tomlinson (2005) notes, in 1995 the House of Commons Education Committee pointed out that the choice policies were having a deleterious effect on education. In particular the flight of the middle classes was creating 'sink' schools, often in deprived areas; inequalities developed between schools of previously equal status. This was reinforced by international and national research which demonstrated the advantages to middle class parents of choice policies and the ensuing decomprehensivisation of secondary schools.

New Labour and school choice

Notably, at this time and until 1994, Labour attacked the Conservative policies of selection and privatisation. They were concerned that a two-tier system of grammar and secondary modern schooling was being created. By the mid-1990s, however, Labour had become equivocal on the subject of selection, grammar and GM schools, with some on the left proposing choice policies themselves. The School Standards and Framework Act (DfEE, 1998a) did, however, require GM schools to become either foundation schools or rejoin the LEA as maintained community schools.

In 1995, and in a break with left wing politics and policy, Stephen Pollard, director at the left wing Fabian Society, argued that inner city schools fail because of poor staff (Pollard, 1995). Further, and in a bid to counter the accusation that the middle classes wish for good local schools, he noted how they are quick to remove their children to private or selective education. Will Hutton (1995) argued that bringing back grammar schools in every town was the only way to win back the middle classes to state education. The policies of the left soon became the politics of the middle classes. Mechanisms that would bring them into the New Labour fold were seen as the way forward. Left-leaning notions of local comprehensive schools soon became a thing of the past as New Labour ushered in policy positions that, in many ways, mirrored those of the Tory Party.

In 1998 the New Labour government legislated so as to alleviate problems associated with an unregulated admissions market. Selection by ability for any reason other than fair banding was ruled out, but selection by aptitude, in a certain area of the curriculum, for example, was permitted. Interviews of parents and children were only permitted for religious schools so that they might determine the religious standing of the applicant and their family. Additionally, selection by aptitude was only permitted for up to 10 per cent of the intake.

The government's first White Paper *Excellence in Schools* (DfEE, 1997) continued the policy of differential school status, with some schools able to act as their own admissions bodies, as per Conservative mandate, through the status of foundation or aided school. The School Standards and Framework Act (DfEE, 1998a) reinforced these divisions and permitted schools to continue to select pupils. Percentages of pupils to be selected were reduced but the wholesale removal of selection was not a Labour priority. Fair funding, via LEAs, for schools was introduced whereby LEAs were required to distribute a certain proportion of their money directly to schools. Tighter controls were put in place to determine how much could be kept back for central services. The services to be provided centrally were: strategic management and access (planning of school places; admissions; transport, etc.); school improvement; and special educational provision. Fair funding was not universally welcomed, however, with many school heads fearing that the requirements placed upon them were far too great and the head teachers of foundation and aided schools became a significant force in arguing for extra funds and special treatment.

In 2001, the government White Paper *Schools: Achieving success* (DfES, 2001) called for a diversified education secondary education system which would guarantee a multiple tier system with schools for achievers. Specialist schools continued to be a major plank of education policy, even though parental demand did not suggest a need. Although such schools seemed to become oversubscribed very quickly, research (Edwards, 1998) seemed to suggest that the specialist status had no bearing on whether parents opted for the school, rather it was the fact that the school was partly selective which gleaned support. It seemed to be the case that parents chose these schools not because of the specialism but because they are 'perceived as being special' (Hirsch, 2002: 20). Initial research did seem to indicate that specialist schools achieved higher GCSE results than other comprehensives. However, such increases may have been due to a number of factors (West and Pennell, 2002):

- the school's ability to select a certain proportion of its pupils based on aptitude;
- funding levels that existed prior to specialism – may have meant that greater facilities were already in place in some schools that converted to specialist status;

■   some form of social selection, which may have been due to parental choice or social segregation in the surrounding geographical area;

■   a lower proportion of pupils eligible for free school meals (FSM) were seen in specialist schools;

■   the school's relative successful position prior to specialising.

Specialist schools were required to work with the local community. In practice this meant that most worked with their feeder primaries. Few worked with other local secondary schools for they were perceived to be in competition and thus allowing such schools to use and benefit from the facilities on offer was seen as detrimental to the future well-being of the specialist school.

Specialist schools

The 2001 White Paper called for half of all secondary schools to become specialist and stated that good schools would be free to pursue their own curriculum and innovate. Furthermore, new schools would be provided by sponsors with running costs met by the state. To convert to specialist status the school needed to raise funds from local business which was then matched by the Department for Education and Employment (DfEE). The level of funding required was initially £100,000, but this was soon reduced to £50,000. The paper called for a marked differentiation between schools in terms of provision, but equally high standards. By 2003 the equivalent of eight new grammar schools had been created through the expansion of numbers in existing schools (Tomlinson, 2005). In addition, the policy of beacon schools was proving controversial. These were schools that were seen to be performing particularly well. Their brief was to work with other schools to share, model and promote best practice. Tomlinson (2005) suggests that such schools were modelling themselves on grammars with attendant notions of education for the middle class.

As Ball (2008: 126) notes, these changes provided for a

> recalibration of the education system to the necessities of international economic competition. Moreover, they [provided] a particular kind of response to middle-class educational aspirations at a time of uncertainty.

It is notable that the very group New Labour wanted to win back from the private sector in order to raise aspirations and standards, the middle classes, are the ones who benefit most from choice policies. As Ball (2008: 196) states, all this was part of 'a new form of liberal individualism with its roots in 19th century notions of "self-making", responsibility, flexibility, choice, family values and entrepreneurship'.

The first five-year strategy for children and learners (DfES, 2004) claimed that personalisation and choice were the keys to driving up standards. In place of the traditional comprehensive, it proposed to create independent specialist schools (Tomlinson, 2005). The specialist school model was seen as the blueprint for secondary education. It also proposed that every school up to standard was to become specialist by 2008 with 3000 separate secondary schools each admitting pupils they chose but nationalised under central control with funding for each school determined by central government. This was individualism in and through policy, evident in the language used and the tactics deployed (Ball, 2008: 196). Further, the Education and Inspections Bill (DfES, 2006) proposed extending and strengthening school choice.

The Coalition and choice

Academies

The first piece of legislation to be enacted by the Coalition government was the Academies Act which received Royal Assent at the end of July 2010. This act extended the role and scope of the previous incarnation of city academies started under New Labour and which were focused on failing schools. The Coalition's view was that all schools should be allowed to convert to academy status, with outstanding schools preapproved for the status. The act removed the right of the LA to take part in the academisation consultation process. It also extended the right to convert to an academy to primary schools, pupil referral units (PRUs) and 16–19 colleges.

Academies are publically funded, privately run schools that are:

- independent of LA control;
- self-governing;
- able to set pay and conditions for staff;
- able to set the length of the school day and holiday times and dates;
- exempt from the National Curriculum, although they do have to teach English, maths and science.

Initially, converter academies as they became known were usually taken over by the school's senior management team (SMT) or governing body. The policy was soon extended to good schools with outstanding features though. Latterly, all schools can now convert if they are part of a group containing a high-performing school or if they join an existing, successful academy trust. It is the case, though, that high-performing schools no longer have to partner with less successful ones. It is notable that due to the changes in application measures new academies are more likely to be high-performing schools.

On the surface it would appear that academies are more successful than maintained schools in raising standards. However, further evidence suggests that the proportion of disadvantaged young students has decreased in academies from 45.3 per cent to 27.8 per cent (Children England, 2011). Whilst it is not the case that someone from a disadvantaged background will necessarily do less well at school, it is the case that social and material deprivation has a significant impact on educational attainment. As most converter academies are high achieving and in areas of low deprivation, it is not surprising that at face value academy status confers with it high standards when in reality all that has happened is the transfer of already high achievement from LA control to the academies programme. On average, most deprived pupils have seen their results increase less quickly than other pupils and the gap between these two groups is wider in academies than it is in maintained schools (Children England, 2011). It also seems to be the case that academy schools are more likely to enter students for GCSE-type qualifications so partially inflating their academic credentials (Children England, 2011).

In July 2012 in a move that was seen to further side-line teacher unions and teacher training institutions, the government announced that academies could have it written into their contract that they do not have to hire qualified teaching staff (Mulholland, 2012). Although the teacher unions described the move as 'perverse' (Mulholland, 2012), the government maintained that it was granting further freedoms to academies to be flexible and creative in how they deliver education to their students, in line with the independent sector. Both the National Union of Teachers (NUT) and the National Association of Schoolmasters Union of Women Teachers (NASUWT) noted that in Sweden where free schools were allowed to hire unqualified staff so that profits could be made from running schools, standards were slipping, whereas in Finland where teachers have to have masters level qualifications before they can teach, standards are high. The moves led Chris Keates, the General Secretary of the NASUWT, to comment that the Coalition is adopting a 'scorched earth policy' (politics.co.uk, 2011). She bemoaned education policy, especially the academies programme, maintaining that the Coalition was 'squandering the legacy of year on year improvement it inherited in 2010' (politics.co.uk, 2011).

Free schools

Free schools have been a controversial Coalition policy since their announcement in the Conservative manifesto. Once again these are local schools funded by the state but which are free from LA control and oversight. Free schools are established by local groups in response to perceived local need and demand. They can take many forms, but in the main they seek to be small providers.

Once in government, Michael Gove maintained that he had received more than 700 expressions of interest from parents, teachers and charities wishing to establish come kind of free school (Thelwell, 2011), this despite the fact that some free schools were being proposed in areas where there was a surplus of school places. As with academies, free schools neither have to hire teachers with qualified teacher status (QTS) nor teach the National Curriculum.

Despite the supposed large number of expressions of interest, the Department for Education (DfE) finally received less than half of these as firm proposals. Of the 323 that applied, only 32 were seriously considered by the department and of these 24 opened in September 2011.

Modelled on Sweden's Free School movement, these schools have been nothing if not controversial, with some maintaining that their effect on existing schools has been deleterious (cf. Allen, 2010). In the main such schools in Sweden have been set up by middle class parents in affluent areas and have increased social segregation and costs with no concomitant increase in pupil attainment (Wiborg, 2010).

At home, opponents have questioned how a small school can act in place of an LA in determining what is needed for a community, town or larger geographical area (Jenkins, 2010). Further concern has been expressed that such schools serve only to permit and facilitate 'white flight' from schools perceived as being in more socially disadvantaged circumstances (Gillard, 2011). Added to this the fact that running a school is a complex activity, and many maintain that most schools would end up being run by private organisations (Wilby, 2010).

Whatever the case, opening up the schools sector to new entrants and to new forms of schooling has occurred under the Coalition government. In some cases such changes have continued the demise of the LA as started under Thatcher and which, to some extent, continued under Blair and New Labour. Prior to the changes it was very difficult to open a new school; under the Coalition, new schools have opened a mere 15 months after the government was formed.

The politics of choice and diversity

As Oría et al. (2007: 92) note, such education policies,

> particularly policies of parental choice, competitive school enrolment, performance league tables and school specialisms and diversity, create an ethical framework which encourages 'personal' values and legitimates parents in the pursuit of competitive familial advantage through education.

In effect, inequality ceased to be the driving cause for change, replaced instead by social exclusion. Gone was the focus on structural causes of underachievement; in their stead was the discourse of culture as the reason for lack of success. Choice and diversity were at the heart of New Labour policy and continue to be at the heart of the Coalition. All of this was not far from 1980s Tory rhetoric.

However, whilst the parental choice mechanisms ushered in by the Tories were centred on neoliberal thinking, New Labour's reforms, based as they were with a more communitarian focus, focused on the co-production of the marketplace: parents may have been given rights, such as the right to choose, but they also had increasing responsibilities. This was said to promote efficiency and equality in the drive to engender the personalisation of public services more broadly: matching education to the needs of the individual child was a key plank of New Labour policy. Personalisation was intended to meet individual pupil and parent needs by extending choice between schools. The main reason for this is a belief that parents want more choice and that it is in their interests. Whilst 1997 saw a discursive shift towards greater inter-school collaboration, the market-state was not dismantled. Rather it evolved to promote competition and collaboration through:

- neoliberal aspects such as league tables, performance management, open-enrolment and funding by pupil numbers;
- Third Way initiatives such as beacon schools, excellence in cities and specialist schools all of which required some form of collaboration and working.

Collaboration and partnership became interwoven with market ideals, an era of 'post-marketisation' (Foskett, 2004: 4). Within the New Labour era, there were inherent contradictions between on the one hand a competitive agenda that sought to pit school against school through the use of league tables, specialisation and academy status, and the social inclusion agenda so widely touted by the government (West and Pennell, 2002). And so local issues took centre stage, eliding the impact that macro-politics can have. New Labour's programme of school improvement systematically extolled the virtues of diversification and choice: specialist schools, academies, trust schools (Oría et al., 2007). Although collaboration was desired in New Labour policies, competition ensued on the ground due to the local situation and schools needed to position themselves favourably in the marketplace: league tables captured the conversation. Although the macro-environmental domain sets the scene for possible responses in the micro-environmental domain, such responses are tempered by the producer and consumer environment. To date it seems that in these respects little has changed since 2010; indeed, some would argue that Gove has gone further. However, time will tell as to the effects such change, mechanisms and policies will have.

At the heart of the choice vision is the desire to see power given to the hands of the users of public services and parental choice was seen as central to these aspirations. Ministers often extolled choice for reasons of user desire. Parents, it was believed, desired to have a say in their child's education through the mechanisms of choice between, and diversity of, schools. There are also arguments for choice in terms of the ways in which neighbourhood schooling reinforces class divisions and thus should be abandoned, for neighbourhood schooling produces sorting by income and ability as parents choose where to live. This benefits the middle classes who have more choice and tend to do better at school. Lack of choice, therefore, makes class segregation quite high. Assigning pupils to schools makes school and neighbourhood sorting quite high. This can be countered by supply-side flexibility, that is, permitting good schools to expand and poor schools to close; only in this way can greater choice be universal and systemic (Burgess et al., 2007). The argument is that choice policies change this and impact positively on neighbourhood and school composition. Additionally, for choice to be truly exercised then subsidised transport costs need to be met and schools need to be willing to expand to meet additional demand (Burgess et al., 2007). A purely choice-based scheme would reduce the benefits of living near to a good school; this would have effects on social mix within residential areas (Burgess et al., 2007). It would also have a knock-on effect on house prices for the premiums attached to houses near good schools would disappear (Burgess et al., 2007).

The problems of choice and diversity

New Labour's changes were not, however, unanimously well received. The House of Commons Select Committee in 2004 and 2005 criticised key New Labour policies on choice which they maintained had actually increased selection. Importantly, they argued, selection by mortgage continued with certain families able to 'buy' their way to good schools through being in a position to move into the catchment of a 'good' school. And this was having a deleterious effect on localities. Geography usually has a role to play in admissions criteria thus having a knock-on effect on the housing market (Burgess et al., 2007). Evidence has emerged that house prices rise in the areas surrounding good schools so narrowing the pool of people who were able to obtain entry to these neighbourhoods and these schools by virtue of catchment. It seems that the geographical argument can be mustered both for and against choice.

Research indicates that attendance at a good school is related to affluence (Burgess et al., 2006): poorer children are less likely to attend a good school. Those pupils eligible for FSM are also less likely to commute to more distant schools whilst at the end of Key Stage Two, higher-scoring children are more likely to switch to a better school. On average, children from poorer families tend to go to less well performing schools, in part because of where they live (Burgess and Briggs, 2006).

It was noted that that even middle class parents were losing out in the race to gain a good place for their child. Battles ensued as to whether grammar schools could remain, with parental ballots being called for with some of the very group New Labour were seeking to appeal to, the middle classes, desiring an end to selective systems. However, the selection and diversification systems promoted by New Labour did little to close the gulf between the 'haves' and 'have-nots'. Such choice policies proved to be divisive in as much as they continued to promote class-based notions of educational advantage, the very effects they were trying to reduce.

In effect what ensued was the fracturing of the system along the lines previously seen in the tripartite era. For schools in the bottom quarter of the national league table a pupil eligible for FSM is 30 per cent more likely to attend their lower-scoring local school that an otherwise identical well-off pupil (Burgess et al., 2006); children from less well-off families are less likely to go to a good school. Location counts for much of this difference, but not all. Factors such as the middle class's ability to 'work the system' come into play (Burgess and Briggs, 2006). Certain behaviours became advantageous in the drive to secure an educational advantage for one's children, behaviours more akin to the language and demeanour of the middle classes. In turn, the middle classes seem to have greater social and cultural capital and are better able to mobilise resources to support their status as 'active choosers' (Bowe et al., 1992). Such resources may be knowledge-based or financial, for example, moving house into the catchment area of a better school or greater access to transport. Burgess et al. (2006) also note that affluent families are more likely to 'bus' their child to school if local schools are of poor quality. This has the effect of increasing travel distances and times, thereby affecting sustainability both environmental and systemic (Waslander et al., 2010).

Notably, Oría et al. (2007) found that whilst the middle class were taking part in activities to bolster opportunities to go to the 'best school' they bemoaned the fact that they had to engage in activities such as moving house or lying in admission procedures; they would have preferred good local schools. Within the study was noted a discourse of contradiction: good parenting vs. good citizenship. For many, choice was seen as a negative for it supported class-based notions already in existence that fragmented society. Knight (1976, cited in Bowe et al., 1992) discusses the ways in which culture, educational advantage and economic opportunity tend to favour increasing opportunity; a self-fulfilling prophecy, whilst Brown (1990, cited in Bowe et al., 1992) maintained that it is parents' wealth and wishes that improve a child's education, not the ability or efforts of pupils. Care must be taken, Brown argues, for the danger is that the 'active choosers' become the ones who drive the system; in turn, the system is in danger of becoming divorced from wider notions of public good. The effect may be that children, young people and families become seen as currency with some carrying more value to the school than others.

Pressure on parents to choose the right school has also put pressure on schools to choose the right families, possibly by engineering the social mix of the school, or by specialist status and hence the ability to choose up to 10 per cent by aptitude in the specialism. The information given to enable choice has often been simplistic, centring on exam scores and little else; in some respects this has narrowed the focus of the school. Whilst performance indicators are a fact of life for schools, it is the case that these are, in the main, what drive school choice for many. For exam results affect a school's league table position which in turn affects its reputation. LEA intervention, for example in the form of support for special measures, has implications for the labelled school and those in the surrounding area. It creates tensions between schools and a perception that all is not well. Choice mechanisms lead to issues of pupil selection and a concentration on exam success at all costs. Exam pressures create an incentive to gain the better positioned parents and children; a more advantaged clientele (Hirsch, 2002). Bowles (1989, cited in Bowe et al., 1992) noted that schools have a need to spend time considering what it is they have to offer, what it is they do well. In effect, they need to engage in some form of cost–benefit analysis against the activities they do and the groups with which they work. If an activity or group does not bring enough rewards then work therein should cease. As Waslander et al. (2010) note, such market mechanisms have engendered supplier-choice, that is, the situation where schools set out enrolment requirements whereby students are admitted to the school. Within-school alterations also occur, such as specialisation and ability setting, so as to attract certain desired groups. Such schemes are not always as neutral as they might be and often favour certain groups of pupils. Importantly the main effect is an attempt to control intake by seeking the most desirable students. In state schools, for example, troublesome pupils have been more likely to be permanently excluded from school and government pressure in the UK was needed to reduce this rise (Hirsch, 2002). Bradley and Taylor (2002) found that good schools, as measured by performance data, tend to have lower percentages of students on FSM, evidence that successful schools tend to become occupied by the middle classes. It is also the case that school composition affects the public measure of school quality which in turn affects parental choice. As non-poor children score more highly in external tests on average (Burgess and Briggs, 2006) schools with a lower proportion of FSM children produce higher average scores.

Gaming behaviour has also occurred to massage league tables. Schools in England tend to favour putting children in for easier tests, so boosting overall performance (Waslander et al., 2010). Selecting and attracting more able pupils was also more likely when raw scores were compared on league tables. Certain schools have also reduced the levels of vocational work undertaken so as to appear more academic in orientation. This is undertaken so as to position the school more favourably in the local hierarchy, thereby more enabling the selection of more able pupils. It seems that specific activities for boosting grades, such as booster classes, are often implemented. It is clear, then, that the choice realised through education policy is generalised and is constrained by a variety of factors (Burgess et al., 2007).

ACTIVITY 6.2

- Is choice illusory?
- Can a system of school choice ever be instigated that is open and fair to all?

Parental choice

Parental choice can be both positive and negative: the choice of a certain school for the education, discipline, etc. it has to offer versus the choice not to go to a certain school where the education, discipline, etc. is believed to be wanting. Choice is not therefore limited to academic success alone and can be based on, and indeed limited by, a number of factors (Bates et al., 2011):

- academic success;
- religious ethos;
- ease of travel;
- facilities;
- reputation;

- school characteristics, for example, large, small; and
- child's happiness and friendship groups.

Goldring and Phillips (2008) found that parents tended to use interpersonal networks to inform their decisions as to which school to send their children. Those with strong and motivated social networks appear to exercise more choice; similarly, those in higher socio-economic groups seem to know how to use and do use data to determine the right school for their child. Importantly, though, the more 'active choosers' seem to use more formal methods such as Ofsted reports, league tables and open days more often (Waslander et al., 2010):

> There is a considerable body of evidence that choice systems in themselves promote inequality in as much as 'choice policies' create social spaces within which class strategies and 'opportunistic behaviours' can flourish and within which the middle classes can use their social and cultural skills and capital advantages to good effect.
>
> (Ball, 2008: 133)

As Hirsch (2002) notes, families use exam results to judge schools, yet not exclusively. Whilst school quality is the main criterion, a portfolio of factors including, for example, a healthy social atmosphere is taken into consideration. Although, exam scores may be used as a proxy for wider issues, social matters are important; who children go to school with matters. In more densely populated areas if a proportion of the middle class do not choose local schools, others follow suit and go elsewhere. Prime movers can influence the social mix of pupils in a school via their activities and lobbying. Internally, schools may group by ability in order to send the message that pupils are with their social peer group. As ability grouping is commonly corre-lated with social class, ability grouping is one way that parents can be surer that their children are with children from similar social groups.

Whatever the mechanism, however, parents do seem to exercise the choices they have, although this is not always the case and there seem to be three main ways that choosers differ (Waslander et al., 2010):

- The well-off seem to exercise choice more fully; choice seems to be a class-based activity. The less well-off are more likely to attend their local school.
- The higher the perceived quality of the school, the more likely parents are to choose the school, or choose to remain at the school. This is related to the perception of the school, however, and not necessarily its actual profile.
- Parents who get more involved in their children's schooling are more likely to express a choice of school. Additionally, the less responsive a school is to parents the less likely parents are to keep their child in the school.

Parental choice is not as straightforward as it seems and stated reasons for choice are not always true indicators of decision-making. As Waslander et al. (2010) note, across Europe, whilst many parents espouse that they choose on quality, they often choose in such a way as to make important variable school composition. It seems that homogeneity is a defining feature and may mean that school composition is used as a proxy for quality. With this in mind, it is not clear that parents always choose the 'best' school available; school composition continues to be a key factor in choice, possibly because it is more visible than performance.

School choice has consequences then: not everyone benefits. In a true market, one's ability to buy goods does not impact on the choice of another whereas in the school system, with a finite number of places in any one area, this is not the case. Choice mechanisms in education ignore the fact that one person's decisions spill over into another's and hence constrain choice for the other (Bowe et al., 1992). Barry (1987: 52, cited in Bowe et al., 1992) writes about humans as 'assiduous calculator' and how this ignores the fact that the ability to choose and make those choices felt is constrained. Some places are inherently more desirable than others and hence attract more interest. But once these are taken, others lose this choice. Burgess et al. (2006) note that actively seeking better schools occurs within all levels of society, but to a much greater extent in the middle classes than the lower classes. Pupils eligible for FSM are 30 per cent more likely to attend their local low-scoring school than otherwise identical pupils from a better-off family (Burgess et al., 2006). This sorting is even more marked in local authorities with a selection policy. In effect, the 'contract' is not the same: the 'products' do the choosing (Trowler, 2003).

Choice and the market

Choice mechanisms have seen varying effects in countries around the globe. The main outcomes have been an increase in 'gaming' behaviour by parents to secure a place for their children in 'better' schools or schools with a specific social composition (Hirsch, 2002). Yet it is notable that in the UK school choice does not expand beyond matters of the selection of school. It is questionable, then, whether this is a true choice market, for wider issues of school reform such as the curriculum, ethos and ways of governing need to be seen as part of the school choice movement. School choice needs to be seen as something much wider than just a choice of school; ability to choose does not, on its own, determine the quality and character of education. It can be argued that the current predilection with *school* choice rather than *education* choice does little to move away from provider capture. Although current school choice mechanisms try to make the system demand driven, it is difficult to see how this can be enacted fully. Further, how much influence children have on the process is class-related, with working class children playing a greater role in choosing their school (Waslander et al., 2010).

With regard to curricular and pedagogic innovation, Lubienski (2009) found that innovation was not causally related to market mechanisms. These areas seem to have stronger links with government intervention: increase this and innovation is more likely to follow. However, in overly accountable systems such innovation is often stymied. This has obvious consequences for the overly performative-based English system. What school choice studies do seem to indicate is that the positive effects on student achievement of market mechanisms such as choice are rather small (Waslander et al., 2010). Indeed, for the UK, competition in the public sector concludes that there is only a small correlation between competition and performance and that this depends on the measurements used (Gibbons et al., 2008). It seems that the results of competition are modest in size:

> if one pattern stands out in the body of research about supply side mechanisms, it is that effects of policies aimed to introduce market mechanisms are differential. That is, they differ according to a range of factors, such as contextual factors including other policies such as accountability measures or possibilities to overtly or covertly control the pupil population; the position of a particular school in the local hierarchy; and responses of neighbouring schools and options to co-operate instead of compete.
>
> (Waslander et al., 2010: 62)

Hirsch (2002) notes issues from the pursuit of choice mechanisms:

■   school choice has proved neither a cure-all nor a catastrophe for the quality of education;

■   school choice can have marked effects on the social polarisation of students;

■   choice creates new possibilities of social exclusion influenced by geography;

■   school popularity, school performance and school quality need to be clearly distinguished.

Conclusion

It is possible to contest the very nature of choice as a mechanism itself. The very notion of choice as envisaged and enacted through the mechanisms involved in education is potentially problematic. The data provided in a sense pre-empt the goals and beliefs of the consumer; consumer notions of what counts become preordained *by the data* rather than decided upon by the consumer herself. It is not that the purchaser chooses freely, rather, they choose based on some already decided upon aspiration for education. We need to ask whether or not such mechanisms truly facilitate choice.

It should be remembered, though, and as Trowler (2003) writes, it is impossible to generalise about the outcome of these or indeed any policies. Often there are unintended consequences and what is the case for one school may not be the case for others. Some aspects of choice policy seem to have had positive effects, in places and for some, whilst in other areas negative effects were seen.

It is notable, though, that choice is a contradictory discourse. On the one hand, selection by ability is still seen as anathema, yet selection by postcode often goes unchallenged. As Hirsch (1997: 163) notes:

> in Britain the dominant view . . . is still that selection of pupils by ability . . . is an insidious route back to elitism . . . , yet selection by residence is acceptable even if it is leading to the concentration of privilege among better-off families living closer to more-desired schools.

Educational choice is a political issue. It forms the cornerstone of party policies from both sides of the political spectrum. The reasons for this are many, but include the fact that politicians are convinced that the populace desires choice above all else. This is, in part, tied to the western ideal of human rights: it is the right of the parent and child to be able to choose where and how they are educated. But this is problematic; for when one person chooses and has her rights met, another may well lose out. It is the case that in a rights-based approach one right may trump another and this may lead to an individual or group not receiving the education they desire. For example, not every parent has the cultural or social capital to access education to its fullest extent. For such groups choice is rather illusory: they do not have the same extent to choose. It is also the case that once one person has successfully chosen, that option is more than likely removed from the options available to another.

It is clear, though, that market-based mechanisms for ordering and organising education hold sway in contemporary society and choice forms a part of this. The Conservatives, the Liberal Democrats and New Labour have adopted choice as a part of their political manifestos and all desire to increase the choice offered to parents both through the types of schools on offer and through the actual mechanisms implemented to place children therein.

But choice is not equal in the way it orders and constructs educational systems. The middle classes have become dominant in this regard and it is they who form the group which is more likely to not only engage in choice but for whom first choice is most likely to manifest. A variety of mechanisms external to the choice apparatus seek to constrain parents' and pupils' ability to choose.

Key points

- Choice mechanisms in western nations are a manifestation, primarily of neoliberal thinking.
- Choice now stands as one of the defining features of English educational policy.
- Choice mechanisms assume that actors engage in purposive action; that is, they actively choose what is best.
- Arguments both in favour of and against choice in education rest on assumptions of equality.
- The Conservatives introduced contemporary notions of choice mechanisms as an aspect of national educational policy.
- For them, parental choice was a cornerstone of their ideological position.
- Choice was introduced both through the diversification of schools and parental right to express a preference of school.
- New Labour continued many of Conservative choice policies, albeit under different guises.
- Their approach adopted neoliberal tendencies but within a Third Way approach.
- Whatever the approach, evidence suggests that the middle classes are advantaged by choice mechanisms.
- Both parents and schools engage in gaming behaviour to position the middle classes more favourably.
- Parental choice is not, however, simple or straightforward.
- Choice seems to have rather limited positive effects on student achievement.
- The Coalition government have continued with the choice and diversity mantra.

Further reading

Burgess, S. and Briggs, A. (2006) *School Assignment, School Choice and Social Mobility*, Working Paper No. 06/157, Bristol: University of Bristol, Centre for Market and Public Organisation (CMPO), available at http://www.bristol.ac.uk/cmpo/publications/papers/2006/wp157.pdf. A discussion of the ways in which choice is mediated by social class.

Coldron, J. (2007) *Parents and the Diversity of Secondary Education: A discussion paper*, London: Research and Information on State Education Trust (RISE) available at http://www.risetrust.org.uk/node/24. A paper that highlights the issues involved in choice systems in secondary schools across England.

Waslander, S., Pater, C. and van der Weide, M. (2010) 'Markets in education: an analytical review of empirical research on market mechanisms in education', OECD Education Working Papers No. 52, OECD Publishing. A paper that discusses the effects of market mechanisms such as choice across a variety of countries.

7

Professionalism

Purpose of this chapter

After reading this chapter you should understand:

- how terms such as professional and professionalism might be defined;
- the way in which teaching was positioned during the welfarist settlement;
- the changes wrought by successive Conservative administrations between 1979 and 1997;
- how New Labour sought to change the professional landscape between 1997 and 2010;
- the changing face of initial teacher education and training;
- how continuous professional development became positioned during the New Labour era;
- how workforce remodelling altered the relationship between teachers and classroom assistants;
- how teacher professionalism has altered to take account of the needs of parents and other stakeholders in education;
- the ways in which Ofsted has contributed to the changing face of teacher professionalism;
- The changes wrought by the Coalition government.

> when I discuss professionals I am talking about groups such as doctors, academics, teachers, accountants, lawyers, engineers, civil servants, etc., that is those groups commonly thought of as professional by the lay public, academics, the professionals themselves and so on.
>
> (Hanlon, 1998: 45)

Notwithstanding Hanlon's position, teaching has never been fully recognised as a profession mainly because of its inability to promote and demonstrate a distinctive expertise (Beck, 2008) and the fact that teachers have never really had the right to determine their own affairs as have medicine and the law (Whitty, 2006). Despite historical moves, teaching has more often than not been cited as a quasi-profession, not enjoying the same status as medicine or law for example, but occupying a space above other 'jobs'. In part this has come about due to the position teaching holds as contributing to the public good: in effect a blend of altruism and intellectual engagement

(Wilkins, 2011). The fact that talk about teaching is usually undertaken in terms of its being a profession so orients it, even if we are not able to tick off the core characteristics prevalent in other professions (Whitty, 2000); the discourse offers the position for teaching to take up.

Professionalism and politics

Such professionalism discussions must be held with political discourses in mind. Driven by the need to 'raise standards' in relation to competitor countries, education in England has been altered from a liberal-humanist tradition to a functionalist, results-driven market (Day, 2002). This is part of an agenda of wider public services reform which started in the mid to late 1970s whereupon the 'New Right' sought to reinvent the public sector. Accordingly, there has been, in the last 25 years, much change globally in the way that teachers work. Many of these changes, however, have led to an increase in workload and compliance (Hargreaves, 2000). As part of this agenda, many activities once carried out at the local authority or national level have been decentralised, whilst others, such as measures of pupil achievement, have been subject to intense government scrutiny and control and compliance with this agenda is now seen as a requirement for the teaching profession. In many respects, such changes have eroded teachers' professional and personal identities (Day, 2002).

Since the 1980s, teachers' work in England has been subject to more government intervention than any other country. Brennan (1996) notes how teachers are now part of 'managerial professionalism' which emphasises the need for teachers to: meet externally set goals and targets; manage students; and, document their and pupil's achievements. In the corporate world of school, teachers work efficiently and effectively, meet standardised criteria and contribute to formal accountability structures. Teachers now seem to be part of a performance culture with high-status accountability requirements (Day and Smethem, 2009).

The golden age for teaching

However, there was a golden age for teacher professionalism and it is generally perceived to have been in the 1950s and 1960s. Then, education was provided by teachers who enjoyed a great deal of autonomy, in schools, locally organised and run with a relatively benign inspectorate, which, in essence, undertook peer review. Teacher education was left to colleges and universities to organise and conceptualise. The curriculum was taught (not delivered) and teacher development was the preserve of the individual member of staff. This was a time where the welfare state and the welfarist settlement were at their zenith and teachers were seen as partners in the social endeavour to ensure a more equal society with opportunities for all. They worked with a 'social service' ethic (Whitty, 2000) to provide a service to their clients. In turn they had considerable *de facto* autonomy (Whitty, 2006) as to what and how they taught and assessed. The state did not intervene in initial teacher education, curriculum, assessment or pedagogy; it was widely accepted that the teacher's role 'included the freedom to decide not only how to teach but also what to teach and assess pupils on and that they had a particular responsibility for curriculum development and innovation' (Furlong, 2005: 120). Throughout this period the state maintained more of a 'hands-off' approach and gave teachers considerable freedom (Shain and Gleeson, 1999). In part this stemmed from a shortage of teachers and meant that the profession was in a good position to defend its licensed autonomy. As the 1960s progressed, teachers' control over matters such as curriculum and pedagogy gradually increased. But the government was increasingly concerned about the rise of militancy in teaching and across the public sector more broadly. This saw efforts by government to appeal to teachers to reject such militancy and achieve greater recognition and pay as a result.

Hargreaves (2000) describes this period as the age of the autonomous professional. Professional judgement was deemed as key to the work of the teacher and in this way 'professional' and 'autonomy' became key-words. From the 1960s debates about pedagogy ensured that teaching was more an ideological position than previously. Child-centredness and traditionalism became the two great meta-narratives (Hargreaves, 2000: 159). Indeed, the 1967 Plowden Report proposed new ways of working that started from the child's point of view and not the subject matter to be taught. However, in practice, many teachers did not move away from more traditional styles of pedagogy. In many ways what ensued was a traditionalist and isolationist approach: individual teachers teaching in their own classrooms in isolation. Problematically, this licensed autonomy 'insulated teachers from the community by keeping teachers on pedestals above the community, it isolated teachers from one another, and it subordinated teachers' professional learning to academic agendas, which often has only tenuous connections to their practice' (Hargreaves, 2000: 161). It offered little in the way of preparation for the dramatic changes that were to be wrought following Callaghan's Ruskin College speech (Callaghan, 1976), which sowed yet more seeds of doubt about the profession.

A right wing backlash

The fact that most teachers retained a more traditional form of pedagogy in their classrooms did not deter the right wing from marking education out as a hotbed of radicalism. In part this stemmed from the fact that throughout the 1970s workers' unions increasingly challenged government and managers over what they saw as unfavourable working conditions and pay. This period saw a rise in trade union power which in turn often pitched those within such organisations against both the government and other parts of the populace.

However, the first Black Paper of 1969 (Cox and Dyson, 1969) sought not to continue the appeal to the 'responsible majority' but rather to denigrate the whole system. This New Right agenda of derision was more to do with a need to liberalise the public sector along private sector lines, in favour of consumers; there was a need to remove power from the producers. Importantly, this agenda saw teaching as a craft with no theoretical underpinning. The final Black Paper (Cox and Boyson, 1977) argued that college work should only be undertaken in subject knowledge, not education; pedagogy, etc. should only be learnt in the classroom. At the time, some even argued that education-related courses were nothing more than nonsense (Anderson, 1982, cited in Ball, 1990).

From the 1970s, then, there was demise in the trust of the welfare state due to economic issues and the belief that it had failed. The New Right belief was that teachers should be called to account along with other public sector employees, and subject to increased competition and surveillance; teachers' motives were called into question. In England, from 1979, Thatcher's government altered the language used about teachers to one of derision: they were portrayed as self-serving and monopolistic. Radical changes were started by the New Right in the 1980s and continued apace throughout the 1990s and into the new century. There have been differences in the discourses deployed in the drive to develop teacher professionalism, but essentially change has moved teaching from autonomy to the post-professional era

(Hargreaves, 2000). But such changes mirror those seen across the globe and can be identified by five common themes (Day, 2002):

- they occur because governments believe that by intervening they can raise levels of attainment and increase economic competitiveness;
- governments wish to stem the decline in personal and social values;
- governments see the need to challenge teachers' existing practices;
- governments have, by default, increased teachers' workload;
- governments do not pay attention to teacher identity in the changes they promote.

The ethos now, in many western countries at least, is neoliberal and follows the doctrine of new public management (NPM). As Day (2002) notes, this requires on-going improvement within a market ethos. Consequently, control has shifted away from professionals towards systems managers. Now, when professionalism is mentioned, it is in relation to the market culture at the heart of the neoliberal agenda. A teacher must now be a

> professional who clearly meets corporate goals, set elsewhere, manages a range of students well and documents their achievements and problems for public accountability purposes. The criteria of the successful professional in this corporate model is [sic] one who works efficiently and effectively in meeting the standardised criteria set for the accomplishment of both students and teachers, as well as contributing to the school's formal accountability processes.
>
> (Brennan, 1996: 22)

This is reminiscent of Sachs' (2003) entrepreneurial professional identity as marked by: efficiency; responsibility; accountability in terms of externally imposed targets; compliance with external mandate; and, high-quality, compliant teaching to meet accountability measures.

However, as Olssen and Peters (2005) state, this is a contradiction, for the very idea of professionalism conveys subject-directed power; the ability of the subject to take decisions in the workplace based on a receipt of power. Control is leveraged by those within the peer group; the levers of power are structured from within. But this is problematic for neoliberalism which sees the professions as

> self-interested groups who indulge in rent-seeking behaviour. In neoliberalism the patterning of power is established on contract, which in turn is premised upon a need for compliance, monitoring, and accountability organised in a management line and established through a purchase contract based upon measurable outputs.
>
> (Olssen and Peters, 2005: 325)

ACTIVITY 7.1

- How are professionalism and being a professional bound up with political decisions and ideology?
- Should the determination of the status 'professional' be a political act?

Professionalism

Before discussing professionalism and derivations thereof, it is worth considering what Beck has to say about the status of the teaching profession.

> Most significantly . . . Teaching in England has long been a *fragmented* profession. It is cross-cut by actual and perceived internal differences of status which are in part the legacy of a class stratified education system, and it has also been chronically divided on the basis of gender. The multiplicity of professional organisations and unions to which different sections of the teaching force have belonged has both reflected and reinforced such divisions.
>
> (Beck, 2008: 121)

It is clear, then, that discussing teacher professionalism, the professional teacher, the teaching profession, etc. is fraught with difficulties, for the history of the project is one of debate, disagreement and, often, derision. The particular views of the professional that people support depend on their values as well as their wider political perspectives and the way they are positioned by reform (Whitty, 2000: 283). Clearly, then, care must be taken when discussing the professionalisation of teaching, or teaching as a profession, for 'profession' is an essentially contested concept; 'there are differing ideologies in informing views of professionalism in teaching' (Poulson, 1998: 419). Despite its widespread use in everyday talk and despite the fact that sociologists, philosophers and historians have attempted definitions, professionalism often eludes common agreement (Hoyle and John, 1995).

Teachers may talk about 'being professional' in terms of their conduct, demeanour and the standards they uphold (Helsby, 1995), and of 'being a professional' in how they feel they are perceived by others. More importantly, attempts to improve teacher status (professionalisation) (Whitty, 2000) are often presented as a complementary project with professionalism (improving practice). It is not clear that such complementarity does always exist, however. Changes to teacher work may engender increased technicisation through the mastery of little more than skills, which, in turn, may well alter the status of the profession from one of autonomy to one of technician. Such views are temporarily defined through discourse and decision, policy and practice.

> Images of and ideas about teacher professionalism, and even about the nature of teaching itself, linger on from other agendas and other times – remaining as real forces to be reckoned with in the imaginations and assumptions of policy-makers, the public and many parts of the teaching profession itself.
>
> (Hargreaves, 2000: 152)

The term 'profession' stands for a set of ideas; a collective symbol; professionalism is a discourse that positions people in relation to other discourses and texts (Robson et al., 2004). However, the three concepts of knowledge, autonomy and responsibility (or altruism) seem to be central to a traditional notion of professionalism and are often cited as being inter-related (Robson et al., 2004); they form the classic professionalism triangle.

Millerson (1964) provides a classic definition of professionalism in terms of these three discourses, whereupon the professional is described because they:

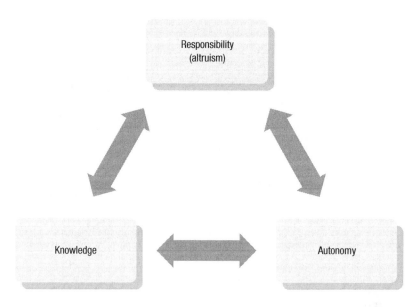

FIGURE 7.1 The classic professionalism triangle

■   use skills based on theoretical knowledge;

■   have an education and training in those skills certified by examination;

■   work within a code of professional conduct oriented towards the 'public good'; and,

■   have a powerful professional organisation.

Such classical ideas stem from the infallible expert view of professionalism (Elliott, 1991: 311) which expects deferential treatment from clients and which acts in terms of one-way communication from professional to client. Specialist knowledge is used exclusively and responses to situations are based on intuition.

Such definitions provide a criterion or essentialist approach to the definition of profession in terms of their 'central social function, length of training, a body of knowledge, high levels of skill, a code of ethical conduct, client-centredness, autonomy, independent decision-making and adaptability, self-governance and the requirement that it play a central role in relevant public policy-making' (Locke et al., 2005: 558). In this vein, Carr (1992) identifies four dimensions of professionalism:

■   procedural: the mastery of technical skills;

■   deontic: teaching being done for others in the light of professional judgement;

■   supererogatory: the way in which teachers carry their professional lives into their personal lives;

■   axiological: the way in which teachers live their personal life is as a role model.

Such classical views can be seen in contrast to what Hargreaves (2000) describes as the pre-professional age. Here teaching was seen as the mastery of certain technical skills related to control and whole class, hand-up instruction. Learning to teach was an apprenticeship; one aligned oneself with a teacher as a novice and learnt from the master. In this age, teaching was seen as 'managerially demanding but technically simple' (Hargreaves, 2000: 156). Traditionally teacher knowledge suffered from being aligned with such common-sense knowledge positions.

Importantly, modern sociological moves call upon the consideration of how professionalism is enacted, not a consideration of a series of definitive statements (Whitty, 2006). It is better to consider teaching in the here and now when discussing professionalism (Whitty, 2000). A social constructionist approach (Troman, 1996) sees the process of professionalisation as a political project or mission (Locke et al., 2005) with differing interpretations. As Fox (1992: 2) notes, 'Professionalism means different things to different people. Without a language police, however, it is unlikely that the term professional (ism) will be used in only one concrete way.'

Holroyd (2000) marks the need to consider the history involved in the changing face of social constructions and Ozga (1995: 22) posits that professionalism is best considered in a policy context. For, as she states, '[c]ritical analyses of professionalism do not stress the qualities inherent in an occupation but explore the value of the service offered by the members of that occupation to those in power.'

New professionalism

With such debates in mind, 'new professionalism' has often been discussed and writers such as Elliott (1991) note the need to consider professionalism in terms of the ways in which teachers have the ability to make informed decisions when working in novel and unpredictable situations. Such images have the following in common (Elliott, 1991: 311):

- collaboration with clients (individuals, groups, communities) in identifying, clarifying and resolving their problem;
- the importance of communication and empathy with clients as a means of understanding situations from their point of view;
- a new emphasis on the holistic understanding of situations as the basis for professional practice, rather than on understanding them exclusively in terms of a particular set of specialist categories;
- self-reflections as a means of overcoming stereotypical judgements and responses.

New professionalism promotes the idea of the professional as reflective practitioner where understanding is a situated endeavour, problem solving is undertaken collaboratively and learning takes place *in situ* (Elliott, 1991). These deeper connections with wider notions of professional training and development Hoyle (1974) terms 'extended Professionality'. In this discourse (Locke et al., 2005) 'the good practitioner is a well-rounded person who can integrate all aspects of their prior knowledge and act in a teaching situation with moral integrity' (Codd, 1997: 140). Such a professional-contextualist position (Locke et al., 2005) notes a number of inherent features:

- the criterion of good practice is one of integrity towards the job and clients;
- the pedagogical aim is to enable the development of diverse human capabilities;
- administrative functions are centred on professional, collaborative leadership and action;

- motivation is intrinsic;
- professional commitment defines the parameters of accountability.

Essentially, New Professionalism seems concerned with the quality of service rather than the simple enhancement of status (Evans, 2008). In this view professionalism seems defined by interplay between the agenda setting activities of those in power and teachers themselves (Boyt et al., 2001).

For Hargreaves (1994) professionalism is about discretionary judgement in the face of uncertainty whilst Robson et al. (2004) note that the environment in which teachers work requires them to have knowledge and autonomy which they discharge responsibly in a client centred manner. Abstract knowledge and technical skills are both of equal importance.

> It is because professionals face complex and unpredictable situations that they need a specialised body of knowledge; if they are to apply that knowledge, it is argued that they need the autonomy to make their own judgements. Given that they have the autonomy, it is essential that they act with responsibility – collectively they need to develop appropriate professional values.
>
> (Robson et al., 2004: 184–185)

For Hall (2004) such teaching is a complex endeavour which has caring, moral, cultural, intellectual and emotional elements. At its heart it

> requires teachers who are not only pedagogically competent and knowledgeable about what they teach, but who are able to enthuse, motivate and engage the learners, who are able to be at their best at all times. To be at their best requires them to be motivated, confident that they can make a positive difference to learning and achievement and that they can be trusted to do so.
>
> (Day and Smethem, 2009: 149)

The idea that professionalism should be discussed in relation to what is happening in the world of education is a powerful one. Resultant typologies often discuss three types for the changing face of professionalism in schools (Wilkins, 2011):

- The Empowered: on the one hand the contradictions inherent between market forces and professional autonomy are disempowering and lead to fractured or contested social identities (Giddens, 1991). On the other, changes to management techniques and leadership styles facilitate professional empowerment.
- The Incorporated: whilst some note that school leadership is now empowering of the professional and enhances collegiality (Gronn, 2000), this view is not widely shared. Most research sees the changes as having eroded autonomy and as having introduced a 'technicist' orientation. In this view teachers have become increasingly de-professionalised and compliant with state mandate (Hatcher, 1994).
- The Activist: this position views professionals as having become adept at using collegiality and a 'democratic discourse' (Sachs, 2003: 134–135) to balance the need for public accountability and professionalism. Teachers, in this position, have a more resistant and transformative agenda, countering and subverting the forces of performativity.

ACTIVITY 7.2

■ Write a definition or paragraph that describes what you think being a professional means.

■ From this paragraph or definition:

    a   Make a list of all of the features that you believe make teaching a profession.
    b   Now make a list of all those features of teaching which mean it is not a profession.

The Conservative era

Notably, Barber (2005) describes the period until the 1980s as one of uninformed profession-alism. In terms of the needs of modern society, teachers, he maintained, lacked appropriate knowledge and pedagogical expertise. However, the 1980s and 1990s saw a systemic upheaval and marketisation of education (Wilkins, 2011). From 1979 Conservative governments started a modernisation project for teacher professionalism the main focus of which was the discrediting of teaching and teachers. The 1980s and 1990s saw continuous neoliberal Conservative gov-ernments who sought to wrest control of schooling away from the teaching profession, whom they saw as complacent, elitist and favouring doctrinaire egalitarianism over pupil attainment (Wilkins, 2011); what ensued was the technicisation of education (Day and Smethem, 2009). This period saw the introduction of monitoring and accountability for performance: these have since become the main planks of contemporary schooling (Day and Smethem, 2009).

Education policy in the 1980s and 1990s sought to increase accountability through cen-tral control and regulation and reform was largely introduced with little, if any, consulta-tion. From the 1980s teachers became seen as a group in need of social and political control and their professional mandate to act in the best interests of the client groups was gradually removed. In Barber's (2005) terms, this amounted to a period of uninformed prescription but for Hargreaves (2000) the changes enacted at the time brought about positive and nega-tive shifts in teacher professionalism. The changes wrought, not only in England but in other western countries, enacted the age of the collegial professional. Educational change at the time meant that teachers were no longer able to simply define the parameters of their own work with no reference to the practices of others. Hargreaves maintains that a number of issues influenced such collaboration:

■ For most of the twentieth century teachers were able to decide what it was they taught and how to do so. Changes such as the advent of the National Curriculum and altera-tions to assessment regimes challenged this and stated, quite clearly, what teachers were supposed to teach. The need was there, then, to know exactly what others had done or were planning to do.

■ Increasingly, teachers became more aware of differing teaching styles and methods and mechanisms for sharing these with others were introduced.

■ The role of the teacher altered: increasingly, their work became 'social work oriented'. Additionally, following the 1981 Education Act (DES, 1981) the identification of and support for children with special educational needs gained an increased focus in the work of teachers in schools and local education authorities (LEA)s.

- The way in which society was becoming ever more diverse and multicultural.
- The ways in which schools were run became a key site for government intervention.

Whilst some teachers complied with government mandate (Troman, 1996), not all embraced such change and, duly, in public, teachers and schools were represented as in need of enforced reform; external accountability was seen to be required. As Poulson (1998: 419) notes, 'Such an emphasis on external accountability has had an impact on the ways in which professionalism has been conceptualised by governments and by teachers themselves in the micro-political contexts of individual schools.' But accountability is ambiguous and has two possible meanings:

- Accountability as self-regulation.

  o   moral obligation; explaining and justifying oneself through dialogue; or

  o   giving solicited information or responding to questions;

- an externally imposed mandate delivered through contract, inspection and testing.

Throughout the 1990s the main thrusts for education policy were to prepare pupils for the workplace and destroy education's potential to undermine the market. Beck (2008) notes three mechanisms by which such change was leveraged:

- Power was devolved to institutions, particularly through mechanisms such as city technology colleges (CTCs) and grant-maintained (GM) status, so that they might operate in a quasi-market.
- The powers of central government were strengthened through the imposition of a national curriculum and national testing at ages 7, 11 and 14. In schools the advent of the National Curriculum is thought to have curtailed teacher autonomy (Robson et al., 2004).
- Change was secured and maintained through an audit culture imposed by the creation of an independent inspectorate.

The Conservative era saw the adoption of the last mechanism for accountability and the systematic undermining of the former as an expression of teacher professionalism. Along with terms such as standards and choice, accountability became a politically driven term. Problematically, accountability always works to constrain professionalism (Locke et al., 2005).

Changes in education are not only affected by political discourse, though; other discursive practices and legislation themselves have an effect. Within the Conservative frame parental choice recast education in terms of commodity production (the commodification of teaching and professionalism) and market forces (the creation of a market which defines what it means to be a teacher and to act professionally). Hence parents were 'cast as consumers whose choice is guided largely by schools' performance in tests or public examinations' (Poulson, 1998: 420). All this positions the teacher as the businessperson; the one who can sell a certain type of education to a certain type of person. Problematically, such a contractual-consumerist model involves specification which is fundamentally at odds with professionalism; to denote exactly what a teacher should do denies them their autonomy (Olssen and Peters, 2005). However, some studies (cf. Poulson, 1998) showed that parents do not automatically adopt this line; they do not necessarily see themselves as consumers or education as a product. Problematically, over time, this situation changed: the language of consumerism came much more to the fore. This may have occurred due to the utilisation of a consumerist line throughout political and social discourse.

Poulson's (1998) work seems to indicate that accountability became a disciplinary technology: a means of teacher control by external forces. Terms such as line management and curriculum audit were used to both demonstrate and justify calls for accountability. However, in fact this gave rise to a multiplicity of identities, for teachers chose their own ways of representing themselves and their work; they used a number of different mechanisms to meet accountability requirements. It was not that teachers specifically acquiesced to reform; rather they carved specific spaces for themselves to work in ways previously held as professional. Traditional ways of working were not simply dropped and replaced; they were positioned by the external forces brought to bear on the profession. The managerial reforms restructured professionalism (Olssen and Peters, 2005).

New Labour's changes

The election of New Labour to power in 1997 initiated a project to respond to globalisation and the knowledge economy (Furlong, 2005). In many ways New Labour maintained the agenda introduced by the Conservatives although it wanted to engender a new model of teacher professionalism. Following election in 1997, they sought to win teachers over by promoting a new form of professional membership and redefined notions of professionalism (Beck, 2008). Whilst the term professional was replete in government literature, they were scornful, however, of models of teaching infused by nurture and ease of relationships; these, they maintained, were inadequate for the new millennium (Hayes, 2001: 43). In support they created new institutions and performance criteria both for training and professional advancement. However, marketisation and centralisation as key drivers for professional improvement continued. But there was a wider emphasis on education as a collective endeavour with the involvement of a range of stakeholders both in terms of initiation into the profession and the ways in which teachers were required to subsequently work (Whitty, 2006). What followed election victory was an

> intensified emphasis upon the raising of standards, with pedagogical prescription (in the form of the Literacy and Numeracy Strategies) added to the prior prescription of the National Curriculum and various auditing mechanisms (league tables of schools' performance in pupil tests, OFSTED inspections, LEA target setting) designed to promote this standards agenda . . .
>
> (Locke et al., 2005: 557)

In the first two terms in office, New Labour was much more assertive in stating what it believed teachers should achieve and their approach was the control of many aspects of teachers' work. They introduced new categories of teacher (post-threshold, advanced skills), performance-related pay (PRP), new definitions and responsibilities for management roles, the National College for School Leadership (NCSL), new frameworks for teaching two of the core subjects, an increase in continuing professional development (CPD) opportunities and the rise of teaching assistants (Day and Smethem, 2009). Entry routes to the profession also diversified and more on-the-job training ensued. From the late 1990s there was a huge investment in information and communications technology (ICT) infrastructure and training. Their control even went so far as to describe ideal lessons for teachers to download from the department website, particularly for literacy and numeracy. The nature of schools changed as well: increases in pupil misbehaviour and violence; and, an increase in workload. Both led to an increase in sick leave and teachers leaving the profession with the most cited reasons being workload, pupil behaviour and government initiatives (Smithers and Robinson, 2003). High levels of poor motivation and high stress continued to be reported, and changes to monitoring and accountability systems led to the intensification of teachers' work. The reforms all contributed to high levels of uncertainty, instability and vulnerability for teachers (Day, 2002).

The first Green Paper, *Teachers: Meeting the challenge of change* (DfEE, 1998b), listed the attributes a professional should have and demonstrated New Labour's corporate management model:

■ high expectations of themselves and their pupils;

■ accepting of accountability;

■ accepting of both a personal and collective responsibility for improving their skills and subject knowledge;

■ using evidence of what works;

■ working in partnership;

■ welcoming the contributions of parents, businesses and others;

■ anticipating change and promote innovation.

This was a new venture for a government; by describing in such detail what it felt should be the main characteristics of a teacher, New Labour initiated a project to centrally define, through government missive, teacher professionalism and action. As Furlong (2005: 120) notes, 'For New Labour, the aim has been to establish forms of professionalism that accept that decisions, about what to teach and how to teach and how to assess children, are made at school and national level rather than by individual teachers themselves.'

Teachers: Meeting the challenge of change (DfEE, 1998b) introduced an element of PRP via a threshold mechanism and the standards for advanced skills teacher. This entailed devising standards for teachers to meet so that they might move to higher levels of pay. Part of these changes involved target setting and performance management and threshold, essentially introducing an element of local pay into what was, previously a national system. In addition, teacher appraisals were introduced. These involved teachers being set targets to achieve so that they can be said to demonstrate both good teaching and year-on-year improvement in the quality of their teaching. Performance became a key feature of the teacher's life, and replaced, in many ways, the nurturing side of primary classroom activity (Hayes, 2001).

Mahony et al. (2004) note how these new systems adopted a regulatory model of performance management and involved:

■ the setting of performance targets linked to student achievement – this became a key feature to gaining promotion over the threshold and into the upper pay spine;

■ a focus on the visible and measurable through the technology of the testing regime;

■ decisions based on scrutiny, judgement and evaluation by line managers;

- a required increase in the capacity for surveillance on the part of managers and others within the system;
- reducing people to measurable 'performances'.

In Mahony et al.'s terms such managerialism involves the reorganisation of the public sector to follow the lines of 'best practice' as found in the commercial world. Worldwide, such managerialism includes 'employee performance measurement; increased demands for public accountability in achieving specified outcomes; and new centralised forms of control and regulation accompanying decentralized responsibility for local management' (Mahony et al., 2004: 137). The emphasis is on compliance and specification: adherence to certain mechanisms for the improvement of educational outcomes as measured through testing. Performance management positions teachers as units of labour to be managed. Such regulatory mechanisms for performance management 'rely on individualistic and competitive notions of motivation, achievement, performance and progressions. In doing so they take it as axiomatic that this version of the teacher will prove to be more "efficient, effective and economical" in relation to the production of desired outcomes' (Mahony et al., 2004: 138).

The introduction of the national literacy and numeracy strategies saw government increase its control over both classroom practice and CPD (Cunningham, 2012). There was an increase in surveillance and control and an increase in the ideas of recipes for success (Day and Smethem, 2009). This was most notable through the deployment of 'what works' as the reason for implementation. Indeed, New Labour was non-ideological in its portrayal of educational improvement: what mattered was that which engendered success. Hayes comments that the pressure on teachers to conform was reminiscent of 'religious sanctification' expressed through the government's view that teachers had let their pupils down. Teachers, he writes, needed to be 'cleansed from depraved ideas and practices' so that they might 'find redemption (notably by means of successful school inspections) through celebrating the "one way" proclaimed through "written oracles" (government directives) from "the Master Educationalist" (the Secretary of State for Education)' (Hayes, 2001: 44).

Adams (2008) notes how certain conceptions of practice became reified through the simplistic aligning of test scores with teacher activity. Here certain specifications for teacher activity, as defined by the likes of Hay McBer (2000), take on *the* defining role for required professional activity. In turn, 'best practice' is identified, to be emulated throughout the teaching profession. Causality between what teachers do and how pupils achieve becomes cemented; what matters, therefore, is not what pupils bring to their education in terms of social class, gender or ethnicity, but rather what teachers do with the pupils in their care. Accordingly, such issues become ignored in the drive to relate pupil attainment to teacher activity; all pupils and teachers were deemed to have an equal starting point. As Osgood (2006) notes, professionalisation became a site for increased governmental control; a means to describe 'correct' or 'best' practice. Essentially, this was a model of social engineering

> characterised by regulation and control through a standards agenda and represents adherence to a mechanistic reductionist project, wherein those who represent the power elite (government departments and agencies) act as regulators of the behaviours of the subordinate (practitioners).
>
> (Osgood, 2006: 6)

Performance and performativity

The aforementioned notes the rise of the performativity discourse (see Chapter 8), but this culture of performativity has unforeseen consequences on the work of teachers. Forrester (2005) notes how, in primary schools, the traditional role of care was reduced. Care became seen as something to be done for legal or administrative purposes rather than as an integral part of the primary school experience. In Noddings' (2002) terms, 'care about' (exam scores, behaviour, league tables) takes precedence over 'care for' (children, community, each other). This delineation of work mirrored that described by Acker (1995) as 'audited and paid for' and that which is 'non-audited and unpaid'. Thus, the ways in which certain activities, particularly those seen as adding to the overall standing of the school become defined as the 'work' of teachers whereas other aspects traditionally part of the fare of the primary school become seen as 'non-work'. Primary teaching seems to lose its Plowden-like feel (see Chapter 4), focusing instead on delivery and standards (Jeffrey, 2002) (see Chapter 8). With regard to relationships, Jeffrey (2002) noted three areas for change:

- Staff–pupil relations: inter-relations became dependent rather than independent, familiar relations became formulised and routinised, and pedagogic relations became preceptive rather than dialogic (Jeffrey, 2002: 536).

- Staff–staff relations: the teacher came to be seen as the expert manager, with some parts of the school seen as 'letting the side down' due to 'poor performance'; an 'us and them' relationship within a managerialist culture. Democratic relations shifted from being consensual to disciplinary, collaborative relations from collegial to hierarchical and personal relations from considerate to confrontational (Jeffrey, 2002: 540). Collaboration was redefined as team-work, where all were dependent on each other for success.

- LEA–school relationships: these changed through the way that the former became seen as conduits for government control.

The performance agenda greatly reduced commitment to the affective, not in terms of desire, but in terms of operation. Importantly, whilst older teachers seemed to have a more holistic vision both for their professionalism and pedagogy, younger teachers seemed more content with managerial creeds and test-based education (Day, 2002). But this demarcation of the generations was particularly problematic. Government mandate often engendered a sense of crisis in the profession, particularly amongst the older generation of teachers. They began to question their worth given that how they had taught for years was now being held up for scorn and ridicule (Hayes, 2001). Duly, many teachers left, and continue to leave, or intend to leave, the profession before they reached retirement age.

Day (2002: 685–686) cites five consequences of the performativity agenda (see Chapter 8). These stem from the continual monitoring of efficiency wherein teachers were expected to implement others' plans for curriculum, teaching and assessment. Performativity, then,

- threatens teachers' sense of agency;
- implicitly encourages teachers to comply uncritically (e.g. teach to the test);
- challenges teachers' substantive identity;
- reduces the time teachers have to connect with, care for and attend to the needs of individual students;
- diminishes teachers' sense of motivation, efficacy and job satisfaction.

The intensification of workload left practitioners too busy and preoccupied with standards to consider and develop their own professional identities. This led to an inability to negotiate and construct their own views of 'being professional' or 'acting professionally'; these were done to them (Osgood, 2006). Regulatory modes of performance management seem, then, to have had a certain defining effect on educational orientation. Policy reform led to 'an intensification of workload with an emphasis on technical competence and performativity' (Osgood, 2006: 6). Conversely, groups such as the School Teachers' Review Body maintained that exam scores were rising and that the quality of education is the reason. They stated that the teaching profession was 'efficient, effective and accountable' (STRB, 2003: vi). However, others questioned this and maintained that the rise in exam scores was not due to some form of re-found professionalism but rather 'teaching to the test' (Day and Smethem, 2009).

Perryman (2006) notes that following 2000 teachers were increasingly controlled by notions of 'productive autonomy', that is:

- the formal auditing of pupil learning;
- student outcomes set and monitored rigorously by senior management;
- the establishment of national strategies and national curricula;
- PRP for career progression linked to pupil outcomes;
- target setting for both staff and pupils.

This posed somewhat of a dilemma for many teachers who, on the one hand, were required to act in ways concordant with new expectations and show how their pupils achieved ever higher test results. On the other hand, though 'they want to fulfil their ambitions to work with children or young people in a generous, enriching environment, where limitations and (even) eccentricities are celebrated and pupils are prepared for life over-and-above academia' (Hayes, 2001: 46).

It seems, then, that the post-1944 'social service' ethic was replaced by a 'commercialised professionalism' which panders to profitability and international competitiveness (Whitty, 2000). This shift from welfarist Bureau-Professionalism, to post-welfare 'new Managerialism' (Gewirtz et al., 1995) is marked by performance measurement, output controls, marketisation and competition. This is a technocratic line where good practice is reduced to a set of predefined skills or competences with little or no acknowledgement of the moral dimension of teaching (Codd, 1997: 140). Locke et al. (2005) note that such technocratic-reductionist conceptions of teaching have the following features:

- Their origins lie in managerial approaches and audit-based, external accountability all of which constrains teacher autonomy.
- Raising standards is measured by test results and is seen as the way to make a difference.
- Working together takes on the form of 'contrived collegiality' whereby surveillance drives the agenda.
- All of this is underpinned by the effective implementation of government designed professional development.

Furlong (2005: 123) notes that under New Labour 'The state has taken a much more assertive role in defining how to teach as well as what to teach; the result has been the establishment of what I would term a more "managed" professionalism.' He further notes, though, that New

Labour also believed in an active state pursuing social programmes. To this end collaborative networks and partnerships ensued within the parameters of a market-based approach. The agenda was one of the best working with those in need. However, for most teachers this translated into interventions that detailed processes for teaching and learning such as the literacy and numeracy strategies, both of which were highly prescriptive. This new age has been termed 'post-professional' (Ball, 2003) where teachers only work to satisfy the requirements of others and with entrepreneurial-competitive identities (Day, 2002). Hayes (2001: 48) notes the contradictions inherent in New Labour's education policy:

> The irony of the political initiatives characterising the end of the 20th century was that despite the wide-eyed protestations from government that educational change had the support of most (sensibly-minded) teachers and was only in response to extensive consultations, the end result was an increase in formal teaching competence at the expense of professional empowerment.

ACTIVITY 7.3

New Labour's focus was on defining the ways in which teachers should work. How do you think this positioned teachers regarding their professional status?

The changing face of teacher education and training

What was certainly notable throughout the 1980s and 1990s was the way in which initial teacher education became a site for political struggle and debate (Furlong et al., 2000). Until the 1980s higher education institutes (HEIs) decided on the constituents of teacher education. In the Conservative years, teacher education was seen as a key part of altering teacher professionalism (Furlong, 2005); the changes started from the premise that changing the nature of teaching was crucial to reform (Furlong et al., 2000). Alterations in training were seen as necessary to construct a new generation of teachers, complete with updated skills, knowledges and professional values and better able to offer an education fit for the modern world. The result was that during the 1980s 'initial teacher education . . . increasingly became a major site for ideological struggle between the government and others' (Furlong et al., 2000: 2). Maintaining a supply of teachers and increasing accountability were, along with influencing professionalism, major policy concerns. This cut against prior, classical notions of professionalism which saw teachers make decisions based on the needs of pupils, as they saw them where professional interpretation and voluntary commitment to good practice were the key.

In 1983 the Council for the Accreditation of Teacher Education (CATE) was created by government. This started the period of greater scrutiny of teachers and teacher education. It was CATE's role to validate university and college courses according to centrally stipulated criteria, including a minimum time students should spend in school. This control was gradually tightened throughout the 1980s and early 1990s. Whitty (2006: 7) notes the effects of such changes:

> And, indeed, in some cases such an approach led to an unduly bureaucratic model of student teacher development that, at its worst, was focused much more upon ticking boxes of statements of competence than upon the real issues related to teaching and learning.

By 1994, CATE had begun to issue guidance that was politically unacceptable and was so replaced by the Teacher Training Agency (TTA) which was directly under ministerial control. Validation criteria were replaced by detailed requirements for courses, adherence to which was the only way to ensure allocation of funds for teacher trainee places (Cunningham, 2012).

Ofsted became responsible for the inspection of initial teacher education and the TTA managed the process. At the same time, teacher training shifted from a competence-based model to a standards-based one, and CPD became centrally defined, practically based and located on the school site (Hargreaves, 2000). However, having the school as the site for CPD dislocated it from academia. Ironically, the constant shifts in requirements often made change less sustainable.

Throughout the 1980s school-based teacher training places began to emerge as a result of a general mistrust of university and college-based courses which were seen to be too theoretical and practice-light (Cunningham, 2012). The government's belief was that higher education was outmoded and outdated; teacher education needed to move out of universities and colleges and into schools. Additionally, headteachers had bemoaned for some time the inability of some newly qualified teachers to control classes, and this gave succour to those who wished to further the craft basis for teacher education and training. The belief was that the emphasis should be on training rather than education and that this training should be more practical in nature. Courses such as School-Centred Initial Teacher Training (SCITT) and Graduate Teacher Programme (GTP) routes emerged throughout the 1990s and were as much an exercise in the emasculation of higher education as they were about preparing teachers for the classroom. They were an attempt to remove provider capture on the part of the universities (that is, the situation whereby universities automatically gained students) and potentially cut costs. The emphasis was on training as a set of competences to demonstrate.

The changes were both neoliberal and neoconservative in orientation. As Furlong et al. (2000) note, both neoliberal market advocates and neoconservative defenders of traditional forms of hierarchy and national culture had a role to play for both are 'critical of egalitarianism and collectivism, which they allege have encouraged an anti-enterprise and permissive culture' (Furlong et al., 2000: 9). Opening up training to the market of schools is a neoliberal line which posits, in turn, that practical matters should be the lot of initial teacher education and that, hence, higher education has little if any role to play. But this orientation goes much further:

> Ideally, there would be a free market in training itself, where schools would be allowed to recruit whomsoever they wanted – trained or untrained. If this were the case then it is assumed that headteachers would favour straightforward graduates over those who had 'suffered' from professional training.
>
> (Furlong et al., 2000: 10)

The move to hold more training in schools, a neoliberal line, was heralded by some as a good move; a coming of age for the profession.

All this change was coupled to the neoconservative doctrine of the control of the content of initial teacher training (ITT). Here the desire was to develop professionals who are experts in subject knowledge; pedagogy plays second fiddle in the drive to ensure good quality teachers. In the neoconservative line canons of knowledge are more important than matters of teaching and learning. The standards for ITT came about as a consequence of neoconservative thinking and a greater push to international competitiveness. The instigation of quasi-market mechanisms was seen as key to educational reform at this time. However the moves should be seen, they were a mixture of devolution and central control. Whatever the view, it can be noted that at this time teachers were still required to decide *how* to teach. However, none of this was achieved through consultation and debate: 'The enhanced role of schools in initial teacher education, and the correspondingly reduced role of higher education, was achieved neither through consensus nor through gradual development: it was achieved through unilateral government intervention of a quite unprecedented kind' (Furlong et al., 2000: ix).

That the two lines shared centre stage is unsurprising. Conservative policy of the 1980s and 1990s was both neoliberal and neoconservative (see Chapter 1). Indeed, both share similar characteristics in that they see teaching as an inherently practical, craft-based activity. The TTA oversaw the gradual removal of 'barmy theory' (Beck, 2008: 136) from teacher training, replacing it instead with school-based practical work structured around a competency model. The noteworthy point here is the use of training and not education in the title for the agency. In this light it is unsurprising that HEIs, throughout the 1980s, made their courses more practically focused; indeed, they were required to do so. Partnership working became a requirement and more time was to be spent in school as a trainee.

Essentially what were defined throughout this period were competency models of teacher development and professionalism; these were the mainstay of government policy throughout the early to mid-1990s. They cut against notions of professionalism which espouse autonomy and were more akin to a tightening of control and regulation regarding the development of the teaching profession (Whitty, 2000) and attest more to the technicisation of teaching. The rise of capitalism as a defining feature for public sector work generally, engendered the role of teacher as technician (Troman, 1996). Teachers' work became specified to a great degree, with the state heavily defining professionalism (the improvement of pay, status and conditions of service) and professionality (the knowledge, skills and procedures teachers deploy in their day-to-day work) (Hoyle, 1974). In addition, new mechanisms for monitoring teachers' work came to the fore.

Following their election, New Labour drew up prescriptive plans to describe both content and pedagogy for the teacher trainee (Furlong, 2005). The initial training curriculum continued to impose a technical rational model of teaching as craft (Cunningham, 2012) and standards for qualified teacher status (QTS) were introduced in 1997. These were over-long, unwieldy and too in-depth (Whitty, 2006) and were widely criticised as instrumental and technicist in orientation; they went into great detail concerning the level of specific knowledge trainee teachers should have mastered before they could be recommended for the award of QTS. Teacher training was refocused onto the standards agenda; the standards for QTS were designed to curtail ITT providers, but they set the tone for training as prescription, not judgement.

In 2002, the national curriculum for teacher education was abandoned and there was a return to a list of standards to be achieved. *Qualifying to Teach* (TTA, 2002) was introduced which significantly slimmed down requirements. It also introduced a section on 'Professional Values and Practice'. This was all broadly welcomed by the profession and other commentators. However, CPD became much more focused on the agenda and mandate of central government especially in the areas of literacy and numeracy. CPD, then, focused specifically on the needs of the school and its pupils in meeting government targets rather than the needs of the individual teacher (Wilkins, 2011). Paradoxically, New Labour seemed to accept that teaching is a research-based profession. One measure which demonstrates this was the creation of Best Practice Research Scholarships (BPRS) which enabled teachers to undertake small-scale pieces of research in their own setting in order to impact on policy and practice and the mooting of sabbaticals and international exchanges; much of this did not appear however. New Labour also further diversified entry routes for teacher training extending, in particular, employment-based routes for experienced individuals and those who had qualified overseas. But is should be recognised that

> the twin strategies of defining 'standards' and the insistence on a range of different 'providers' has done more than maintain a market; together, they have also ensured that teacher education has now become narrowly functional; an entirely 'technical rationalist' enterprise. Technical rationality in education . . . creates the impression of disinterestedness and objectivity. It implies that there is a common framework for people, with fixed goals.
>
> (Furlong, 2005: 127)

In 2005 the TTA became the Training and Development Agency for Schools (TDA); prior ideals concerning the training of teachers did not disappear though and the standards-based approach continued. It was the TDA which sanctioned 'approved' ways of advancing teachers' careers. Other routes to achieving further qualifications were open to teachers, but these were often self-funded. It was the government, through the TDA, which defined the funded professional development courses to be accessed.

ACTIVITY 7.4

- How might the alteration of initial teacher education to initial teacher training be viewed with regard to professionalism?
- Does it make a difference which term is used?
- Which term should be used?
- Which term do you think is most appropriate to the current orientation for the preparation of teachers?

Continuing professional development

The changes in 2007 in the awards for QTS also saw the introduction of standards defining the various career stages of teachers. For the first time the requirements to access the post-threshold payments or the status for advanced skills teacher, or even post-induction year were all amalgamated into one document designed to define the route a classroom teacher might take as they progress in their career. These were designed to offer a progression route for staff who did not wish to progress to the leadership pay spine; they defined the following stages:

- QTS and entry to the profession;
- core (following the first year of teaching);
- post-threshold (transfer to an upper pay scale, usually after five years);

- excellent teacher (the ability to improve school effectiveness);
- advanced skills teacher (required to contribute to school improvement in schools additional to their own).

Some of the positions had existed prior to this time, but the key issue was the way in which they were presented as a mechanism to ensure that classroom teachers could be rewarded for their work (Wilkins, 2011). However, in effect, the new standards promoted and defined both what a teacher *should do* and what he or she *is*. The statements were very subjective: how, for example, is 'effective' defined; against whose criteria? In reality, such measures usually related to performance against national standards. In effect, the new criteria continued to promote teachers as technicians of the state (Wilkins, 2011). In 2007, and in support of the view that teaching should gradually become a higher level profession; a new Masters in Teaching and Learning (MTL) was proposed and the 'post-threshold' standards were seen as being in line with MTL requirements. Problematically, this was seen as a possible way to entrench 'professional development as an arm of performance management' (Wilkins, 2011: 406).

That professional standards for teachers could be seen as a mandate for continuous professional development is not in doubt. However, Wilkins (2011) suggests that the views of beginning teachers note that accountability is the key to improving professional practice. In turn career aspirations were seen to be in contradistinction to being in the classroom; the former undermines the latter. The beginning teachers in his study were sanguine about the performative element of their work; they were more in keeping with the empowered professional who accepts accountability *because it works*. For Wilkins, such a post-performative identity suggests that the 'improvement agenda' is accepted: it is a given; it has pervaded the lives of beginning teachers. It is for such reasons that Reid et al. (2004: 263) note that the focus of training

> has not been on equipping teachers with the skills to engage in professional self-development, to develop evidence-based practice, to run educational teams, to innovate or facilitate, but rather to prepare a generation of teachers as technicians or deliverers of set strategies.

What has occurred is the refocusing of initial teacher training and of teacher in-service training towards the standards agenda with competences for teachers at all stages of their career tightly defined (Locke et al., 2005). Over the years, CPD has gradually found itself beholden to government political priorities. Teacher education at all levels became identified as training and was technicist and rationalist in orientation (Day, 2002). Hall (2004: 37) comments most notably in this matter:

> A whole raft of policy initiatives on teacher education appears to have been framed specifically to change the nature of teacher professionalism and to increase a focus upon craft skills at the expense of reflection and professional understanding. By emphasising competencies the dominant discourse of liberal humanism is undermined and replaced with a discourse of technical rationality; technicians are preferred to reflective practitioners whose skills are theoretically underpinned. Whilst central government holds on tightly to strategic control it relies increasingly on intermediary agencies like Ofsted and the TTA, headed up by government appointees, to implement and facilitate its vision.

In 2003 'Excellence and Enjoyment' (DfES, 2003c; see Chapter 4) announced the dropping of targets from 2004 in response to head teachers' complaints about excessive pressure; schools and teachers were promised more autonomy. However, significant cohorts of teachers knew nothing other than government imposed mandate. According to Cunningham (2012), what has ensued over the past two decades is an increase in the performance culture, whereby teachers perform in order to survive inspections. He notes that performance rather than learning seem to have taken centre stage in primary schools. Further, the National Curriculum has continued to dominate and has brought about a culture of recipe following rather than the exercise of professional judgement.

Workforce remodelling

Labour's third term saw renewed emphasis on workforce remodelling rather than a concentration on initial teacher education as a site for intervention and was coupled with 'tightly prescribed national standards' (Furlong, 2005: 131). Here there has been a dramatic increase in the number of support staff in schools, whereas at the same time the increase in qualified teachers has been more modest. Between 1997 and 2005 the number of teaching assistants almost trebled from 35,500 to just under 100,000 whilst the number of teachers increased by just 4000 in the same period.

The introduction of teaching assistants was initially construed as a politically sensitive move. The profession had, until the Second World War, a system of pupil apprentices and this use of unqualified ancillary staff had been fought against during the formative years of the welfarist settlement (Cunningham, 2012). The way in which the policy was introduced was also to blame: the Secretary of State for Education, John Patten, described a 'mums' army'. Questions were asked as to whether this was undertaken to assist teachers or cut costs; to aid professionalism or replace it.

Nevertheless, teaching assistants as extant members of staff continued to grow in number throughout the 1990s, albeit at a small rate. However, that rate grew exponentially from 1997 under New Labour. Also, the nature of teaching assistants' work changed dramatically as well, from essentially a welfare position to direct support for learning and assessment. That the introduction of classroom assistant was designed to ease teacher workload was enshrined in the 2003 workforce agreement, signed by all unions (except the National Union of Teachers, NUT) and the government. This mandated that certain administrative and secretarial tasks should be undertaken by classroom assistants not teachers. It also allowed for planning, preparation and assessment (PPA) time with a guarantee of 10 per cent of time out of the classroom to undertake such activities. By 2006 teaching assistants represented a quarter of all teaching staff in schools. Their 'vital' role was recognised by the establishment of the Higher Level Teaching Assistant (HLTA) award. This allowed teaching assistants to pursue a level 5 qualification and gain higher rates of pay. In return they were expected to take on more responsibility, including working with whole classes. The teacher unions were divided in their support for these changes. In particular, the NUT was opposed to the blurring of the distinctions between teaching assistants and teachers and the extra roles teaching assistants could take on which had previously been undertaken by teachers.

Notably, the workforce agreement and the increase in the use of teaching assistants were seen both as a threat to teacher professionalism and an enhancement to it. Some (Whitty, 2006) maintained that all these changes amounted to re-professionalisation: teachers were seen as part of the agenda for change. This new form of professionalism is a form of 'democratic professionalism' which seeks to engender a partnership approach between teachers, pupils, parents and the community, thus indicating that the teacher's role is wider than just the classroom. By requiring teachers to help young people to become fully autonomous and learn key skills rather than memorise information, teachers are required to develop more collaborative and constructive approaches to learning (Beard, 2008: 5). This re-professionalisation sought to demystify professional work and build alliances between various members of the school community (Whitty, 2006):

> A democratic professionalism thus encourages the development of collaborative cultures in the broadest sense, rather than exclusive ones. It certainly suggests that the teacher has a responsibility that extends beyond the single classroom – including contributing to the school, other students and the wider educational system, as well as to the collective responsibilities of teachers themselves to a broader social agenda. Indeed, under democratic professionalism, this broader agenda becomes part and parcel of the professional agenda rather than being counterposed to it.
>
> (Whitty, 2006: 14)

Barber (2005) suggests that the period from 1997 to 2005 was one of informed prescription, whereas post-2005, teachers were able to work with informed professionalism whereby teachers have appropriate, knowledge so that the government can grant them licensed autonomy. This has been questioned, however, particularly the latter phase where the imposition of prescribed ways to teach and national targets is seen to constrain teachers. What is evident, though, is the paradox of, essentially, a free market where schools are able to control, to a large degree, their own affairs and act as autonomous, independent businesses, alongside a strong state which controls what is taught and how it is assessed (Whitty, 2006).

In 2000 the General Teaching Council for England (GTCE) was created in an effort to instil professional status for teachers of the kind enjoyed by other professions such as those in medicine. The instigation of the GTCE could be seen as an attempt to satisfy the trait theory of professionalism (Webb et al., 2004). It drew up codes of conduct and was the official qualifying association for state teachers. The GTCE dealt with matters of professional misconduct, but could only advise government on issues such as assessment and curriculum.

The GTCE was not independent of government, however, and had no role in negotiating pay or conditions; rather it was set up to ensure high professional standards and accountability. It serviced a register of qualified teachers which all teachers were obliged to join so that they might be able to continue to teach and gave government advice regarding teaching and learning. Most notably, the GTCE dealt with disciplinary cases.

The creation of a coalition government

The general election of 2010 saw a raft of policy proposals from all three of the main political parties regarding professional development and initial teacher education and training. At the heart of Conservative plans was the belief that teachers were the main answer to education's problems. Accordingly they promised to 'take steps to enhance the status of the teaching profession and ensure it attracts the best people' (Conservative Party, 2010: 51).

To achieve this end, they proposed to expand Teach First, a programme which took top graduates and trained them on the job in some of the most challenging schools. They proposed a new programme called Teach Now which would attract career changers. They also planned a new training pathway for ex-service men and women called Troops into Teaching. To further raise the status of the profession five additional steps were proposed:

- raising the entry requirement for teacher training;
- expecting entrants for postgraduate training to have a 2:2 or above to qualify for state funding;
- paying the student loans of top maths and science graduates;
- protecting teachers from false accusations;
- strengthening home–school behaviour contracts.

The main plank of Liberal Democrat policy in this area was recognition that government interference in education was unhelpful. They noted that '[t]eachers are held back by constant government interference which distracts from teaching' (Liberal Democrats, 2010: 37). They proposed to increase the size of the GTP, which allowed trainees to train on the job. In addition they planned to expand Teach First. An improvement in CPD was also promised. They planned to remove national pay and conditions rules and give schools freedoms to innovate, whilst ensuring that all teachers receive the minimum national pay award. Increased spending on frontline staff was proposed: an additional 41,000 teachers and 120,000 teaching assistants. Professionalism was to be heavily invested in with a new right for every teacher to have CPD. In turn, though, every teacher would have to demonstrate high standards of teaching to maintain their licence to practice.

The Labour Party desired to get the best people into teaching and for this reason they also planned to expand Teach First. They promoted the idea of new teacher training academies and the introduction of £10,000 golden handcuffs to attract the best into teaching. But all this was countered by recognition that spending would not rise as fast as in previous years due to the on-going financial crisis.

One of the common themes in all three parties' 2010 electoral promises was the expansion of the school-based provider of ITT, Teach First. Once in power the Coalition put this into practice, pledging more funding for the charity and expanding the number of training places it would receive. In addition a new School Direct training programme started in September 2010. Under this scheme schools train graduates as they see fit working in conjunction with accredited providers of initial teacher education. Such providers might be universities or they might be a partnership collected together under a teaching school umbrella. More than 900 places were allocated to the programme initially but numbers are expected to rise as the programme expands over the next few years (Robinson, 2012). The government has also closed down the GTP, replacing it instead with a new employment-based route, a strand of School Direct, for those who have at least three years of employment experience in other fields. Initially, 5000 places for 'high-calibre career changers' have been earmarked for this development from 2013 (DfE, 2012).

In essence this programme saw the beginning of the relocation of teacher training to schools. The rhetoric from government was one of mistrust of university-based courses. Their view was that too many trainees received training in institutions graded as satisfactory only and that the involvement of schools is minimal (DfE, 2012). This belief is not borne out by the evidence, however; schools play a major role in all ITT courses from having students spend the majority of their courses *in situ* to being involved with interviews and the wider selection process. But government view is that universities are no longer expected to play the role they once had. Indeed, the Department for Eduction (DfE) is clear that by the end of the parliament in 2015 as many as 10,000 places are expected to be offered on school-based training routes, including in schools that have training status in the manner currently given to universities (DfE, 2012). This meshes with Gove's view that teaching is a 'craft' and that theory has little if any place in the work of a teacher (Adams, 2011b).

In addition to these plans the government set out to (DfE, 2012):

- attract more primary maths teachers with an additional £2,000 for those who have a grade B or above in A level maths;
- incentivise trainees into working in the most challenging schools through the provision of additional bursaries to those training via a school-based route;
- offer graduates in maths, physics, chemistry or a modern foreign language up to £20,000 to train as a teacher if they have a first class honours degree;
- increase the difficulty of the literacy and numeracy tests students have to take and reducing the number of attempts they can make to pass the tests;
- remove centrally funded training places from those institutions deemed as requiring improvement. Only those intuitions rated by Ofsted as outstanding would see their numbers remain constant; there would be a reduction in numbers for those rated good.

Many of the changes are far-reaching in terms of the involvement of schools and the provision of bursaries for shortage subjects. However, much of the thinking is based on outdated conceptions of the ways in which schools work with higher education and the nature of teaching. The view that trainees would be better off in school flies in the face of Ofsted evidence that more university provision is rated outstanding than school-based (Ofsted, 2010). But the view that teaching is only a craft matches the traditional view of education held by Gove and other ministers, whereby knowledge alone coupled with traditional methods of teaching and learning are what matters. For Gove, academic and emotional intelligence are what make a good teacher; there is no room for educational theory in this model. Such opinions are captured by a government source who stated that 'For too long left-wing training colleges have imbued teachers with useless teaching theories that don't work and actively damage children's education' (cited in Paton, 2012b). This is notable given that since the 1990s ITT has been prescribed and effectively proscribed by successive governments who have sought to control the ITT curriculum. The fact is that such work is not routinely covered in ITT courses in universities and has not been studied for many years, if it ever was. The Coalition is clear: only 12 per cent of GTP students (primary) and 10 per cent of GTP students (secondary) saw their training as too theoretical, against 46 per cent of Bachelor of Education (BEd) students and 33 per cent and 19 per cent of primary and secondary Postgraduate Certificate of Education (PGCE) students, respectively (DfE 2010b, 9). This, it believes, is a mandate for change: theory has little to offer the teacher; it is skills and craft that matter: 'It is crucial that during the period of training and induction, teachers are given plenty of opportunity to practise skills, that they are exposed to outstanding skills and receive plenty of feedback and coaching' (DfE, 2010b: 9).

Possibly the biggest change to teachers' pay and conditions was the wholesale introduction of PRP (STRB, 2012). This replaced the previous system whereby teachers automatically progressed up the pay spine according to their length of service until they reach the threshold levels. The new measures were to be linked to a teacher's performance targets and their annual appraisal. The DfE sought to increase flexibility so that schools might develop their own pay policies tailored to their particular needs (DfE, 2013). It identified factors that a school might consider when determining the pay levels of teaching staff. These included (DfE, 2013):

- impact on pupil progress;
- impact on wider outcomes for pupils;
- contribution to improvements in other areas (e.g. pupils' behaviour or lesson planning);
- professional and career development;
- wider contribution to the work of the school, for instance their involvement in school business outside the classroom.

The changes were roundly condemned by the teaching unions. The new measures were introduced in the academic year 2013 to 2014 despite the Chief Inspector of Schools Sir Michael Wilshaw announcing that some schools would have to have larger classes if they were to pay their teachers more (Garner, 2013).

Conclusion

It can be seen, then, that teacher professionalism has altered considerably in the last 30 years. The post-war welfarist settlement afforded teachers a great deal of autonomy, and whilst they might not have been professionals in the classic sense of the term, they had considerable professional status. The advent of neoliberal and consumerist discourses throughout the 1980s and 1990s meant that the teacher's position was challenged. No longer were they seen to be the holder of some elevated status replete with the ability to make their own decisions on matters curricular and pedagogic. The changes of the Conservative era altered the positions from which teachers could operate as well as changing the very essence of what it meant to be a classroom professional. Government mandate increasingly occupied teachers' time and with it a raft of new measures designed to ensure external accountability came to the fore.

The New Labour era saw a ratcheting of accountability measures through the auspices of national targets for literacy and numeracy and the designation of standards to achieve both to qualify as a teacher and to move through the professional structure. In essence teaching became 'individualistic, competitive, controlling and regulative, externally defined and standards-led' (Day, 2002: 681). Research seems to suggest that New Labour reforms have led to a decrease in job satisfaction and a feeling of diminished autonomy amongst teachers (Wilkins, 2011). Such was the product of the neoliberal, performative, market agenda. The marking out of acceptable performance in such acute terms notes the controlling feature inherent within New Labour policy. But such control supposedly did not stem from espoused ideological positions, rather New Labour's way was non-ideological; but in a sense this is what makes it so problematic. In describing professionalism in prescriptive terms, the government attempted to identify and get teachers to operate according to 'what works'. But such a position has at its heart a value position: in determining what works one has to identify the measures by which one judges. Thus, New Labour designed its educational effectiveness programme according to absolute scores in national tests and international comparisons. In essence, then, what was described was a position from which the government could judge worth, and in so doing, both cognitive and affective domains for teachers' work would have to be defined. All of the policies would have been challenging to someone at such time and in this way the success or otherwise of reform depended on the extent to which they challenged existing identities:

> This interplay between the private and public, the personal and professional lives of teachers is a key factor in their sense of identity and job satisfaction and, by inference, in their capacity to maintain their effectiveness as teachers.
>
> (Day, 2002: 684)

Despite this, Day and Smethem (2009: 152) found that some teachers taught creatively despite the government's agenda. Their

> work was founded upon hope, a sense of agency, and a belief that they could continue to make a positive contribution to the learning and achievement of their pupils. They had refused to allow economic considerations to overwhelm their moral and ethical purposes, or to subordinate themselves to the 'epidemic' of educational policy.

This must be remembered when considering changes to professionalism, for to be a professional entails working with affective as well as cognitive and skills-based attributes. Whether consecutive governments have carried the profession with them is debatable, for not everyone is convinced that the changes implemented since the 1980s have improved the quality of English education. Certainly, the Coalition has continued to set itself against the teaching profession in many ways and has sought to marginalise traditional ways of entering teaching. Questions continue to be asked as to whether or not this can continue, but for now it seems that change with performance in mind is the order of the day.

Key points

- In England since the 1980s, teachers have been subject to more government intervention than in any other country in the world.
- The 1950s and 1960s were seen as a golden age for teacher professionalism.
- The 1970s saw the start of the demise in trust of the teaching profession.
- Neoliberalism is a defining feature for professionalism.
- Professionalism is an essentially contested concept.
- Classic notions of professionalism cite responsibility (altruism), knowledge and autonomy as key features.
- New professionalism is concerned with the quality of service rather than the enhancement of status.
- The 1980s and 1990s saw increasing attacks on teacher professionalism.
- New Labour oversaw the constraining of teacher autonomy through the adoption of prescriptive ways of working.
- Initial teacher education has seen many changes since the 1980s, from a school-based competency model to a predominantly school-based standards driven system.

- Since 2002, teacher training and CPD have become more concerned with meeting government mandate than the instigation of professionalism. Teacher training became a technical endeavour.

- The role of teaching assistants has altered greatly and their numbers have increased dramatically.

- The creation of the GTCE was not universally welcomed, mainly due to the impoverished input the body could have on matters such as curriculum and assessment.

Further reading

Cunningham, P. (2012) *Politics and the Primary Teacher*, London: Routledge (Chapter 6). This chapter discusses the politics behind professional reform.

Hargreaves, L., Cunningham, M., Hansen, A., McIntyre, D. and Oliver, C. (2007) 'The status of teachers and the teaching profession in England: view from inside and outside the profession', *Final Report of the Teacher Status Project Research Report RR831A*, Nottingham: DfES Publications. This report discusses the findings of a project to determine public and individual teachers' perceptions of the status of teachers and teaching.

Thomas, L. (2012) *Re-thinking the Importance of Teaching: Curriculum and collaboration in an era of localism*, London: RSA. This report considers the interplay between teaching and the curriculum and the implications for teacher professionalism.

8

Performance and accountability

Purpose of this chapter

After reading this chapter you should understand:

- that there is history of performance and accountability matters in UK education;
- how performance and accountability came to be viewed under the auspices of the New Right in the 1980s and 1990s;
- the role New Labour played in the maintenance of a performance and accountability regime;
- the ways in which the Coalition government have used performance measures;
- about the role that testing has played in driving forward the performance and accountability agenda in education;
- about performativity.

What is meant by performance?

The word performance conjures up images of literary and dramatic aptitude and ability, yet the word has become part and parcel of educational parlance in recent years. Certainly the performance of teachers, of head teachers and of schools, colleges and universities is now under considerable scrutiny. It is not unheard of for politicians to bemoan the current state of educational performance at a variety of levels or even for them to hold up as beacons of success certain schools or even individual teachers due to the levels of attainment pupils achieve. To use the term performance in an educational sense seems to present no real challenge for ministers and other commentators, yet the term carries with it notions of acting out, of doing tasks in order to please a certain audience. Indeed, this 'acting out' element of performance-based notions is captured well by Elam when discussing teacher education:

> By contrast, in performance based [teacher education] programs (sic) performance goals are specified, and agreed to, in rigorous detail in advance of instruction. The student must either be able to demonstrate his ability to promote desirable learning or exhibit behaviours known to promote it . . . Emphasis is on demonstrated product or output.
>
> (Elam, 1971: 1–2)

There is a need to question whether such ideas are feasible in education though. Is it right that teachers act in ways that overtly please through, for example, the maximisation of exam performance, or should they be concentrating on teaching practices that develop the whole child and which are more nebulous and difficult to pin down? Even though contemporary education seems fixated on the performance of a range of individuals and organisations in the educational process, performance measures are not a new entity.

Performance throughout history

In 1862 'payment by results' through the Revised Code was introduced. This process detailed how schools were to be paid according to the numbers of pupils who reached specified standards in identified subjects. Pupils' answers to questions on the 'three Rs' determined the level of grant to be given to the school and hence the teacher's salary. Schools were paid 4 shillings (20p) per year for each pupil with satisfactory attendance and 8 shillings (40p) if the child passed the examinations in reading, writing and arithmetic (Cunningham, 2012). Payment by results was relaxed in 1895 and at the start of the twentieth century a new breed of enlightened Her Majesty's Inspectorate of Schools (HMI) sought to encourage more risk-taking and responsiveness in teaching. But this was an all-pervasive technology that had far-reaching results; the effect of the changes was to reduce state spending on education and reduce the number of students in teachers' colleges. The curriculum became hugely narrowed and the aims for education became instrumentalised. More importantly, as teachers' salaries were tied to results cheating was commonplace. As the chief inspector pointed out:

> The mode of teaching in the primary schools has certainly fallen off in intelligence, spirit and inventiveness during the four or five years which have elapsed since my last report. It could not well be otherwise. In a country where everyone is prone to rely too much on mechanical processes and too little on intelligence, a change in the Education Department's regulations, which, by making two-thirds of the government grant depend upon a mechanical examination, inevitably gives a mechanical turn to the school teaching, a mechanical turn to the inspection, is and must be trying to the intellectual life of a school.
>
> (Maclure, 1973: 81)

This situation was not to remain and throughout the twentieth century teachers in the UK gradually came to enjoy greater professional freedoms. Indeed, in what has been described as the 'golden age' for teaching, from the 1950s to the late 1970s, teachers had 'relative autonomy'. A system of reflection and peer review was developed which, it was believed, would promote professional behaviour and improve the quality of teaching and learning in schools. Evidence to support this was usually informal and professional judgement prevailed.

ACTIVITY 8.1

- How do such performance ideals square with notions of teaching and learning?
- Is teaching something that can be performed and thereby judged?
- How might the adoption of such 'performance' measures as a method to determine quality present problems for education?

The rise of contemporary performance and accountability discourses

The current ubiquity of performance and accountability in the UK seems to stem from the late 1970s/early 1980s and in particular the great debate sparked by the 1976 Labour Prime Minister James Callaghan in his Ruskin College speech. One of the features of this debate was a consideration of the role for teachers in the new educational era and in particular how education was to be judged. Held up for scrutiny was education's role in developing and advancing the economy, and into this mix teachers were thrown, required to give an account of themselves through the auspices of the performance of education itself: 'what is the proper way of monitoring the uses of resources in order to maintain a proper national standard of performance' (Callaghan, 1976).

As Ball notes, questions were asked in the national press about the 'value for money of educational spending and unsatisfactory standards of school performance' (2008: 73). The election to power of Margaret Thatcher's government in 1979 saw a ratcheting up of such rhetoric and the start of the performance era. The 1980s saw the introduction of a system of 'controlled autonomy' (Perryman, 2006). It was no surprise, then, that Thatcher's government desired to control education more tightly than previously seen. In keeping with the view that public services were inefficient and ineffective and with more than a nod to a marketplace discourse, measures were put in place to attempt to define and control the outputs of education. Such definitions and control were in the monitoring and surveillance of exam scores, teacher practices and measures for whole school evaluation. Under the twin discourse of accountability and performance, education policy began to cast its gaze over the outputs of education in ways not seen for many years. Following the Education Reform Act (DES, 1988) there has been a steady and sustained shift away from professional judgement to accountability to agencies external to the school; government-decided reform of the system was required, and was then monitored by increased surveillance (Perryman, 2006).

To monitor this new accountability the Conservative government created the Office for Standards in Education (Ofsted). This new body was responsible for inspecting all state-maintained schools. Rather than reporting directly to the Secretary of State for Education, as had been the case with HMI, Ofsted was required to report directly to parliament. Even today it still champions its independence and impartiality (Ofsted, 2011). Created by the 1992 Education Act, Ofsted acts as a privatised system. Teams bid for contracts and use a criteria-based system to make judgments of schools.

This was a change in the way inspections were to be conducted from that which had been in place, in different guises, since 1833. The introduction of Ofsted marked a watershed moment for it oversaw the monitoring of performance indicators in ways not seen for over a century.

ACTIVITY 8.2

■   Download the current inspection and regulation forms and guides from the Ofsted website.

■   In what ways might these contribute to the idea that education is about performing?

Performance and New Labour

It was the Conservative era, then, that ushered in substantial accountability measures through its procurement of a market-driven strategy for education. However, in 1997 New Labour swept to victory. Whilst it might have been expected that much of the discourse of the New Right would be dismissed, as we have seen in previous chapters, it was soon very clear that this was not to be the case. For New Labour the standards agenda was to become a defining feature of their term in office. They very quickly upped the ante with regard to accountability measures. Shortly after coming to power, the new Secretary of State for Education, David Blunkett, named and shamed those schools seen to be failing. This naming and shaming was based upon exam results and Ofsted inspections and demonstrated the line that would be taken in subsequent years. There was to be intensified support *and* intervention: support for those schools seen to be improving at a fast enough rate, and intervention for those who were not. Accountability came to be seen as a 'good thing', and the mechanisms through which accountability was achieved were increasingly accepted as part of the education system; critics of such a regime were seen as being against progress (Perryman, 2006: 149).

New Labour certainly ratcheted up the use of Ofsted and in particular the devices of naming and shaming and special measures. Through such measures, effectively the mechanisms of sanction and reward, the state defined its obligations to ensure that school performance was appropriate. In this way, inspection requires schools to adhere to defined criteria identified as descriptors of successful schools. In turn, these become mechanisms for dictating normality. However, questions need to be asked about how such normality is constructed; school effectiveness criteria seem to suggest a self-fulfilling prophecy: successful schools are successful (Perryman, 2006).

It is when things 'go wrong' that the potential for inspection as a legitimising force becomes more obvious. Poor performance in an Ofsted inspection can lead to a school being placed in special measures, a category which explicitly states that the school is not performing to required, acceptable standards. The mechanisms by which to move out of special measures are to follow a predetermined path to success. Certain behaviours need to be exhibited by the school against established and explicit criteria (Perryman, 2006). But as Perryman notes, this process of normalisation effectively pathologises the 'sick' school; those that do not run according to predetermined criteria require 'treatment'. Although audit is supposed to be neutral, in effect it shapes the very behaviour it is supposed to identify and measure. And Ofsted also ignores local, contextual factors when making judgements, even though they allude to them as 'facts' in the inspection report. This effectively removes issues such as poverty from the education debate (Perryman, 2006). For such schools, the inspection process and category of special measures identifies ways in which their offering is 'substandard'. This is a limiting category in that it defines what is to be done and how. The school is no longer deemed to be able to run its own affairs without intervention and increased inspection which both lead to the adoption of certain behaviours for success. As Perryman notes:

> The discourse of Ofsted involves standards, quality, efficiency, value for money and performance. In order to be successful in a special measures regime, schools need to accept that this discourse is the way forward. There is no room within special measures regimes for schools to 'do their own thing' in terms of improvement. If a school is to be removed from special measures, it must demonstrate that it has normalized against pre-determined criteria set with which to judge a school, irrespective of the socio-economic environment.
>
> (Perryman, 2006: 152)

Schools that are placed into special measures go through a process of change that marks the inspection out as a force for the legitimation of certain features marked as effective and necessary, which can, in turn, affect their focus and reason for existence. For example, due to the frequency of inspections under special measures teachers come to work as though they are constantly being inspected: 'the disciplinary mechanism is internalised' (Perryman, 2006: 155). Perversely though, this surveillance can result in less risk taking and the use of 'steady' or 'safe' lessons which do little to enhance learning. In effect, special measures schools can come to exist purely to pass an inspection.

School performance

Ofsted was not the only way in which New Labour effected a performance and accountability culture. It was through measures such as the National Literacy Strategy (NLS) and National Numeracy Strategy (NNS; see Chapter 4) that New Labour defined legitimate ways of working. Teachers were, in effect, given legitimised scripts by which they might work; the setting of professional requirements was achieved. And such requirements became the mantra against which all professional activity was to be judged. Thus, teachers and pupils were required to act in ways consistent with these requirements. In effect, performative accounts were to be given that demonstrated both teaching quality and pupil attainment.

But the state also had to control for quality. The apparatus of the Department for Education and Skills (DfES) had been attuned to the need for certain scripts to be written, scripts such as NNS and NLS but also the National Curriculum (see Chapter 4), professional standards for the award of qualified teacher status (QTS) (TTA, 1997) (see Chapter 7) and the Key Stage Three strategy of the early 2000s. These were designed to remove, as far as possible, decision-making from the hands of school professionals, concentrating it instead in organisations such as the DfES, the Qualifications and Curriculum Authority, which wrote and published the National Curriculum, and the Teacher Training Agency (TTA, then the Training and Development Agency for Schools, TDA) which published standards for the award of QTS. Decision-making was centralised, augmented into a machine that would churn out missive after missive in the drive to improve the performance of schools, teachers and pupils. Here were attempts at predictability also; measures were put in place to control outputs so that they 'will be the same over time and in all locales' (Ritzer, 2011: 15).

Teacher performance

An additional plank of New Labour policy relates to the development of certain forms of professionalism. As was seen in Chapter 7, measures designed to usher in new forms of professionalism were part of the drive for accountability and educational development. Part of this was a marked rise in the use of pedagogic control by New Labour. In addition to specific interventions in the arena of literacy and numeracy there were more general moves toward defining teaching performance. Indeed, to support the drive for an increase in teacher effectiveness New Labour placed great store in reports that seemed to demonstrate how better teaching leads to better pupil learning, the assumption being that increased test success provides appropriate evidence for both. Thus, those teachers deemed 'effective' become those whose practice was held up as observably good, *against certain predefined criteria*. What was noticeable was a shift in emphasis from 1997 towards the use of test data to laud certain teaching actions and activities. The outcome was the emergence of terms such as 'best practice' defined as that which elevates 'successful' teacher performance to the level of the objectively outstanding. Teacher performance was seen as a direct causal factor for pupil learning with the latter evidenced through the testing regime.

One such piece of research was that of the consulting group Hay McBer (2000), which analysed the behaviour of a small number of teachers judged to be 'outstanding' (Flecknoe, 2005). From these behaviours, generalisations about the professional qualities required to improve schools were extrapolated. The report subsequently played a significant part in directing professional activity in English schools, interwoven as it was with the analysis of quantifiable test data.

It is enough to note here that teacher behaviour became judged through the lens of 'effective teaching skills'. In effect what came to be promoted was the application of a raft of technical behaviours, focused entirely on what teachers do. Judging a teacher was aligned with the observable; the technicality of teaching. That craft which resulted in increased levels of pupil performance became that which garnered respect. The assumptions inherent in such measures are twofold. First, that the quality of teaching is what determines the amount of pupil learning. Second, and following on from the first point, it is thus teacher time and activity which should command attention; get the inputs right and the outputs necessarily follow. However, what both of these do is obviate the psychological, the cultural, the historical and the sociological as elements of school improvement.

ACTIVITY 8.3

- In what ways might it be possible to identify and capture the skills involved in teaching?
- What makes it difficult for this to occur? In what ways is teaching not able to be defined and monitored?

Pupil performance

The way in which New Labour drove the development of education was not a purely British endeavour. Indeed, such developments have been seen the world over. What is noticeable is the way in which quantitative measures hold sway in the drive to ensure performance and accountability. Measurability is key here; the ability to determine not only whether improvements have been made, but by how much. That held up to scrutiny is that which can, by its very nature, be quantified. Hence the measures themselves become oriented towards key indicator sets derived from a particular view of education and associated measurement. And so New Labour focused on the objectively empirical:

> One of the oddest things in debating education policy is that people often debate it as if no empirical evidence at all existed, as to what works and what doesn't. Actually it is reasonably clear, at least up to a point . . .
>
> (Blair, 2006)

Indeed, a relentless focus on 'what works' is a manifestation of this orientation; a mode of working that deploys certain accolades in its drive to secure performative success. This was New Labour's focus: a concentration on success as derived through specific, measureable means:

> One of our prime needs is to be able to measure the size of the effect of A on B. This is genuine social science and reliable answers can only be reached if social scientists are willing to engage in this endeavour. We are not interested in worthless correlations based on small samples from which it is impossible to draw generalisable conclusions.
>
> (Blunkett, 2000: 20)

And so New Labour started its time in office in 1997 with the announcement that by 2002 80 per cent of 11-year-olds should have gained a level 4 in the end of the Key Stage Two English standard assessment tests (SATs). A similar target of 75 per cent was announced for the maths SATs. Duly, all maintained schools were required to set targets that met with the requirements handed down to local education authorities (LEAs) by central government. The targets for individual pupils were set three years in advance at the level of the school, to be reviewed annually. Pupil progress against these targets was expected to be monitored by parents, teachers and pupils.

Measuring accountability

Measures to monitor accountability were, and still are, built upon the twin measures of efficiency and calculability. But it should be remembered here that efficiency is ultimately an economic argument and that human beings gain more worth with more education. Thus Human Capital Theory stands on the idea of individual contribution; contribution defined by the person's individual credentials:

> the forms of efficiency which were imposed on schooling and higher education systems were motivated more by goals of cost cutting, a desire to vocationalise the curriculum and a desire to impose an ethos of business style principles upon publically funded education systems, often during times of financial uncertainty.
>
> (Welch, 1998: 157)

In the drive to improve intended and desired outputs, measures are put in place to realise the achievement of such outputs by the most efficient means; that is, maximising output by maximising the effect of input. For example, to improve the numbers of young people attaining five or more A★ to C grades at GCSE, accountability measures were designed that would monitor not only the output from such endeavours, but also the ways and means by which such measures could be gleaned. Hand-in-hand with such measures was an emphasis on the use of measurable data to describe and extol the virtues of undertaking certain tasks. Thus, the numbers of young people achieving the aforementioned five or more qualifications became seen as the measure of success. In part this was chosen as GCSEs were, and still are, the natural end of compulsory schooling. However, the measure was also chosen because it permitted sound bite, that is, it permitted the political exhortation of successful schools and the denigration of those deemed to be underperforming. Although schools had been required to publish their examination results in the 1980s, in the 1990s the press began to create local 'league tables' of school results. Originally constructed from data about the results of GCSEs these tables, it was believed, would provide the consumer (parents) with benchmarks against which they could judge the performance of schools in their locale. When added to the fact that parents were, by this time, able to express a preference as to which school their child should attend, it was soon the case that the performance tables became more than just a means by which judgements might be passed. It was very clear early on that schools were changing the way that they operated so that they could glean the best position in the league tables. There was a belief that such measures were being taken seriously by parents in their efforts to place their children in the best possible school. This was despite the evidence that less than half of parents, mainly well-educated ones, find the tables helpful (Bates et al., 2011).

Pupil results have proved crucial in the extent to which schools do well in their Ofsted inspections; the proportion of young people attaining the magic standard was seen as a limiting factor, that is, a means by which good or better judgements in other areas of school provision are discounted.

Such attempts at accountability meshed well with the Conservative drive to establish a market in education. However, they also formed a major plank of the New Labour time in office. The publication of key performance data in a form that can be readily manipulated by the press offered a ready mechanism by which parents can base their preference. Despite evidence that it is schools not parents who do the choosing (Bates et al., 2011) this plank of Conservative and New Labour policy was heralded by both as the best way in which to improve the education system. It was believed that competition between schools on a narrow range of measures (exam scores and inspection reports) would both concentrate the minds of educationalists on delivering an observably efficient product and help parents to exercise their democratic right to choose. As Jeffrey (2002) notes, performance has become the focus for schools. Efficiency and effectiveness have become the main criteria for judging success. Inspection reports and results on national tests take on a new importance. Success in this new culture increases opportunities for the recruitment of the 'right' kind of staff and pupils. The National Curriculum, SATs and Ofsted inspections saw the start of the performativity discourse. The publicity that surrounds these events holds schools up to public scrutiny and account. Performance is a discourse in that it is

> about what can be said and thought, but also about who can speak and with what authority. Discourses embody meaning and social relations, they constitute both subjectivity and power relations.
>
> (Ball, 1990: 2)

Performativity

Clearly, then, the drive for a performance orientation in education has its genesis around 1976, developed during the Conservative years of 1979 to 1997 and continued apace during New Labour's reign. These changes were mirrored throughout the public sector and throughout social policy. Essentially that which teachers and pupils do measures and demonstrates the worth not only of the individual involved but also the organisation in which they operated. The overt performance they give marks out, as successful or otherwise, their being within the organisation. Ball describes this as performativity and defines it thus:

> The performances (of individual subjects or organizations) serve as measures of productivity or output, or displays of 'quality', or 'moments' of promotion or inspection. As such they stand for, encapsulate or represent the worth, quality or value of an individual or organization within a field of judgement.
>
> (Ball, 2003: 216)

Wilkins (2011) notes that, as a discourse, performativity has three features:

- *An audit/target culture*: advocates for performance-driven mechanisms argue for its effectiveness, but critics maintain that such an orientation strips education of meaning and extols a 'what works' rationale coupled to a 'top-down' reform agenda.

- *Interventionist regulation*: school inspections are undertaken by Ofsted which replaced the rather benign HMI. Ofsted undertakes inspections and during its early years was believed by many to be a policy driver rather than a commentator on educational standards. From the late 2000s, schools engaged in school self-evaluation, in effect they inspect themselves. Their views are then subject to scrutiny by Ofsted at regular intervals. This mechanism was widely touted as a means to increase professional decision-making, autonomy and teacher control. However, many have highlighted the panoptic effect of such mechanisms in the way that they overlaid a self-surveillance mechanism onto professional judgement. In effect, schools are constantly inspected with school managers adopting the inspector's role. Since publically observable data often impact upon rolls, schools are increasingly required to adopt government rhetoric and guidance as a matter of course.

- *A market environment*: in this frame, parents are constructed as consumers (see Chapter 5). This encourages the deployment of performativity measures in an effort to win custom (schools) and make the right choices (parents). This, coupled with an admissions-based funding formal has made 'market-share' an increasingly important issue.

ACTIVITY 8.4

- How might these three features drive the work of schools and teachers?
- In what ways might this be positive?
- In what ways negative?

In effect, rather than be judged in their own right, value is assigned through the quantitative uplift teachers and pupils provide to an organisation's relative standing (schools in relation to schools) and absolute success (schools as measured by Ofsted inspections and against national targets). As Maddock et al. state:

> the source of energy in schools is more often the powerful principle of accountability, in its thousands of daily manifestations, the pressure not just to do it right, but to be seen to be doing it right. This is the source of the energy that goes into creating and sustaining a quiet class, a busy hum, a brisk pace and the satisfying completion of each orchestrated movement of the school day. The pressure to complete activities on time, the necessity of sticking to the complex choreography of the timetable: these are forces powerful enough to preclude the possibility of desire.
>
> (2007: 53)

What was deployed was a 'regime of accountability that employ[ed] judgements, comparisons and displays as means of control, attrition and change' (Ball, 2008: 49). What ensued was the value-ascription of certain forms of judgement that in turn both utilised certain measures and became their slave. In an effort to achieve efficiency and effectiveness performativity is concerned with the maximisation of outputs and the minimisation of inputs. Education became quantified and controlled by central mandate and missive and the increasing of surveillance and accountability mechanisms. This is a global feature.

> Pursuing progress in education means, for example, pursuing higher performance scores in science and technology, more students entering higher education, more scientific researchers, more job-related adult learning, more externally funded research, more international mobility, more academic publications, etc. The more the better; the maximum is the optimum. The 'evidence-based' educational policy of transnational institutions is fully penetrated by the logic of quantification which defines their perception of progress in education.
>
> (Moutsios, 2010: 134)

But this is also tied to the rise of the managerial and market state. For here can be seen the links between performativity and education, the ways in which the former influences and drives the latter as a means to achieve success in the business oriented ways of the modern state:

> The rise of a performativity discourse in education in England emanates from the importation of an economic 'market' structure for schools in order to improve the effectiveness and efficiency of the outputs of learning and to increase the opportunity of choice for the 'consumers' of education (Ball, 1998).
>
> (Jeffrey, 2002: 531)

In turn four things occurred (Ball, 2008):

- The judgement of political advisers and departmental heads, many of whom had no background in education, became elevated over the views and judgements of teachers.
- Myriad judgements were made about education, all of which were made through quantifiable measures: money spent; exam scores gleaned; lessons rated good and so on.

- Such information was published, held up for public scrutiny so defining expectations, future indicators and shifting demands.

- Individuals became responsible for monitoring themselves so that they might be responsive and flexible.

It is business interests that are increasingly influential on school governing bodies. As Welch (1998: 172) notes, under such influences institutions are 'pressed to be more efficient: to work better, do more with less, be responsive to market forces, engage in entrepreneurial activities and engage in ongoing (indeed endless) processes of so-called quality improvement, via techniques of self-assessment and regulation'.

It is this auditing that is so crucial, for it is this which orients teaching and learning as performances, rewarded through the auspices of 'effective teaching skills' (Hay McBer, 2000), performance-related pay for teachers and success in national tests for pupils. Such instrumentalisation is the predominant force (Jeffrey, 2003) and led to practices such as a concentration on borderline pupils, i.e. those who were predicted to get a grade D at GCSE but who, with intensive support, could get a grade C. The same happened in primary schools with those pupils judged to be working at level 3 but who could, with additional help, attain level 4. Such concentration meant that other groups, the less able, the more able, became sidelined. Individual desire is shaped by the mechanisms of surveillance, for example, the desire for a good school through the auspices of the Ofsted report. The 'social state' is replaced by the 'enabling state', whereby services traditionally offered by the state are still offered, and are still desired to be offered, but by individuals, firms or organisations (Davies and Bansel, 2007).

Performativity, then, has effects on the workings of the school. The ways in which teachers are positioned in the discourse leads to certain mechanisms for action being adopted and extolled as virtuous. Professional actions and activity become governed in new ways and towards new ends. But it is not only teachers who are so affected. Pupils too demonstrate the effects of a performativity discourse. For as Pollard and Triggs (2000: 297) note, 'a significant proportion of pupils seem to have become instrumentally concerned with "playing the system", with superficial learning and trying to avoid boredom'. This view of learning and school is mirrored in other quarters. Carnell (2005) writes of the general passivity of pupils and the way in which they define the good pupil as one who listens and does their work and of the way in which pupils view themselves as akin to 'empty vessels' who see learning as 'getting taught'. The identification is one of 'pupil' that is as 'other' to the teacher: the lines are drawn and a learning as a partnership is not seen to be required. For the pupils, learning is seen to be unsatisfying, unmotivating and uncomfortable (Pollard and Triggs, 2000) with the main aim of the lesson to find out what is required and respond. It is little wonder, however, that pupils are so outcomes driven when the very orientation of education itself is towards the demonstration of performance indicators:

> with the increasing dominance of the performativity discourse, relations between teachers, colleagues and local inspectors have become less humanistic as they each take up a more defined role. Teachers are defined as deliverer, team player and performer. Children are redefined as pupils, colleagues as competitors, team members, experts and 'weak or strong links' and inspectors are now examiners and authoritative coaches. Equal and open negotiative relations have been superseded by hierarchical, dependent and deferential relations.
>
> (Jeffrey, 2002: 544)

Performativity can be seen as a process of normalisation which effectively pathologises the 'sick' school: those that do not run according to predetermined criteria are identified by Ofsted and require 'treatment'. Although audit is supposed to be neutral, in effect it shapes the very behaviour it is supposed to identify and measure. Thus schools come to work as performance-driven organisations, seeking to maximise ways to demonstrate their success in simplistic and measurable ways. Those unable to do this become marked as having 'serious weaknesses' or requiring of 'special measures'. Performativity serves the ends of improving the performance of the system.

League tables

The most obvious manifestation of the quasi-market is the introduction of league tables. Those in favour argue that they empower parents by giving them simple, quantitative data by which to judge a school's success or otherwise. It should be noted, though, that the raw data are published by schools and local authorities but that the media construct the league tables themselves. For those on the political right, any objections result from attempts by the teaching profession to hide incompetency. It is notable, though, that the professional body is overwhelmingly opposed to league tables and the publication of such simplistic data. Critics cite three main problems with league tables (Power and Frandji, 2010):

- Reductionism: league tables dehumanise education and make it nothing more than a technical endeavour. This has led to a loss of focus on what really matters in school in favour of simplistic measurements.
- Misleading attribution of outcomes: others argue that league tables in effect show out-of-school factors not internal ones; they hold up for scrutiny those issues that lie outside of the school's control. This seems to be borne out by the nature of those schools at the top of the tables (predominantly selective or in high socio-economic areas) and those at the bottom.
- Collateral damage: some believe that league tables damage the reputation of schools.
- The belief is that league tables give rise to economic and cultural injustices. Those at the bottom end of the tables suffer more than other schools, especially as they become displayed in the media. More importantly, externally seen 'failure' may become internalised in the schools processes and mechanisms.

ACTIVITY 8.5

- Look at the league tables for your local area and compare them with another location.
- What do the tables tell you about the schools they cite?
- What other information would you require if you were a parent choosing a school for your child?

New Labour did go some way to reducing the impact of league tables, however. By recognising a broad range of qualifications, many of which were vocational in orientation, and by measuring schools according to institutional improvement they established a system of accountability that identified achievement in a much broader way than previously. Added to this was their introduction of value-added league tables to show how schools developed their pupils according to their baseline position on entry to the school. The removal of simplistic raw score evaluations was a productive move in that it created a 'new politics of recognition' (Power and Frandji, 2010: 390); what was to be celebrated was progress rather than simple attainment. However, at the same time New Labour continued to cite level 4 as the average level for all 11-year-olds to achieve in their SATs scores. But even value-added measures are not without their problems (Power and Frandji, 2010):

- *The impossibility of separating a school from its context:* value-added measures are problematic as they attempt to separate 'internal' and 'external' factors. But such external 'noise' cannot be easily factored out. In effect they ignore that fact that inequalities are 'constituted through the interaction between school and society' (p. 391).

- *The displacement of a politics of redistribution:* the politics of recognition replaced the politics of redistribution; a sense that economic injustices, which so heavily impact on educational outcome, are not being dealt with. Instead cultural practices are the only area of inequality being considered. Celebrating the success of poor schools in effect diverts attention from their poverty and material disadvantage. Recognition does nothing to tackle the root causes of failure: inequality and economic deprivation.

- *The naturalisation of educational failure:* this accepts as natural the inferiority of certain schools.

Value-added is not inherently better, then, than raw score tables; both have their problems. Indeed, the former draw attention away from structural and systematic constraints on educational achievement through their measurement and subsequent neutralisation through the auspices of 'taking them into consideration' (Power and Frandji, 2010). Consequently, matters such as social deprivation become elided for they are reduced to simple constraining factors which can be accounted for. The politics of recognition thus serves to maintain the ecology of a marketised education system. However, what adjusted league tables do show is how well pupils have progressed against defined norms. Schools are able to counterbalance their overall raw data by the way in which they provide for uplift in the expected progress of their pupils. What such league tables show are schools which produce below, at and above expectations. Conversely, unadjusted league tables exacerbate stigmatisation and negatively impact through their simplistic assumption that exam results are a measure, simply, of what occurs within school.

The Coalition

Following the 2010 general election, a Liberal–Conservative coalition formed the government. Whilst there were similarities in some of the Conservative and Liberal Democrat pre-election manifestos, there was much to separate them as well. What are interesting, though, are the policies they have embraced since joining forces in 2010. In *The Importance of Teaching* (DfE, 2010a) the Coalition indicated its views concerning the performance of education and the performance of teachers and pupils. From the outset, the paper set out its stall in terms of the part to be played by international performance indicators:

but what really matters is how we're doing compared with our international competitors. That is what will define our economic growth and our country's future.

(DfE, 2010a: 3)

In *The Case for Change* (DfE, 2010b) the Coalition government echoes this concentration on key performance data. Citing international comparisons, this document, the partner to *The Importance of Teaching*, notes that accountability is a feature of all high-performing systems. This is particularly the case where external measures are deployed, for these, it is believed, are 'more reliable indicators of future progress and success than teacher assessment' (DfE 2010b: 22). What are particularly notable, though, are the assertions that teacher assessment tends to downplay the successes of poorer children and those from minority groups.

On the other hand, the Coalition's position in such matters is not simply a continuance of New Labour. Importantly, the White Paper proposes to end the use of contextual value added (CVA) measures and concentrate instead on raw scores alone, the argument being that it is difficult for the public to judge a school's worth based on how far it improves pupils' attainment relative to other schools in similar circumstances. The White Paper also details, quite extensively, the ways in which the previous administration's concentration on test scores drove the development of a pedagogy concerned with little more than narrow test results. Indeed, they bemoan the 'gaming behaviour' undertaken by a significant proportion of primary schools through the over-rehearsing of tests (DfE, 2010b: 12–13) to a point that went beyond 'what would be sensible familiarisation with the tests into excessive rehearsal and repeated practice . . . [which] . . . eats into valuable teaching time' (DfE, 2010b: 16). They are clear: such measures fall short of meeting the needs of pupils.

Measures would continue to hold education to account so that the performance might not only be compared between schools, but also between countries. The system of accountability was to be altered: Ofsted would focus more clearly on teaching and learning and the performance measures used to hold schools to account would be strengthened. Yet they also noted that 'clear performance information and good comparative data are positive features of our system' (DfE, 2010a: 12). It is notable, though, that the coalition bemoans the 'gaming' behaviour of schools whereby, in secondary schools, certain qualifications have grown in popularity, not because they are valued by employers and universities but because they carry a higher value in league tables, and in primary schools, over-rehearsing for tests occurs.

It is not only schools that are engaged in such behaviour. In December 2011 the Secretary of State for Education, Michael Gove, announced an investigation by OFQUAL, the regulator for the examinations system, following evidence that examiners from some of the examining boards, private companies in their own right, were giving teachers information about which topics to teach and what questions would and would not come up on forthcoming GCSE and A level test papers (Watt et al., 2011). It seems that even exam boards feel the strain of the performative culture: for if more students gain higher grades then more business goes to the exam board as more schools opt to use their product.

It is clear that performance and accountability measures are to stay. The Coalition has signalled its intent to ensure that standards rise and to do so testing data would be rigorously used. Indeed, Michael Gove was quick to set a school floor-standard of 60 per cent of pupils reaching level four in each of literacy and numeracy in the end of Key Stage Two SATs. Performance and accountability were part of the solution, then, to engendering a world class education system.

This concentration on international test scores has not been without criticism. The UK Statistics Authority has cast doubt over whether or not the line taken by Michael Gove and

Sir Michael Wilshaw that England has plunged down the international league table is in fact robust (Stewart, 2012). Their line is that from 2000 the number of UK schools taking the OECD's Programme for International Student Assessment (Pisa) is too small to use as a reliable indicator of international standing. Despite this, missives concerning the parlous state of English education can often be heard emanating from either the DfE or Ofsted.

Conclusion

Performance and accountability are, then, features of the state education system in England. The worth of individual pupils, teachers and schools is marked out by the levels of attainment they get in a number of performative measures. Pupils are expected to attain certain grades in national tests and teachers are expected not only to ensure that their pupils hit such expectations, but also to teach in ways designated as outstanding by Ofsted. In effect what is created is a technology of performance. Such technology is all-pervasive in its reach: pedagogy is tightly defined and outputs are closely and vigorously monitored. In the drive to perform, attributes are marked as desirable and the system does all it can to ensure that these are met. Yet this technology is not without its problems. A reorientation of teachers' work has taken place, a reorientation that can be said to have skewed the aims of education away from wider notions of achievement and love of learning, and towards a view that success in a narrow range of measures is what should command attention. The basis for interpersonal relationships has changed, as has the way in which schools see the relationship between the curriculum and broader educational concerns. Questions also need to be asked concerning who such changes and accountability is for:

> In theory the new culture of accountability and audit makes professionals and institutions more accountable to the public. This is supposedly done by publishing targets and levels of attainment in league tables . . . But underlying this ostensible aim of accountability to the public the real requirements are for accountability to regulators, to departments of government . . . The new forms of accountability impose forms of central control quite often indeed a range of different and mutually inconsistent forms of central control.
>
> (O'Neill, 2002: 52–53)

This orientation is not without success. Since the introduction of Key Stage Two SATs targets the proportion of pupils achieving level 4 has increased to a current plateau. Similarly, each year brings stories of an increase in GCSE and A Level passes and the proportion of pupils attaining the highest grades. Undoubtedly one aspect of education is to prepare pupils for the future, and success in exams marks individuals out for increased chances of increased income and position. But the drive to concentrate on performance is not a simplistic one; it is a complex interaction of politics and education. On the one hand is the need to be seen to have a world-class education system, whilst on the other hand individual pupil and teacher needs must be paramount.

Key points

- Notions of performance and accountability based teaching have a history in the Revised Code of 1862.

- Contemporary ideas about performance and accountability originate in the late 1970s and early 1980s.

- Currently, Ofsted monitors and inspects schools and judges the quality of their education. Part of this judgement is performance-based.

- If any school is judged to be inadequate then it can be placed in an Ofsted category. This effectively requires the school to work in certain ways to demonstrate that the education they offer is at least good.

- NNS, NLS, the National Curriculum and standards for QTS all also offered mechanisms for both performance and accountability.

- New Labour sought to control pedagogy so that performance and accountability might be maintained, through the definition of terms such as 'best practice'.

- New Labour desired to be able to measure educational performance objectively and quantifiably.

- Certain targets were defined which would indicate whether or not the education system, and by default teachers and pupils, were performing adequately.

- Performativity is a system of monitoring and control that seeks to ensure that certain features are put into practice. In these ways the quality or worth of an organisation or individual is represented.

- Such mechanisms are not confined to the UK, however; this system of reward and control is manifest across the world.

- The performativity discourse has negative effects for both pupils and teachers.

- League tables offer a quantifiable mechanism by which parents and others may judge the success of a school.

- The Coalition government has continued to use performance measures to determine the success of the education system, despite criticism of some of its conclusions.

Further reading

Adams, P. (2008) 'Considering "Best Practice": the social construction of teacher-activity and pupil-learning as performance', *Cambridge Journal of Education*, **38**(3), 375–392. This paper challenges the idea that effective teaching skills can contribute to a definition of 'best practice'.

Ball, S.J. (2006) *Education Policy and Social Class*, London: Routledge (Chapter 10). This chapter introduces the idea of performativity and question the ways in which such mechanisms are helpful to the education profession.

Cunningham, P. (2012) *Politics and the Primary Teacher*, London: Routldege (Chapter 5). This chapter considers the idea that pedagogy is an inherently political act through an examination of government policy.

9

The future?

Purpose of this chapter

After reading this chapter you should understand:

■ some of the more recent changes in education policy enacted by the Coalition government;

■ some of the possible outcomes for these changes.

Continuity or change?

As previously noted, it is clear that the Coalition government has continued with the market-based approach started since the 1980s. With regard to the ways in which market forces can be said to be part of the educational landscape, it seems that matters such as private finance have taken on a renewed emphasis since 2010. The ways in which academy chains have expanded since then means that business has a large role to play in the delivery of education, certainly in England's schools. What has occurred is a wholesale demarcation between private and public. Although this started under the Tories in the 1980s, it was New Labour which extended this trend. The Coalition government has extended it even further by bringing in private providers on a hitherto unseen scale.

Writing to further the work of Allen and Burgess (2010), the Institute for Government (2012) has identified five conditions for ensuring that a quasi-market will improve educational outcomes and use these to identify whether or not the Coalition's policies are likely to affect such improvement.

Schools must have autonomy over the drivers of educational outcomes or there must be a variety of school types

It is certainly the case that more schools now enjoy more autonomy than under New Labour. The increase in the number of academies and free schools that sit outside of local authority control and that do not have to employ qualified teachers, pay staff according to national pay scales or teach the National Curriculum means that more schools than ever before have the freedom to innovate. It is questionable, though, how far such innovation will go. For example, will such schools vary the terms and conditions of staff dramatically, and will such alterations be to the benefit of pupils? Similarly, if the National Curriculum is slimmed down, will the freedom not to teach to this affect a school's curriculum in any meaningful way?

It is not at all clear whether or not such freedoms will be wholeheartedly embraced, or whether such options will mean more tinkering around the edges. For example, the government announced that schools no longer had to pay heed to the term dates set by the local authority. This was a position held by free schools and academies anyway, but on 1 July 2013 the right a school had to set its own term and holiday dates was extended to all schools. Whilst there are a small number of schools that wish to use such innovative powers to make changes, the immediate response from schools and unions was that local consultation between schools and between schools and parents must take place so that families are not disadvantaged. It is one thing to grant extra powers, but the education system has run in its present form for over 150 years and change takes time.

Parents must value and be able to correctly identify educational success

The decision to remove contextual value added as the mechanisms by which schools are to be judged was a bold one. In its place, the Coalition wishes to create a series of performance tables whereby similar ability pupils will be judged against each other. In some respects this does form a clearer picture of the progress a pupil is making. However, it is also the case that the tables continue to be reductionist in orientation and concentrate on a small part of the work of a school. The introduction of floor targets for both secondary and primary schools signals intent to concentrate, once again, on performance measures. But will such measures enable parents to be able to judge whether or not their child is getting the education they require and to which they are entitled? For different groups of parents different issues will be uppermost in their mind when considering the education their child will get. For example, parents with a child who has special educational needs (SEN) may be less concerned with test scores and more concerned with the ethos of the school and its SEN provision. It is not clear that the new Ofsted framework, concentrating as it does on a reduced set of criteria or the newly introduced floor targets will necessarily inform parents in the way they would wish to be informed.

Parental choice must be meaningful and capable of affecting the allocation of pupils to schools

Even though school choice has supposedly been extended it is still the case that for many parents the options are limited due to financial and/or geographical reasons. It is the case that in instances of over-subscription the mechanism by which school places are allocated is often geographical proximity. In addition, it is often the case that a successful school will push up the house prices in the neighbourhood so reducing the pool of people who are able to attend the local school.

Whilst such matters are not pertinent for free schools or academies, it is the case that local organisation of schools is hampered by the advent of these institutions operating outside of the local authority remit. In fact, free schools (called 'Additional Schools' in the Academies Act (DfE, 2010c)) are wholly designed to be created in addition to the places already in existence in the local authority. Whilst some argue that this forces local authority schools to improve, many are unconvinced by the Coalition policy. The National Union of Teachers (NUT, 2010) is against the move to create extra school places in this way. They cite five reasons why free schools should be opposed:

- They undermine local democracy.
- They will damage funding to other schools.
- Choice and competition are ideological and do nothing to raise standards.
- They could lead to other schools closing.
- They lead to privatisation and profit-making.

Machin and Vernoit (2010) found that under New Labour those disadvantaged schools which converted to academy status saw increased gains in the number of pupils gaining five or more A* to C grades at GCSE providing they had been academies for at least two years. However, they also note that the Coalition's policies are in danger of exacerbating the disadvantage gap, because new converters following the 2010 general election were those schools already deemed outstanding. As such, these schools were mostly to be found in less disadvantaged areas; the concern was that these conversions might well increase the disadvantage seen before academy status.

Schools must find it beneficial to be popular and to grow

The main incentive for business to grow is profit. However, it is currently illegal for profit to be made from running a school. This is not to say that services cannot be offered at a profit, however. The Coalition is not, however, ideologically opposed to ending this situation. It may, therefore, be the case that schools will be run by business and seek to make a profit. Given that funding is relatively fixed for schools, extra resources to provide profit will have to be found by offering services outside of the traditional remit of a school and charging for them, or by cutting costs elsewhere, possibly via pay and resourcing. It remains to be seen whether schools will wish to expand.

The best way for schools to be popular must be to raise the quality of teaching and learning

Ofsted now concentrates its efforts on four areas of school life, one of which is teaching and learning. It is notable that such moves have been coupled with an increase in the difficulty of gaining an outstanding Ofsted grade. Certainly the Coalition is determined to ensure that the quality of teaching improves. Measures to operationalise this have been put into place and include yearly targets for teachers some of which need to be based around the performance of pupils. It remains to be seen whether this actually improves teaching quality, however, or whether teachers become even more adept at teaching to the test.

Professionalism

As stated in Chapter 7, the Coalition government has embarked on an ambitious project to renew teacher professionalism. As part of this drive a number of changes have been instigated:

- A removal of the requirement to have qualified teacher status to be employed in a free school or an academy.
- An extension of the performance-related pay initiative brought in by New Labour. This means that teachers must have their performance monitored against identified targets with

their pay being contingent upon meeting the requirements set. Whereas previously teachers on the main professional grade would automatically see their pay increase up to the top of the scale for the amount of service they had accrued, the government has removed this. Now, pay awards are wholly determined by whether or not targets have been met.

■ Teacher training is now in the process of moving out of universities and into schools. Whilst PGCEs still remain, it is the case that matters such as School Direct and Teach First have seen a large increase in their recruits. This has meant that places have been lost in universities. Indeed, the government has signalled its intention only to offer places to the best performing higher education institutions.

What is clear is that the Coalition is determined to break the perceived monopoly held by local authorities, teacher unions and universities. The changes amount to an increase in market-based functions for teacher professionalism. As Surman (2010: 6) notes, 'the Coalition Government has reframed the discussion in general, and teacher training in particular.' In its pamphlet *In Defence of Teacher Education*, the Standing Committee for the Education and Training of Teachers (2010) signalled its opposition to the moves undertaken by government in the area of initial teacher preparation. In particular the 'ideology of teaching as craft' and the primacy of prior academic qualifications as an indicator of teaching quality highlighted by Gove and others were challenged.

The Coalition position certainly raises challenges for teacher education and professional development as well as the general professional standing of teachers. Questions need to be asked concerning the ways in which initial teacher education and training are being organised. It is clear that to move training into schools requires a considerable sea-change and reorganisation. Whereas under the previous system of higher education-based courses with small numbers of school-based routes, planning and organisation could be effected more easily, it will surely be the case that under the new regime central planning will be more difficult. To control the supply of teachers from a relatively small number of higher education institutes (HEIs) is relatively easy in comparison with controlling supply from thousands of schools of differing sizes and locations.

It is also important to question just how effective will be performance management. The government, in its White Paper *The Importance of Teaching* (DfE, 2010a), bemoaned the gaming behaviour used by schools to ensure favourable scores on national tests and positions in league tables. If teachers' pay is now to be determined by whether or not certain grades are achieved by pupils then this calls into question whether or not a broad and balanced curriculum in primary schools can be maintained and whether or not simply teaching to the test will occur both here and in secondary schools. This, coupled with the fact that floor standards have been set for both sectors, means that teachers will be under increased pressure to maximise exam performance. Notably, Hobby (2010) states that bad habits and behaviours that lead to unhelpful professional characteristics can be difficult to change. If new teachers start their professional life with the mindset that what matters is performance alone, then it may not necessarily bode well for the future of the profession.

Conclusion

It is still too early to tell what the effects of the Coalition government's policies will be. Three years into their tenure, much has been achieved by Gove and the Department for Education.

The introduction of new schools and new providers into education marks a change in the way in which education is run and organised in England. Other matters are still to be resolved, for example the on-going review of the primary and secondary National Curricula.

What is known, though, is the way in which neoliberal agendas have shaped the educational landscape of today. Opening up education to the marketplace, which started with Callaghan's Ruskin College speech in 1976, has clearly been the major agenda item. Whether this will continue is unknown, but the signs are that it will. This coupled with the changes to teachers' working practices mean that education is positioned on the cusp of change that may well prove extremely difficult to unravel. Just as the tenor of the changes wrought in the 1980s has been continued with ever since, it might well be that the introduction of for-profit providers and the dismantling of national pay and conditions might well be the brave new world of education. It might also be that organising schooling locally according to local need is seen as anathema to the marketplace. It might be that the individual parent is required to be the local authority for their child. But we have seen in preceding chapters that access to education is in part determined by the social and cultural capital held by parents and pupils. To require families to act in this way may prove beyond the ability of some. Where then does the state step in?

What can be said with some certainty about the future is that there will be further change and development. It stands to reason that a new government of whatever political hue will wish to stamp its authority on both the profession and the system. It would also seem that parties of all persuasion are enamoured by the promise of the marketplace. All three of the main political parties see the extension of the quasi-market, in some cases into a full market, as the way to ensure that education will prosper. Only time will tell.

ACTIVITY 9.1

Peter Mortimore (2010) wrote:

> Over my years in the education service, I have witnessed the policies of 28 secretaries of state. I have observed the work of scores of local authority education officers, hundreds of heads and thousands of teachers, teacher trainers and pupils in many different countries.
>
> I have seen great progress: British teachers today are amongst the best I have seen anywhere. But the improvements to the system, so obvious in the first half of my career, have not kept pace. Anthony Crosland's request to local authorities to go comprehensive, the raising of the school leaving age from 15 to 16, the Plowden Committee's concern for the disadvantaged, the merging of the GCE and CSE into the GCSE and the abolition of corporal punishment pointed the way to a modern education system.
>
> Regrettably, the influence of the anti-progressive Black Papers, the wasted opportunity of James Callaghan's Great Debate and the systematic rubbishing of the comprehensive ideal by both Tories and New Labour have stymied progress. In addition, the downgrading of local government and the creation of new types of schools – from Kenneth Baker's city technology colleges to Michael Gove's free schools – have fashioned a deeply fragmented English education service. Add to this the haughty control and command of New Labour's classroom diktats, and small wonder that – despite the dedication of those who work in schools – the system is a mess.

Do you think the education system is in a mess?

Key points

- The first White Paper *The Importance of Teaching* signalled the direction and intent of the Coalition.

- The Lib–Con Coalition, once established, set about reforming school organisation. An Academies Act was passed and outstanding schools were pre-approved for conversion to academy status.

- Invitations were extended to groups who wished to establish free schools.

- Proposals were set out that would greatly increase the numbers of trainee teachers training on the job in schools, rather than in institutes of higher education.

- Performance matters have continued to take centre stage through Coalition policies, especially in the area of pupil and teacher performance target setting and achievement.

Further reading

Abbott, I., Rathbone, M. and Whitehead, P. (2013) *Education Policy*, London: Sage (Chapter 10). Gives a good overview of the first two years in power and includes an interesting interview with Michael Gove, Secretary of State for Education.

Adams, P. (2011) '(Dis)continuity and the coalition: primary pedagogy as craft and primary pedagogy as performance', *Educational Review*, **63**(4), 467-483. Details the ways in which the Coalition is adopting a craft-based approach to pedagogical matters.

References

Abbott, I., Rathbone, M. and Whitehead, P. (2013) *Education Policy*, London: Sage.

Acker, S. (1995) 'Carry on caring: the work of women teachers', *British Journal of Sociology of Education*, **16**(1), 21–36.

Adams, P. (2007) 'Learning and caring in the age of the five outcomes', *Education 3–13*, **35**(3), 225–237.

Adams, P. (2008) 'Considering "Best Practice": the social construction of teacher-activity and pupil-learning as performance', *Cambridge Journal of Education*, **38**(3), 375–392.

Adams, P. (2011a) 'From "Ritual" to "Mindfulness": policy and pedagogic positioning', *Discourse: Studies in the Cultural Politics of Education*, **32**(1), 57–69.

Adams, P. (2011b) '(Dis)continuity and the coalition: primary pedagogy as craft and primary pedagogy as performance', *Educational Review*, **63**(4), 467–483.

Adams, P. and Calvert, M. (2007) 'Breaking the curriculum code: citizenship education in England since 2002', in B. Ravn and N. Kruger (Eds.) *Learning Beyond Cognition*, Copenhagen: Danish University of Education, 149–166.

Adams, P. and Tucker, S. A. (2007) 'Every Child Matters: change for children in schools', *Education 3–13*, **35**(3), 209–211.

Ainley, P. (2004) 'The new "market-state" and education', *Journal of Education Policy*, **19**(4), 497–514.

Alexander, R. (2004) 'Still no pedagogy? Principle, pragmatism and compliance in primary education', *Cambridge Journal of Education*, **34**(1), 7–33.

Alexander, R. (2010) Children, *Their World, Their Education: Final Report and Recommendations of the Cambridge Primary Review*, London: Routledge.

Alexander, R., Rose, J. and Woodhead, C. (1992) *Curriculum Organisation and Classroom Practice in Primary Schools*, London: DES.

Allen, R. (2010) 'Replicating Swedish "free school" reforms in England', *Research in Public Policy*, Summer, 4–7.

Allen, R. and Burgess, S. (2010) 'The future of competition and accountability in education', 2020 Public Services Trust at the RSA, available at: http://clients.squareeye.net/uploads/2020/documents/ESRC_Allan%20and%20Burgess_FINAL.pdf [accessed 9 September 2013].

Apple, M.W. (2009) 'Understanding and interrupting Neoliberalism and Neoconservatism in education', *Pedagogies: An International Journal*, **1**(1), 21–26.

Apple, M.W. (2013) *Knowledge, Power and Education: The Selected Works of Michael W. Apple*, Abingdon: Routledge.

Bacchi, C. (2000) 'Policy as discourse: What does it mean? Where does it get us?', *Discourse: Studies in the Cultural Politics of Education*, **21**, 45–57.

Bagley, C. (2006) 'School choice and competition: a public-market in education revisited', *Oxford Review of Education*, **32**(3), 347–362.

Ball, S.J. (1990) *Politics and Policy Making in Education: Explorations in policy sociology*, London: Routledge.

Ball, S.J. (2001) 'Labour, learning and the economy: a "policy sociology" perspective', *Cambridge Journal of Education*, **29**(2), 195–206.

Ball, S.J. (2003) 'The teacher's soul and the terrors of performativity', *Journal of Education Policy*, **18**(2), 215–28.

Ball, S.J. (2003) 'The risks of social reproduction: the middle class and education markets', *London Review of Education*, **1**(3), 163–175.

Ball, S.J. (2006) *Education Policy and Social Class*, London: Routledge.

Ball, S.J. (2008) *The Education Debate*, Bristol: The Policy Press.

Ball, S.J., Maguire, M. and Braun, A. (2012) *How Schools Do Policy: Policy enactments in secondary schools*, London: Routledge.

Bangs, J., Macbeath, J. and Galton, M. (2011) *Reinventing Schools, Reforming Teaching: From political visions to classroom reality*, London: Routledge.

Barber, M. (2001) 'Large-scale education reform in England: a work in progress', paper for the Managing Education Reform Conference, Moscow, 29–30 October.

Barber, M. (2005) 'Informed professionalism: realising the potential', presentation to a conference of the Association of Teachers and Lecturers, London, 1 June.

Bartlett, S. and Burton, D. (2012) *Introduction to Education Studies* (3rd edn), London: Sage.

Bates, J. Lewis, S. and Pickard, A. (2011) *Education Policy, Practice and the Professional*, London: Continuum.

Beard, R. (2008) 'What is the role of the teacher today?', paper presented at the EPP-ED Hearing on Teacher Quality: does it really matter?, Brussels, Belgium.

Beck, J. (2008) 'Governmental professionalism: re-professionalising or de-professionalising teachers in England', *British Journal of Educational Studies*, **56**(2) 119–143.

Bentley, T. (1998) *Learning Beyond the Classroom: Education for a changing world*, London: Routledge.

Best, R. (2003) 'New bottles for old wine? Affective education and the "citizenship revolution" in English schools', *Pastoral Care in Education*, **21**(4), 14–21.

Blair, T. (2006) Speech given to the Annual Conference of the Specialist Schools and Academic Trust, 30 November, Birmingham.

Blair, T. (2008) *Socialism*, Fabian Pamphlet 565, London: The Fabian Society.

Blunkett, D. (2000) 'Influence or irrelevance: how can social science improve government?', *Research Intelligence*, **71**, 12–21.

Bobbitt, P. (2002) *The Shield of Achilles, War, Peace and the Course of History*, London: Allen Lane.

Bonal, X. (2003) 'The neoliberal educational agenda and the legitimation crisis: old and new state strategies', *British Journal of Sociology of Education*, **24**(2), 159–175.

Bottery, M. (2005) 'The individualisation of consumption, a Trojan Horse in the destruction of the public sector', *Educational Management Administration and Leadership*, **33**(3), 267–288.

Bowe, R., Ball, S.J., and Gold, A. (1992) *Reforming Education and Changing Schools: Case studies in policy sociology*, London: Routledge.

Boyt, T. E., Lusch, R. F. and Naylor, G. (2001) 'The role of professionalism in determining job satisfaction in professional services: a study of marketing researchers', *Journal of Service Research*, **3**(4), 321–330.

Bradley, S. and Taylor, J. (2002) 'The effect of the quasi-market on the efficiency–equity trade-off in the secondary school sector', *Bulletin of Economic Research*, **54**(3), 295–314.

Brehony, K.J. (2005) 'Primary schooling under New Labour: the irresolvable contradiction of excellence and enjoyment', *Oxford Review of Education*, **31**(1), 29–46.

Brennan, M. (1996) *Multiple Professionalisms for Australian Teachers in an Important Age*, New York: American Educational Research Association.

Brown, P. (1995) 'Cultural capital and social exclusion: some observations on recent trends in education, employment and the labour market', *Work, Employment and Society*, **9**(1), 29–51.

Burgess, B., Briggs, A., McConnell, B. and Slater, H. (2006) *School Choice in England: Background facts*, Working Paper No. 06/159, Bristol: University of Bristol, Centre for Market and Public Organisation (CMPO), available at http://www.bristol.ac.uk/cmpo/publications/papers/2006/wp159.pdf [accessed 21 December 2011].

Burgess, S. and Briggs, A. (2006) *School Assignment, School Choice and Social Mobility*, Working Paper No. 06/157, Bristol: University of Bristol, Centre for Market and Public Organisation (CMPO), available at http://www.bristol.ac.uk/cmpo/publications/papers/2006/wp157.pdf [accessed 2 January 2012].

Burgess, S., Propper, C. and Wilson, D. (2007) 'The impact of school choice in England implications from the economic evidence', *Policy Studies*, **28**(2), 129–143.

Cabinet Office (2010) *The Coalition: Our programme for government*, London: Cabinet Office.

Callaghan, J. (1976) Speech delivered at a foundation stone-laying ceremony at Ruskin College, Oxford, 18 October, available at http://education.guardian.co.uk/thegreatdebate/story/0,,574645,00.html [accessed 26 September 2013].

Carnell, E. (2005) 'Understanding and enriching young people's learning: issues, complexities and challenges', *Improving Schools*, **8**(3), 269–284.

Carr, D. (1992) 'Four dimensions of educational professionalism', *Westminster Studies in Education*, **15**(1), 19–31.

Children England (2011) *School Reforms*, London: Children England.

Chowdry, H. and Sibieta, L. (2011) 'Trends in education and schools spending', IFS Briefing note BN121, available at http://www.ifs.org.uk/bns/bn121.pdf [accessed 27/11/2012].

Codd, J. (1997) 'Knowledge, qualifications and higher education: a critical view', in M. Olssen and K. Morris Matthews (Eds) *Education Policy in New Zealand: The 1990s and beyond*, Palmerston North, New Zealand: Dunmore Press, 130–144.

Coldron, J. (2007) 'Parents and the diversity of secondary education: a discussion paper', London: Research and Information on State Education Trust (RISE), available at http://www.risetrust.org.uk/node/24 [accessed 26 September 2013].

Conservative Party (2010) 'Invitation to Join the Government of Britain' (election manifesto), London: The Conservative Party.

Cox, C.B. and Boyson, R. (Eds.) (1977) *Black Paper 5, Black Paper 1977*, London: Temple Smith.

Cox, C.B. and Dyson, A.E. (Eds.) (1969) *Black Paper 1, Fight for Education*, London: Critical Quarterly Society.

Croxford, L. and Raffe, D. (2007) 'Education markets and social class inequality: a comparison of trends in England, Scotland and Wales', in R. Teese, S. Lamb and M. Duru-Bellat (Eds.) *Educational Theory and Public Policy*, International Studies in Educational Inequality, Theory and Policy, Volume 3, London: Springer, 39–66.

Crozier, M., Huntington, S.P. and Watanuki, J. (1975) *The Crisis of Democracy: Report on the governability of democracies*, New York: New York University Press.

Cunningham, P. (2012) *Politics and the Primary Teacher*, London: Routledge.

Dadds, M. (2001) 'The politics of pedagogy', *Teachers and Teaching: Theory and Practice*, **7**(1), 43–58.

Davies, B. and Bansel, P. (2007) 'Neoliberalism and education', *International Journal of Qualitative Studies in Education*, **20**(3), 247–259.

Day, C. (2002) 'School reform and transitions in teacher professionalism and identity', *International Journal of Educational Research*, **37**(8), 677–692.

Day, C. and Smethem, L. (2009) 'The effects of reform: have teachers really lost their sense of professionalism?', *Journal of Educational Change*, **10**(2–3), 141–157.

DBIS (2011) *Students at the Heart of the System*, London: Department for Business, Innovation and Skills.

DCSF (2007) *The Children's Plan: Building brighter futures*, Cmnd 7280, London: HMSO.

DCSF (2008) *Independent Review of the Primary Curriculum: Final report*, London: Department for Children, Schools and Families.

DCSF (2009a) *A School Report Card: Prospectus*, London: Department for Children, Schools and Families.

DCSF (2009b) *The Children's Plan Two Years On: A progress report*, London: HMSO.

Dearing (1994) *The National Curriculum and Its Assessment*, Final Report, London: School Curriculum and Assessment Authority.

DES (1980) Education Act 1980, London: HMSO.

DES (1981) Education Act 1981, London: HMSO.

DES (1986) Education Act 1986, London: HMSO.

DES (1988) Education Reform Act 1988, London: HMSO.

DfE (1992a) Education (Schools) Act, London: HMSO.

DfE (1992b) *Choice and Diversity*, White Paper, London: HMSO.

DfE (2010a) *The Importance of Teaching*, Schools White Paper, Norwich: TSO.

DfE (2010b) *The Case for Change*, Norwich: TSO.

DfE (2010c) The Academies Act 2010, Chapter 32, London: TSO.

DfE (2012) New school-led teacher training programme announced, available at http://education.gov.uk/inthenews/inthenews/a00210288/new-school-led-teacher-training-programme-announced [accessed 5 November 2012].

DfE (2013) New advice to help schools set performance-related pay, available at https://www.gov.uk/government/news/new-advice-to-help-schools-set-performance-related-pay [accessed 15 June 2013].

DfEE (1997) *Excellence in Schools*, Cmnd 2681, London: TSO.

DfEE (1998a) School Standards and Framework Act 1998, London: HMSO.

DfEE (1998b) *Teachers: Meeting the challenge of change*, Green Paper, London: Department for Education and Employment.

DfEE (1998c) *The National Literacy Strategy: Framework for teaching*, London: Department for Education and Employment.

DfEE (1999) *The National Numeracy Strategy*, London: Department for Education and Employment.

DfES (2001) *Schools: Achieving success*, London: HMSO.

DfES (2002) *14–19: Extending opportunities, rising standards*, London: HMSO.

DfES (2003a) *21st Century Skills: Realising Our Potential: Individuals, Employers, Nation*, Cmnd 5810, London: HMSO.

DfES (2003b) *Every Child Matters*, Cmnd 586, London: HMSO.

DfES (2003c) *Excellence and Enjoyment: A strategy for primary schools*, the Primary National Strategy, London: Department for Education and Skills.

DfES (2004) *A Five-Year Strategy for Children and Learners: Putting people at the heart of public services*, Cmnd 6272, London: TSO.

DfES (2005) *Higher Standards, Better Schools for All: More choice for parents and pupils*, London: TSO.

DfES (2006) Education and Inspections Act 2006, London: HMSO.

Dronkers, J., Felouzis, G. and van Zanten, A. (2010) 'Education markets and school choice', *Educational Research and Evaluation: An International Journal on Theory and Practice*, **16**(2), 99–105.

Dye, T. (1992) *Understanding Public Policy* (7th edn), Englewood Cliffs, NJ: Prentice Hall.

Earl, L., Watson, N., Levin, B., Leithwood, K., Fullan, M., Torrance, N., Jantzi, D., Mascall, B. and Volante, L. (2003) *Watching and Learning 3. Executive Summary*, Final Report of the External Evaluation of England's National Literacy and Numeracy Strategies, Nottingham: Department for Education and Skills.

Edwards, T. (1998) *Specialisation without Selection*, Rise Briefing no. 1, London: Research and Information on State Education Trust.

Elam, S. (1971) *Performance Based Teacher Education: What is the state of the art?*, Washington, DC: American Association of Colleges for Teacher Education.

Elliott, J. (1991) 'A model of professionalism and its implications for teacher education', *British Educational Research Journal*, **17**(4), 309–318.

Etzioni, A. (1995) *The Spirit of Community, Rights, Responsibilities and the Communitarian Agenda*, London: Fontana.

European Trade Union Institute (2001) 'Activation policies for young people in international perspective: monitoring the European employment strategy', seminar organised in cooperation with the group ESC Toulouse, Brussels, 8–9 November.

Evans, L. (2008) 'Professionalism, professionality and the development of education professionals', *British Journal of Educational Studies*, **56**(1), 20–38.

Flecknoe, M. (2001) 'Target setting: will it help to raise achievement?', *Educational Management and Administration*, **29**(2), 217–228.

Flecknoe, M. (2005) 'The changes that count in securing school improvement', *School Effectiveness and School Improvement*, **16**(4), 425–443.

Forrester, G. (2005) 'All in a day's work: primary teachers "performing" and "caring"', *Gender and Education*, **17**(3), 271–287.

Foskett, N. (2004) 'Markets and cultural evolution in schools: an international comparison', paper presented at the American Educational Research Association Annual Conference, San Diego, 13 April.

Foucault (1977) *The Archeology of Knowledge*, London: Tavistock.

Fox, C. J. (1992) 'What do we mean when we say professionalism? A language usage analysis for public administration', *The American Review of Public Administration*, **22**(1), 1–17.

Furlong, J. (2005) 'New Labour and teacher education: the end of an era', *Oxford Review of Education*, **31**(1), 119–134.

Furlong, J., Barton, L., Miles, S. Whiting, C. and Whitty, G. (2000) *Teacher Education in Transition. Re-forming Professionalism?*, Buckingham: Open University Press.

Galton, M. (2007) 'New Labour and education: an evidence-based analysis', *Forum*, **49**(1&2), 157–177.

Garner, R. (2013) 'Reforms to teachers' pay "will mean bigger class sizes"', *The Independent*, 22 May.

Garratt, D. and Forrester, G. (2012) *Education Policy Unravelled*, London: Continuum.

Gergen, K.J. (1995) 'Social construction and the educational process', in L.P. Steffe and J. Gale (Eds.) *Constructivism in Education*, Hillsdale, NJ: Lawrence Erlbaum, pp. 17–39.

Gewirtz, S. (2002) *The Managerial School, Post-welfarism and Social Justice in Education*, London: Routledge.

Gewirtz, S. and Ball, S. (2000) 'From "Welfarism" to "New Managerialism": shifting discourses of school headship in the education marketplace', *Discourse: Studies in the Cultural Politics of Education*, **21**(3), 253–268.

Gewirtz, S., Ball, S. and Bowe, R. (1995) *Markets, Choice and Equity in Education*, Buckingham: Open University Press.

Gibbons, S., Machin, S. and Silva, O. (2008) 'Choice, competition, and pupil achievement', *Journal of the European Economic Association*, **6**(4), 912–947.

Giddens, A. (1991) *Modernity and Self-Identity: Self and society in the last modern age*, Cambridge: Polity.

Giddens, A. (1998) *The Third Way: The renewal of social democracy*, London: Wiley.

Gillard (2011) 'Education in England: A Brief History', available at http://www.educationengland.org.uk/ [accessed 12 December 2012].

Giroux, H.A. (2002) 'Neoliberalism, corporate culture and the promise of higher education: the university as a democratic public sphere', *Harvard Educational Review*, **72**(4), 425–463.

Glennerster, H. (1991) 'Quasi-markets for education?', *The Economic Journal*, **101**(408), 1268–1276.

Goldring, E.B. and Phillips, K.J.R. (2008) 'Parent preference and parent choices: the public-private decision about school choice', *Journal of Education Policy*, **23**(3), 209–230.

Gorard, S. and Fitz, J. (1998) 'The more things change . . . the missing impact of marketisation?', *British Journal of Sociology of Education*, **19**(3), 365–376.

Gorard, S. and Taylor, C. (2002) 'Market forces and standards in education: a preliminary consideration', *British Journal of Sociology of Education*, **23**(1), 5–18.

Gray, J., Hussey, S., Schagen, I. and Charles, M. (2003) 'The primary side of the transfer divide: heads' perceptions and pupil progress', in M. Galton, J. Gray and J. Ruddock, *Transfer and Transitions in the Middle Years of Schooling (7–14): Continuities and discontinuities in learning*, Research Report 443, Nottingham: DfES Publications.

Gronn, P. (2000) 'Distributed properties: a new architecture for leadership', *Educational Management Administration and Leadership*, **28**(3), 317–338.

Hall, K. (2004) *Literacy and Schooling: Towards renewal in primary education policy,* Aldershot, Ashgate.

Hanlon, G. (1998) 'Professionalism as enterprise: service class politics and the redefinition of professionalism', *Sociology*, **32**(1), 43–63.

Hargreaves, A. (1994) *Changing Teachers, Changing Times: Teachers' work and culture in the postmodern age*, London: Cassell.

Hargreaves, A. (2000) 'Four ages of professionalism and professional learning', *Teachers and Teaching: History and Practice*, **6**(2), 151–182.

Hartley, D. (2003) 'New economy, new pedagogy?', *Oxford Review of Education*, **29**(1), 81–94.

Hartley, D. (2008) 'Education, markets and the pedagogy of personalisation', *British Journal of Educational Studies*, **56**(4), 365–381.

Hartley, J.F. (1983) 'Ideology and organizational behavior', *International Studies of Management and Organization*, **13**(3), 7–34.

Harvey, D. (2005) *A Brief History of Neoliberalism*, Oxford: Oxford University Press.

Hasan, M. (2012) 'Gove's stealthy school reforms could become as toxic as the NHS bill', *New Statesman*, 16 February.

Hatcher, R. (1994) 'Market relationships and the management of teachers', *British Journal of Sociology of Education*, **15**(1), 41–61.

Hay McBer (2000, June) 'Research into teacher effectiveness: A model of teacher effectiveness', Report by Hay McBer to the Department for Education and Employment, available at http://webarchive.nationalarchives.gov.uk/20130401151715/https://www.education.gov.uk/publications/eorderingdownload/rr216.pdf [accessed 24 September 2013].

Hayes, D. (2001) 'Professional status and an emerging culture of conformity amongst teachers in England', *Education 3–13*, **29**(1), 43–49.

Heckman, J.J and Smith, J.A. (1998) 'Evaluating the welfare state', NBER Working Paper 6542, Cambridge, MA: National Bureau of Economic Research, available from http://www.nber.org/papers/w6542.pdf?new_window=1 [accessed 14 May 2013].

Heclo, H.H. (1972) 'Policy analysis', *British Journal of Political Science*, **2**(1), 83–108.

Helm, T. and Colman J. (2012) 'Key policy "comes across as waffle", says archbishop of Canterbury in valedictory bombshell', *The Observer*, 24 June.

Helsby, G. (1995) 'Teachers' Construction of Professionalism in England in the 1990s', *Journal of Education for Teaching*, **21**(3), 317–332.

Henkel, M. (1991) 'The new "Evaluative State"', *Public Administration*, **69**(1), 121–136.

Higgins, D. (1998) 'The National Literacy Project: a case study into status quo and change', MA Dissertation, Norwich: Centre for Applied Research in Education, University of East Anglia.

Hirsch, D. (1997) 'What can Britain learn from abroad?', in R. Glatter, P. Woods and C. Bagley (Eds) *Choice and Diversity in Schooling: Perspectives and prospect*, London: Routledge.

Hirsch, D. (2002) 'What works in innovation in education – school: a choice of directions', OECD/CERI, available at http://www.oecd.org/dataoecd/21/0/2755749.pdf [accessed 13 December 2011].

Hobby, R. (2010) in Standing Committee for the Education and Training of Teachers (2010) 'In defence of teacher education', available at http://www.scett.org.uk/media/3583/in_defence_of_teacher_education_scett_march_2011.pdf [accessed 25 June 2013].

Hogwood, B.W. and Gunn, L.A. (1984) *Policy Analysis for the Real World*, Oxford: Oxford University Press.

Holroyd, C. (2000) 'Are assessors professional?', *Active Learning in Higher Education*, **1**(1), 28–44.

Hoyle, E. (1974) 'Professionality, professionalism and control in teaching', *London Education Review*, **3**(2), 13–19.

Hoyle, E. and John, P. D. (1995) 'The idea of a profession', in E. Hoyle and P. D. John (Eds) *Professional Knowledge and Professional Practice*, London: Cassell, pp. 1–15.

Hutton, W. (1995) *The State We're In*, London: Cape.

Institute for Government (2012) 'The development of quasi-markets in secondary education', available at http://www.instituteforgovernment.org.uk/sites/default/files/publications/The%20Development%20of%20Quasi-Markets%20in%20Education%20final.pdf [accessed 25 June 2013].

Jeffrey, B. (2002) 'Performativity and primary teacher relations', *Journal of Education Policy*, **17**(5), 531–546.

Jeffrey, B. (2003) 'Countering learner "instrumentalism" through creative mediation', *British Educational Research Journal*, **29**(4), 489–503.

Jenkins, S. (2010) 'Gove's claim to be "freeing" schools is a cloak for more control from the centre', *The Guardian*, 27 May.

Jenkins, W.I. (1978) *Policy Analysis: A political and organizational perspective*, London: Martin Robertson.

Jongbloed, B. (2003) 'Marketisation in higher education: Clark's Triangle and the essential ingredients of markets', *Higher Education Quarterly*, **57**(2), 110–135.

Kelly, A. (2009) 'Globalisation and education: a review of conflicting perspectives and their effect on policy and professional practice in the UK', *Globalisation, Societies and Education*, **7**(1), 51–68.

Kendall, I. and Holloway, D. (2001) 'Education policy', in S.P Savage and R. Atkinson (Eds.) *Public Policy Under Blair*, Basingstoke: Palgrave, pp. 154–173.

Labour Party (1997) New Labour. Because Britain Deserves Better (election manifesto), London: The Labour Party.

Labour Party (2010) A Fair Future for All (election manifesto), London: The Labour Party.

Lawton, D. (1994) *The Tory Mind on Education 1979–94*, London: Falmer.

Liberal Democrats (2010) Change That Works for You. Building a Better Britain (election manifesto), London: The Liberal Democrats.

Locke, T., Vulliamy, G., Webb, R. and Hill, M. (2005) 'Being a "professional" primary school teacher at the beginning of the 21st century: a comparative analysis of primary teacher professionalism in New Zealand and England', *Journal of Education Policy*, **20**(5), 555–581.

Lubienski, C. (2009) 'Do quasi-markets foster innovation in education?: A comparative perspective', OECD Education Working Papers No. 25.

Lynch, K. (2006) 'Neo-liberalism and marketisation: the implications for higher education', *European Educational Research Journal*, **5**(1), 1–17.

Machin, S. and Vernoit, J. (2010) 'Academy schools: who benefits?', *CentrePiece*, Autumn, Centre for Economic Performance, available at http://cep.lse.ac.uk/pubs/download/cp325.pdf [accessed 25 June 2013].

Maclure, J.S. (1973) *Educational Documents England and Wales 1816 to the Present Day* (3rd edn), London, Methuen.

Maddock, M., Drummond, M.J., Koralek, B. and Nathan, I. (2007) 'Doing school differently: creative practitioners at work', *Education 3–13*, **35**(1), 47–58.

Mahony, P., Hextall, I. and Menter, I. (2004) 'Threshold assessment and performance management: modernizing or masculinising teaching in England?', *Gender and Education*, **16**(2), 131–149.

McMurtry, J. (1991) 'Education and the market model', *Journal of Philosophy of Education*, **25**(2), 209–217.

McPherson, A. and Raab, C. (1988) 'Exit, choice and loyalty', *Education Policy*, **3**(2), 155–179.

Meighan, R. and Siraj-Blatchford, I. (1997) *A Sociology of Educating*, London: Continuum.

Millerson, G. (1964) *The Qualifying Association*, London: Routledge & Kegan Paul.

Mortimore P (2010) 'Fight Gove's big sell-off of public education', *The Guardian*, 7 December.

Moser, M. (2006) 'Primary school choice in a rural locale: a "right, good, local" school', paper presented at the British Educational Research Association Annual Conference, University of Warwick, 6–9 September.

Moutsios, S. (2010) 'Power, politics and transnational policy-making in education', *Globalisation, Societies and Education*, **8**(1), 121–141.

Mulholland, H. (2012) 'Michael Gove tells academies they can hire unqualified teaching staff', *The Guardian*, 27 July.

Newman, J. and Clarke, J. (1995) 'Going about our business?: The managerialization of public service', in J. Clarke, A. Cochrane and E. McLaughlin (Eds.) *Managing Social Policy*, London: Sage.

Newman, S. and Jahdi, K. (2009) 'Marketisation of education: marketing, rhetoric and reality', *Journal of Further and Higher Education*, **33**(1), 1–11.

Noddings, N. (2002) *Starting at Home: Caring and social policy*, Berkeley: University of California Press.

Norman, J. (2010) *The Big Society*, Buckingham: University of Buckingham Press.

Norwood Committee (1943) *Curriculum and Examinations in Secondary Schools (Norwood Report)*, London: Ministry of Education.

NUT (2010) Free Schools, Beyond the Spin of Government Policy, available at https://sites.google.com/a/antiacademies.org.uk/aaa/Home/teachers/nutbriefing-freeschoolsbeyondthespinofgovernmentpolicy [accessed 26 September 2013].

Ofsted (2002) *National Literacy Strategy: The first four years 1998–2002*, London: Ofsted.

Ofsted (2010) *The Annual Report of Her Majesty's Chief Inspector of Education, Children's Services and Skills 2010/11*, London: TSO.

Ofsted (2011) available at www.ofsted.gov.uk/about-us [accessed 16 November 2011].

Olssen, M. and Peters, M.A. (2005) 'Neoliberalism, higher education and the knowledge economy: from the free market to knowledge capitalism', *Journal of Education Policy*, **20**(3), 313–345.

Olssen, M., Codd, J. and O'Neill, A-M. (2004) *Education Policy: Globalisation, citizenship and democracy*, London: Sage.

O'Neill, O. (2002) *A Question of Trust*, The BBC Reith Lectures 2002, Cambridge: Cambridge University Press.

Oría, A., Cardini, A., Ball, S., Stamou, E., Kolokitha, M., Vertigan, S. and Flores-Moreno, C. (2007) 'Urban education, the middle classes and their dilemmas of school choice', *Journal of Education Policy*, **22**(1), 91–105.

Osborne, D. and Gaebler, T. (1993) *Reinventing Government: How the entrepreneurial spirit is transforming the public sector*, New York: Penguin.

Osgood, J. (2006) 'Deconstructing professionalism in early childhood: resisting the regulatory gaze', *Contemporary Issues in Early Childhood*, **7**(1), 5–14.

Ozga (1995) 'Deskilling and profession: professionalism, de-professionalism and the new managerialism', in H. Busher and R. Saran (Eds.) *Managing Teachers as Professionals in Schools*, London: Kogan Page.

Paterson, L. (2003) 'The three educational ideologies of the British Labour Party, 1997–2001', *Oxford Review of Education*, **29**(2), 165–186.

Paton, G. (2012a) 'Government adviser attacks "fatally flawed" curriculum', *The Telegraph*, 12 June.

Paton, G. (2012b) 'Top graduates to get £25,000 to teach in tough schools', *The Telegraph*, 14 June.

Paton, G. (2013) 'Michael Gove attacks headteachers over no confidence vote', *The Telegraph*, 18 May.

Perryman, J. (2006) 'Panoptic performativity and school inspection regimes: disciplinary mechanisms and life under special measures', *Journal of Education Policy*, **21**(2), 147–161.

Pick, D. and Taylor, J. (2009) ' "Economic rewards are the driving factor": neo-liberalism, globalisation and work attitudes of young graduates in Australia', *Globalisation, Societies and Education*, **7**(1), 69–82.

Politics.co.uk (2011) 'NASUWT: The coalition is adopting a "scorched earth" education policy', available at http://www.politics.co.uk/opinion-formers/nasuwt-the-teachers-union/article/nasuwt-the-coalition-is-adopting-a-scorched-earth-education [accessed 13 November 2012].

Pollard, A. and Triggs, P., with Broadfoot, P., McNess, E. and Osborn, M. (2000) *What Pupils Say: Changing policy and practice in primary education*, London: Continuum.

Pollard, S. (1995) *Schools, Selection and the Market*, Memorandum no. 16, London: Social Market Foundation.

Pollit, C. (1990) *Managerialism and the Public Services: The Anglo-American experience*, London: John Wiley and Sons.

Poulson, L. (1998) 'Accountability, teacher professionalism and education reform in England', *Teacher Development: An International Journal of Teachers' Professional Development*, **2**(3), 419–432.

Power, S. and Frandji, D. (2010) 'Education markets, the new politics of recognition and the increasing fatalism towards inequality', *Journal of Education Policy*, **25**(3), 385–396.

Power, S. and Whitty, G. (1999) 'New Labour's education policy: first, second or third way?', *Journal of Education Policy*, **14**(5), 535–546.

Pring, R. (2005) 'Labour government policy 14–19', *Oxford Review of Education*, **31**(1), 71–85.

Reay, D. (2008) 'Tony Blair, the promotion of the "active" educational citizen, and middle class hegemony', *Oxford Review of Education*, **34**(6), 639–650.

Reid, I., Brain, K. and Comerford Boyes, L. (2004) 'Teachers or learning leaders? Where have all the teachers gone? Gone to be leaders everyone', *Educational Studies*, **30**(3), 251–264.

Rein, M. (1983) *From Policy to Practice*, London: Macmillan.

Ritzer, G. (2011) *The McDonaldization of Society 6*, London: Sage.

Rizvi, F. and Lingard, B. (2010) *Globalizing Education Policy*, London: Routledge.

Robinson, G. (2012) 'Gove announces "revolutionary" changes to initial teacher training', TES (online), availableathttp://newteachers.tes.co.uk/news/gove-announces-%E2%80%98revolutionary%E2%80%99-changes-initial-teacher-training/46372 [accessed 13 November 2012].

Robson, J., Bailey, B. and Larkin, S. (2004) 'Adding value: investigating the discourse of professionalism adopted by vocational teachers in further education colleges', *Journal of Education and Work*, **17**(2), 183–195.

Roche, J. and Tucker, S. A. (2007) 'Every Child Matters: "tinkering" or "reforming" – an analysis of the development of the Children Act (2004) from an educational perspective', *Education 3–13*, **35**(3), 213–223.

Sachs, J. (2003) *The Activist Professional*, Buckingham: Open University Press.

Savage, S.P. and Atkinson, R. (2001) *Public Policy Under Blair,* Basingstoke: Palgrave Macmillan.

School Teachers' Review Body (STRB) (2003) School teachers' review body, 12th report CM5715. London: TSO.

School Teachers' Review Body (STRB) (2012) School teachers' review body, 21st report CM8487. London: TSO.

Shain, F. and Gleeson, D. (1999) 'Under new management: changing conceptions of teacher professionalism and policy in the further education sector', *Journal of Education Policy*, **14**(4), 445–462.

Shepherd, J. (2013) 'Tougher targets mean hundreds more primary schools risk failure', *The Guardian*, 5 March.

Simon, B. (1991) *Education and the Social Order (1940–1990)*, London: Lawrence and Wishart.

Smith, B.C. (1976) *Policy Making in British Government*, London: Martin Robertson.

Smithers, A. and Robinson, P. (2003) 'Factors affecting teachers' decisions to leave the profession', DfES Research Report RR430, London: Department for Education and Skills.

Standing Committee for the Education and Training of Teachers (2010) 'In defence of teacher education', available at http://www.scett.org.uk/media/3583/in_defence_of__teacher_education_scett_march_2011.pdf [accessed 25 June 2013].

Stewart, W. (2012) 'Gove accused of building on shaky Pisa foundations', *The Times Education Supplement (TES)*, 11 November.

Surman, R. (2010) in Standing Committee for the Education and Training of Teachers (2010) 'In defence of teacher education', available at http://www.scett.org.uk/media/3583/in_defence_of_teacher_education_scett_march_2011.pdf [accessed 25 June 2013].

Swaine, J. (2009) 'Pupils disqualified from SATs after teachers cheated', *The Telegraph*, 28 July.

TTA (1997) *Standards for the Award of Qualified Teacher Status*, London: Teacher Training Agency.

TTA (2002) *Qualifying to Teach: Professional standards for qualified teacher status and requirements for initial teacher training*, London: Teacher Training Agency.

Thelwell (2011) 'Free Schools: revolution or retreat?', The FactCheck Blog, Channel 4 News, available at http://blogs.channel4.com/factcheck/free-schools-revolution-or-retreat/6753 [accessed 13 November 2012].

Tomlinson, S. (2005) *Education in a Post-Welfare Society* (2nd edn), Maidenhead: Open University Press.

Troman, G. (1996) 'The rise of the new professionals? The restructuring of primary teachers' work and professionalism', *British Journal of Sociology of Education*, **17**(4), 473–487.

Trowler, P. (2003) *Education Policy* (2nd edn), London: Routledge.

Tucker, S. A. (1999) 'Making the link: dual "problematization", discourse and work with young people', *Journal of Youth Studies*, **2**(3), 283–295.

Tymms, P. and Coe, R. (2003) 'Celebration of the success of distributed research with schools: the CEM Centre, Durham', *British Journal of Educational Research*, **29**(5), 639–654.

Tymms, P. and Fitz-Gibbon, C. (2001) 'Standards, achievement and educational Performance: a cause for celebration?', in R. Phillips and J. Furlong (Eds.) *Education Reform and the State: 25 years of politics, policy and practice*, London: Routledge.

Ward, S. and Eden, C. (2009) *Key Issues in Education Policy*, London: Sage.

Waslander, S., Pater, C. and van der Weide, M. (2010) 'Markets in education: an analytical review of empirical research on market mechanisms in education', OECD Education Working Papers No. 52.

Watkins, C. (1999) 'Personal–social education: beyond the National Curriculum', *British Journal of Guidance & Counselling*, **27**(1), 71–84.

Watt, H., Newell, C., Winnett, R. and Paton, G. (2011) 'Exam boards: how examiners tip off teachers to help students pass', *The Telegraph*, 7 December.

Webb, R., Vulliamy, G., Hämäläinen, S., Sarja, A., Kimonen, E. and Nevalainen, R. (2004) 'A comparative analysis of primary teacher professionalism in England and Finland', *Comparative Education*, **40**(1), 83–107.

Welch, A. R. (1998) 'The cult of efficiency in education: comparative reflections on the reality and the rhetoric', *Comparative Education*, **34**(2), 157–175.

West, A. and Pennell, H. (2002) 'How new is New Labour? The quasi-market and English schools 1997 to 2001' [online], London: LSE Research online, available at http://eprints.lse.ac.uk/archive/00000214 [accessed 21 March 2012].

Whitty, G. (2000) 'Teacher professionalism in new times', *Journal of In-Service Education*, **26**(2), 281–295.

Whitty, G. (2006) 'Teacher professionalism in a new era', paper presented at the First General Teaching Council for Northern Ireland Annual Lecture, Belfast, March.

Whitty, G. (2008) 'Twenty years of progress? English education policy 1988 to the present', *Educational Management, Administration and Leadership*, **36**(2), 165–184.

Wiborg, S. (2010) 'Learning lessons from the Swedish model', *Forum*, **52**(3), 279–284.

Wilby P (2010) 'Private companies will run "free schools"', *The Guardian*, 25 May.

Wilkins, C. (2011) 'Professionalism and the post-performative teacher: new teachers reflect on autonomy and accountability in the English school system', *Professional Development in Education*, **37**(3), 389–409.

Wrigley, T. (2003) 'Is "school effectiveness" anti-democratic?', *British Journal of Educational Studies*, **51**(2), 89–112

Index